Exceeding the Standards:

Teaching with Pride, Poise, and Passion

- Pride in Performance
- Poise in Professionalism
- Passion for Perfection

Bill Collar

Exceeding the Standards: Teaching with Pride, Poise, and Passion
© 2005 by Bill Collar

Library of Congress Copyright Registration Number: TX-6-212-772

ISBN   1-59971-308-X

Bill Collar
"All The Way With PMA!"
421 Keune St.
Seymour, WI 54165
(920) 833-6064
www.billcollar.com
pma@billcollar.com

Printed and Bound by Publishers' Graphics, LLC

Preface

Why is this book titled *Exceeding the Standards*? It is a tribute to all the educators I have known who made the commitment to perform at a level of excellence that was beyond what was required. They were driven by a desire to provide the best education possible for their students. These individuals were task oriented as opposed to time driven and perceived themselves as integral components in the daily operation of the school. It was before the days of formal "standards," but because of their commitment, caring, and concern they exceeded the standards of any era.

"Teaching is like holding a dove in your hand, if you squeeze it too tightly you will kill it, if you don't squeeze tight enough it will get away from you." Somewhere along the way that advice was passed on to me. During my teaching career the challenge was to discover the proper way to handle each student. Fortunately, I interacted with many talented people who exhibited pride in their performance, poise in their professionalism, and possessed a passion for perfection. They were impressive role models and mentors who took classes and workshops without being coerced, managed their classrooms with perfection, and found the time to coach or advise in extracurricular activities.

These people believed in doing everything possible to reach all of their students. Being dedicated professionals they were excellent communicators, planned unique lessons, and knew how to test and assess. Most of all they worked together as a team and valued the contributions of everyone ranging from the custodial staff to the teacher down the hall. This book is a result of the inspiration provided by numerous colleagues and friends who demonstrated what was necessary in order to exceed the standards. Indeed, they taught with pride, poise, and passion.

"The nature of the relationship of the adults in a school has
more impact on learning than any other factor."
Roland Barth, Harvard educator and author

Contents

Acknowledgments

My first teachers were my parents Elmer and Mary Collar. Mother provided me with caring and understanding, while my gregarious father was instrumental in influencing my personality development. I appreciate the unwavering support of my wife, Holly, who dedicated herself to teaching our daughters sound values while I was spending endless hours at school. We were blessed with three daughters, Susan, Angela, and Sarah, who are all teachers. They have made us proud by living the principles under which they were raised.

My high school teacher and coach, Bob Newhouse, modeled the lifestyle I hoped to emulate and influenced me to attend college. Numerous other educators provided inspiration and guidance critical to my vocational choice. Dr. George Gilkey, an exceptional European history teacher at UW-La Crosse, demonstrated the ability to make history come alive by utilizing poignant stories and appropriate humor. Bill Merwin, my student teaching supervisor, was relentless in challenging me to vary my instruction and experiment with different methodologies.

In the sports world, Coach Bill Vickroy, my college football coach, embraced the values of integrity, commitment and self-respect. Gordy Schofield, the head football coach at Antigo, took this raw assistant under his wing and laid the groundwork for future success. Roger Harring, head coach at UW-La Crosse, spent endless hours sharing his knowledge. I also wish to thank all the assistant coaches who played such a vital role in our success at Seymour.

At UW-La Crosse, I had the opportunity to work with Dick Koehler, the personable Director of Housing, and Don Staats, an Assistant Dean of Men. Working with them was as good as taking a course in human relations. During my early years at Seymour, Lyle Martens, Dick Tepp, and John Peterson provided support during challenging times. Peterson, the principal, provided me with the materials and academic freedom to employ unique instructional strategies.

I've had the occasion to learn from many colleagues at Teacher World, the Wisconsin Teacher Forum, the Turning the Tide workshops, football camps, and numerous professional conferences. It is impossible to mention everyone who has contributed to making this book possible. I've always believed in being a life-long learner and thank everyone, including my students and colleagues, who helped me enjoy 35 years of teaching and coaching.

A special thank you to my teaching partner Jane Eberly. Her organizational skill and attention to detail made working with her a delight. I'm grateful for her assistance in reading the manuscript and making suggestions.

**If your students don't learn the
way you teach, teach the way they learn.**

Introduction

In August 1966, at Antigo Junior High School in northern Wisconsin, I began a 35-year teaching career. I was hired to teach U.S. History and serve as an assistant football coach. My wife, Holly, taught seventh grade just down the hall. We started the school year filled with eager anticipation and confidence that this was the beginning of a long and fruitful association with the Antigo School District. Our co-workers gave us a warm welcome and made the two newlyweds feel comfortable in their new community.

Reflecting on those years, it is amazing to realize we were simply given our teaching assignments and then allowed to sink or swim on our own. Fortunately, I had an excellent student teaching experience the previous spring and was well prepared for the challenge.

College Administration

My wife and I were very happy at Antigo, but after two years we received a phone call from the dean of men at UW-La Crosse. At the young age of 25, I was offered a position in the university student personnel office. I would coordinate five men's residence halls and the student staff. He was looking for a former resident assistant with strong leadership skills and felt I fit the bill. After considerable thought we decided to take advantage of the opportunity. For the next four years I was the assistant director of housing at UW-La Crosse and offensive line coach in football.

There is something special about working on a college campus. I had the chance to interact with a number of highly talented individuals. Through participation in faculty social outings, committee work, and daily job responsibilities, my communication skills improved, and I experienced much personal growth. While I enjoyed the people and was encouraged to get a PhD in student personnel work, high school teaching was my first love, and I yearned to get back to the classroom. Against the advice of many people, I "stepped down" to high school and spent the next 29 years as a history teacher, football coach, and assistant track coach at Seymour High School.

Back to High School

Seymour was a progressive district, with a number of insightful administrators who believed in providing in-house opportunities for staff development. While at Seymour I was fortunate enough to be recognized as Wisconsin Social Studies Teacher of the Year, Wisconsin Teacher of the Year, and Wisconsin Football Coach of the Year. Of course, no honor is earned – or deserved – without the support of others, in my case, my students and colleagues.

Being active in numerous professional organizations, I interacted with outstanding educators and helped organize Teacher World and the Wisconsin Teacher Forum. I was a member of the executive board of the Wisconsin Council for Social Studies, and served as president of the Wisconsin Football Coaches Association. Not bad for a kid who was told by his high school teacher, "If you graduate from college, it will be a miracle."

Purpose of the Book

The purpose of this book is to share my educational philosophy and materials with other educators. It is an attempt to compile and assemble the resources necessary to experience success as a teacher and coach. I realize everyone has different strengths and weaknesses, but certain common threads need to be woven together to provide the foundation for success. I've always loved quotations and subscribe to Winston Churchill's statement, "The more distant we look into the past, the farther we can see into the future." This book is a result of all the experiences I've had and the influence of numerous people with whom I have interacted. All educators must not only teach students, but also network and share with each other. As Sir Isaac Newton said, "If I have seen further than others, it was by standing on the shoulders of giants."

> **The book is meant to be a reference manual for educators.** In order to excel as an educator, one must first excel as a person. Consequently much is said about peak performance and personal growth. No differentiation is made between teaching and coaching since common attributes are needed for success at both.

> **Much of the book refers directly to my experiences.** At times this may seem self-serving and border on braggadocio, but please keep in mind that the reference is being made to emphasize or illustrate a key point. Those of us who have been in the classroom for years have been humbled countless times!

How to Use this Book

> **The chapters are somewhat independent of each other.** You need not read from front to back. If you are most interested in "Goal Setting," start with Chapter Five. If you are looking for humor in the classroom go to Chapter Nine. Because of this, some cross-references are included and critical attributes may be repeated.

> **A number of self-evaluations and summary sheets are incorporated in the book.** Feel free to reproduce these as desired. They are printed in a format suitable for duplication and included in the appendix.

> **If you have some question about the identity of the author of a quote, check the list of people in the appendix.** All people who are quoted are listed in alphabetical order in the back of the book.

> **Over 100 experienced educators completed surveys for the book.** The survey results are incorporated in the last two chapters. Interviews with eight educators who have been recognized for excellence are also included. Their comments provide valuable insight. I've also included a number of excerpts from other veteran teachers.

Please Keep in Mind

> **The information about peak performance, motivation, communication, goal setting and personal growth relates to educators at all grade levels.** The teaching tips pertain predominantly to the middle school and high school levels. I have visited elementary classrooms, and have great respect for primary teachers, but I've had no experience teaching at that level.

> As I travel around the Midwest speaking with educators, they often ask where more information can found about the topics presented. While this book will serve as a good resource, a recommended reading list follows the appendix.

As a young teacher I often struggled and questioned my vocational choice, especially when working weekends and 12-hour days correcting papers and preparing lessons. In fact, at the insistence of my wife, one year during football season, I tabulated the hours spent at school for one week and the total was 82 hours. That may seem excessive, but I did what had to be done. During the week, work ran from 6:00 AM to 6:00 PM and usually a couple nights a week and most of the weekend. Finally we agreed that I would have to organize my time better and one day a weekend would be reserved for the family. If you have not yet scheduled specific time for your family, make sure to do it now!

Celebrate Your Profession

It is normal to question the time commitment and the limited wages. I often thought, "What would the return be if I was in sales or business and put in the same amount of time and energy?" Then I got certified to sell all types of insurance and had an offer to be a partner with a local businessman. After working part time for six months, the financial potential was intriguing, but I just didn't get the positive feeling received from teaching and coaching. That's when I concluded teaching is a calling. It takes a very special person to make the commitment necessary to make a difference everyday in the lives of students.

Babe Didrikson Zaharias said, "All my life I've always had the urge to do things better than anybody else." I hope my experiences provide you with some practical pointers, add depth to your knowledge, challenge you with different perspectives, and help you become a better educator. The process of writing was a humbling experience. Reflecting on 35 years as a teacher and coach made me realize how often I failed. But as John Wooden said, "Success is never final, just as failure is never fatal." To those of you pleased with your personal and professional growth, I offer this thought: "Even the best lumberjack in the woods has to sharpen his ax once in awhile."

Anyone who has been in the field of education for some time realizes no one right way to teach or coach exists. Each of us has certain gifts that make us unique. There is no one exactly like you. Keep improving and continue the great work helping young people discover more about themselves and life. Be proud to echo Christa McAuliffe's statement, "I touch the future, I teach!"

Perhaps this story passed on to me by my friend Jim Flora sums up our profession the best. *A number of professionals were having dinner and discussing life. They were comparing job responsibilities and financial rewards, and finally a business executive asked the lone teacher, "What do you make?" The teacher thought for a minute and replied, "I make kids wonder, I make kids think, I make kids question, I make a difference!" Silence prevailed.*

Keep making a difference everyday!

In Pursuit of Peak Performance

Chapter 1

Nice Leisure Suit! 1970's

➢ **"The more distant we look into the past, the farther we can see into the future."**
   Winston Churchill

➢ **"I don't know anyone who has gotten to the top without hard work. That is the recipe."**
   Margaret Thatcher

➢ **"Whatever your mind can conceive and believe it can achieve."**
   Napoleon Hill

Objectives

- **To explain the formula for teacher success in the classroom**
- **To identify the principles of peak performance and personal growth**
- **To provide methods for self evaluation and student feedback**
- **To relate personal experiences citing the application of the above**

In Pursuit of Peak Performance

"View life as a continuous learning experience"
Denis Waitley

During 35 years as a teacher/coach I was challenged to reach as many students as possible. At the end of the day, I would reflect and ask, "Did I make a difference today? Did I engage as many students as possible? Was I fair? Was I understanding? Did I take the time to get the most out of each student?" Unfortunately the answer wasn't always "yes." Especially early in my teaching career patience was lacking, and I had little tolerance for students who were reluctant learners. My leadership style was authoritarian and I had little regard for individual differences. While classroom discipline was fine, students followed policy more out of fear than respect.

> *"The older I get the more I realize that there is but one wealth, one security, on this earth and that is found in the ability of a person to perform a task well. And first and foremost this ability must start with knowledge."*
>
> **Abraham Lincoln**

During the early 1970's, it seemed the primary concern of school administrators was classroom discipline. As long as the teacher had the class under control, the principal assumed learning was taking place. Certainly, well developed classroom management skills are essential, but other methods can earn the support of the students other than threats or intimidation. Veteran teachers often offered advice such as, "Start out really tough. You can always loosen up." Following that advice was helpful, and it became apparent the teachers who were having the most difficulty with control were those who wanted to be the "friend" of the students. However, I thought there must be some middle ground where the teacher would earn the respect of the students without making threats. After many years of teaching juniors, I determined in order to perform at a peak level; I needed to abide by certain success principles.

The Success Formula

Since a teacher must have the students' attention in order for them to learn, the teacher must hold in high regard the ability to maintain student interest. After several years of teaching, I discovered that the more students were treated with respect, the more they respected the teacher.

> *"To the degree you give others what they need, they will give you what you need."*
> **Robert Conklin**

This formula included a number of fundamental educational principles. With a little adjustment, the principles apply at all grade levels.

- **Clear expectations** – To live up to the expectations of the teacher, the students must understand what behavior is expected of them. Individual teachers have different guidelines, and too often the particular classroom policy is not made clear. This is why each teacher must take the time to introduce and periodically review proper classroom behavior.

- **Be firm and fair** – Once the guidelines for proper behavior are established and conveyed, they must be enforced. Example: If the policy is "Listen when another person is speaking," the teacher must insist on proper listening. Usually a look or simple reminder is sufficient to correct the behavior. Ignoring an indiscretion is not firm enough, and sending a student to the office or assigning a detention is not fair enough.

- **Communicate privately with the individual** – The answer to dealing with the student who is continually disruptive is to sit down in a private setting and explain what behavior is expected. An effective explanation might include, "I feel you are mature enough to behave properly, and I know you will make the necessary adjustments to conform to classroom policies." If the student is resistant or obnoxious, go into more detail and explain the logical consequences of continual disruption.

- **Conflict resolution** – Mutual respect is enhanced when you make the effort to communicate directly with the student to work out a solution to a behavior problem. Too often when the student is referred to the principal or if the parent is contacted immediately, the student may lose respect for the teacher and become a bigger problem when he/she returns to the classroom. This is especially true at the senior high level.

- **Have a predetermined plan to handle behavior problems** – The teacher can best deal with a situation when the reaction to the event has been thought out in advance. By mentally rehearsing the solutions to a variety of problems, the teacher is more likely to respond in the proper manner.

- **Time on task** – By keeping students engaged, their opportunity for foolishness is  lessened. It is important to be organized to the point where students have work to do from the time they arrive in class until the end of the period. When students are reading, working on projects, or involved in class discussion, learning is taking place. It is the teacher's responsibility to organize the class in a manner that insures everyone is engaged in learning.

- **Build a broad knowledge base** – Being a life-long learner, the teacher continually adds to a reservoir of knowledge that may be tapped as needed. This provides the educator with the tools necessary to monitor and adjust as necessary. When supervising student teachers, I observed most behavior problems developed when students were not active.

- **Support student activities** – By relating with the teacher in a setting outside of the classroom, the student concludes the teacher is interested in them as a person and not just his/her performance. Over the years I attended many concerts, plays, athletic events, agricultural exhibits, art shows and technical displays. It always impressed me how my students greeted me warmly when they realized I made a special effort to witness their achievements outside the classroom.

- **Meet and greet students daily** – By being cordial and welcoming, the teacher makes the classroom a friendly, inviting place. Calling students by their names provides them with a sense of belonging and a willingness to cooperate.

- **Lead by example** – Student respect is earned when the teacher exhibits the behavior expected of the student. Labeling, stereotyping, sarcasm, and ridicule all destroy a positive relationship and must be avoided. If the teacher doesn't allow drinking soda in class, he/she shouldn't have a can of soda on the desk. If the educator expects students to listen when others are speaking, the teacher must demonstrate good listening skills. Since students are expected to be on time, the teacher must be on time for class.

While these principles may sound pretty basic, in 35 years of teaching/coaching I saw them violated often. The teacher who complains about students being in the hallway after the bell often is the same individual who returns late to his/her classroom. The educator who is consistently removing students from class and sending them to the principal may be the same individual who sits in the lounge and complains about the lack of discipline and no administrative support. When teachers are standing in the hallway with a foot up on the wall with complete disregard for the maintenance staff, how can we expect students to respect the physical plant? During my first year in education, a veteran teacher actually advised me to, "Volunteer as little as possible because the more you do the more they expect you to do." While that may be true, school would be a pretty miserable place if all teachers had that attitude.

> *When teachers are standing in the hallway with a foot up on the wall with complete disregard for the maintenance staff, how can we expect students to respect the physical plant?*

Living History

Much can be learned about peak performance by studying the lives of great achievers. One of the reasons I became a history teacher was my interest in what made people tick, how they overcame adversity, and how they reacted to different situations. I became fascinated with people like Theodore Roosevelt, who in spite of being born into wealth, was faced with many struggles that he met and overcame. He had severe asthma as a child. He was virtually blind in one eye. When he was just a young man, both his beautiful young wife and his mother died in the same house on the same day. Certainly it took strength of character to triumph over these and other adversities.

As a peak performer, Elizabeth Cady Stanton intrigued me. What drove this woman to call for a national women's rights convention way back in 1848, and take a stand "that all men and women are created equal?" Why was Martin Luther King willing to give his life for a cause he believed in? How did Frances Perkins manage to have such an impact when she served in a cabinet surrounded by men? Why did Carnegie transform from an insensitive industrialist to a philanthropist? To me teaching history was studying about people and events and what we can learn from the past to build a better future.

Personal Growth

Consistent with this theme I wondered, "What can I do to be the best at my profession?" I began to set aside 30 minutes a day for professional reading. I started reading biographies of historical personalities whom I admired. Most of the great people in history seemed to experience considerable adversity on their way to achievement. This is when I began to subscribe to the belief that it isn't how seldom a person fails that counts, but it's how often one gets up and goes again after failure. The next logical question was, "How might history class become a stimulating and exciting experience where students can learn life-long lessons?" It was challenging and enjoyable to find examples of peak performance in history and devise interactive ways to have students learn the concept in class. I also wondered what lessons I can learn from the study of history that will help build the confidence and commitment to help take our football team from the bottom of the conference to the top?

Earl Nightingale

My introduction to the concept of peak performance came via the radio and the inspirational messages of Earl Nightingale. His daily five-minute programs, delivered with a distinctive husky voice, offered a variety of tips for personal improvement. His motivational moments provided a boost to the spirit as he reminded the listener about keeping a positive attitude and how the subconscious mind controls our daily actions. That is where I first heard a work by Max Ehrmann titled "Desiderata" or collection of things that are needed. This reminded me to keep problems in perspective and enjoy each day to its fullest. Nightingale concluded with the comment, "If each hung up his pack of troubles on the wall and looked around at those of others, he would quickly run to grab his own."

Desiderata

"Go placidly amid the noise and haste, and remember what peace there may be in silence. As far as possible, without surrender, be on good terms with all persons. Speak your truth quietly and clearly; and listen to others even to the dull and the ignorant; they too have their story.

"Avoid loud and aggressive persons; they are vexations to the spirit. If you compare yourself with others, you may become bitter or vain, for always there will be greater and lesser persons than yourself...

"Be yourself. Especially do not feign affection. Neither be cynical about love; for in the face of all aridity and disenchantment, it is as perennial as grass. Take kindly the counsel of the years, gracefully surrendering the things of youth. Nurture strength of spirit to shield you in sudden misfortune. But do not distress yourself with dark imaginings. Many fears are born of fatigue and loneliness..."

"And whatever your labors and aspirations, in the noisy confusion of life, keep peace in your soul. With all its broken dreams, it is still a beautiful world. Be cheerful. Strive to be happy."

I taped a copy of "Desiderata" to the top of my classroom desk and even highlighted several of the passages that were most meaningful. I remember when I first read, "Avoid loud and aggressive persons; they are vexations to the spirit," thinking, "Is that me?" The advice about the perils of comparison to others also made a big impression.

Napoleon Hill

My foundation in peak performance was shaped by Napoleon Hill. In one of Nightingale's programs, he told the story of Hill, who was contracted by Andrew Carnegie to discover the secrets of what makes people successful. Carnegie commissioned Hill to interview over 500 millionaires to find a success formula that could be used by the average person. The interviewees included Theodore Roosevelt, Woodrow Wilson, John D. Rockefeller, Thomas Edison, Alexander Graham Bell, Henry Ford, F. W. Woolworth, and many other political figures and business leaders. Hill took over 20 years to produce his book, a classic in the peak performance field titled *Think and Grow Rich*. The book, published in 1937, is sexist by today's standards and is occasionally politically incorrect, but it served as a foundation for future books on personal development.

Cassette Learning

Impressed with the messages conveyed by Earl Nightingale, my appetite for more learning in the field of peak performance became insatiable. Books and cassette tapes by Denis Waitley, Maxwell Maltz, Brian Tracey, Dale Carnegie, Norman Vincent Peale, Thomas Peters, Wayne Dyer, Roger von Oech, Charles Garfield, Og Mandino, Robert Conklin, Zig Ziglar, Tony Robbins, Steven

Covey, and other leading names in the field of personal development were purchased. Reading with renewed vigor and perspective, I gained more significance from the writings of Benjamin Franklin, Thoreau, and Emerson. The cassette tapes were invaluable and a unique way to learn as I traveled in my car to various speaking engagements, classes, workshops and even football camp. I had come the full circle. When in college I would skip classes because the content or professor didn't seem relevant, and now I couldn't get enough learning and was listening to motivational tapes instead of Johnny Cash or rock and roll. In fact, I had to make an agreement with my daughters not to listen to "that weird stuff" when they were in the car.

Denis Waitley and Charles Garfield

My increased knowledge of peak performance provided me with the confidence to apply the principles of motivation and personal growth to the classroom and athletics. Then I discovered that both Denis Waitley and Charles Garfield not only worked with the space program as a psychologist and computer analyst, but they applied the lessons learned in performance and productivity to the sports world. Waitley guided Olympic athletes and Super Bowl teams. Garfield's research was widely accepted in sports competition, and being an accomplished weightlifter, he practiced the powerful tool of visualization and the value of concentration and focusing on the task at hand. Of particular interest was a video he made getting a world-class weightlifter "in the zone" for a peak performance. Since my interests were similar, everything they authored was consumed with enthusiasm. I knew the same principles could be applied in working with young people.

Garfield on Peak Performance

After reading Garfield's book on peak performance, viewing his video, and listening to his cassette series, I decided to use his research as the foundation to my approach in teaching and coaching. Garfield did research for 16 years and conducted over 1,500 in-depth interviews of peak performers in various pursuits. He identified the specific attitudes and skills that enabled top achievers to excel consistently in business, arts, science and sports. In his introduction to the cassette series, Garfield says, "The difference between peak performers and everybody else is much smaller than 'everyone else' thinks. Even more encouragingly, the special qualities of peak performers are learnable;

> *"The difference between peak performers and everyone else is much smaller than 'everyone else" thinks."*
> *Charles Garfield*

they are not reserved for only a lucky few who have been blessed by genetic good fortune."

Self-Evaluation

The highest form of evaluation is self-evaluation. The truly reflective teacher is continually assessing and reassessing his/her performance. While administrative evaluation, appraisal, review, (or whatever euphemistic term is used), may satisfy requirements, they seldom provide sufficient feedback to make a significant difference in teaching effectiveness. I

> *The highest form of evaluation is self-evaluation.*

found Garfield's research provided an excellent basis for personal appraisal and improvement. I took his main points and modified them so they would relate directly to teaching. The simple checklist was used as a self-evaluation tool and it assisted me in focusing on the critical attributes of personal peak performance. I've included it here for your convenience and a form suitable for reproduction may be found in the appendix.

Peak Performance Appraisal

Consider your approach to teaching/coaching, read each description and rank yourself from 1 (low) to 5 (high). This activity will help you identify your strengths and weaknesses.

_____ 1. **Foresight and the ability to carry out effective planning.**
   Do you set goals and develop a plan to reach those goals? Do you always have a teaching/practice plan? A game plan?

_____ 2. **A drive toward transcending previous levels of accomplishment.**
   Are you willing to commit yourself to rise above previous performances? Do your classes/ teams show consistent improvement as the year/season progresses?

_____ 3. **High levels of self-confidence and self-worth.**
   Do you view yourself as an effective teacher/coach? Would you be difficult to replace?

_____ 4. **A high need for responsibility and control.**
   Do you like to take action and be in charge? Do you enjoy competition and the opportunity to make critical decisions?

_____ 5. **Well developed communication skills in both personal and professional areas.**
   Are you capable of effectively communicating your ideas? Do your students/players understand what you expect of them?

_____ 6. **An effective use of mental rehearsal.**
   Do you visualize the process and desired outcome of your task? Do your students/players understand how to practice visualization for success?

_____ 7. **Little need of outside praise or recognition.**
   You must have an internal feeling of accomplishment. Are you driven by attitude motivation rather than fear or reward?

_____ 8. **A superior ability to take risks.**
   Are you willing to break out of the comfort zone? Do you welcome new challenges? Do you experiment and challenge your students/players with new ideas?

_____ 9. **The ability to accept feedback and to self-correct.**
   Are you able to use information from respected sources to improve? Do you attend classes, clinics and conferences for personal improvement?

_____10. **A willingness to accept ownership of creative ideas.**
   Are you willing to "go for it" and initiate action on your ideas? Do you take the time to consider all options and make proper adjustments?

The purpose of this exercise is to identify your strengths and weaknesses. Don't be concerned if you rank low in several areas. Where you are now is not so important; more important is the direction in which you are heading. To make the best use of this instrument, identify your strengths and use them to build up your weaknesses. Pick an area that you have ranked one or two, and make a commitment to show improvement within the next several months. Actually develop a written plan to build this weakness into a strength.

In other words, if you rank high in number one, "planning ability," but low in number seven, "little need for recognition," use your planning and organizational skills to affirm that you are doing a great job teaching. Human nature wants positive feedback and recognition for performing with excellence. This was an area of personal concern since several principals I worked with were reluctant to give out praise and were more likely to dwell on what needed improvement. Also, one of the most difficult aspects of education is that you never see a tangible finished product. For years during the summer, I did construction work. I took great pride in being able to step back and look at a finished sidewalk or building and realize I played a role in its construction. In education the feedback usually doesn't come until years later.

You will note that number eight in the peak performance guide is "a superior ability to take risks" and number nine is "the ability to accept feedback and self-correct." In order for me to transcend previous levels of accomplishment (number two), I had to have the confidence and self-worth (number three) to see the plan through. Number ten emphasizes the need to take ownership of creative ideas. Eventually I concluded the path to personal improvement was full of hurdles and I had to attack each one with courage and determination.

> *"Teachers are the guardians of civilization."*
> *Bertrand Russell*

Something Missing

After experiencing administrative evaluation and engaging in self-evaluation, I still felt something was missing. The challenge was to design a succinct and relevant teacher evaluation form to be completed by the students. My enthusiasm for the idea was tempered when several coworkers tried to discourage me by saying the students were too immature to deal with the issue in a responsible manner.

At the time that I decided to design the student evaluation form I was teaching five classes of U.S. History. Even though there was no grouping, two of the classes exhibited a greater degree of maturity. After speaking with several of the students and getting some feedback on how to administer the instrument, I decided to experiment with those two classes. Certainly there was concern about the ability of the students to keep a serious attitude, but my motivation remained strong as I realized peak performers have to do some creative risk taking.

Hot Tip! *Use the goal-setting guide located in Chapter 5 to get started on a personal improvement plan for peak performance. Check with your area technical college for classes on goal setting and motivation. Scan the bibliography for some of the best books on reaching your full potential. You will feel great about launching a personal improvement plan and remember, "Attitudes are Contagious!"*

The Student Evaluation Instrument

The student evaluation instrument had to be something that could be completed in 10–15 minutes and yet provide an opportunity for open-ended student comments. Over the years the form was modified some. The version reproduced in the appendix on page 210 represents the final copy. Students were asked to rank me as either poor, fair, average, good or excellent in twelve categories. Prior to administering the form, I explained why the junior students were being asked to complete it. I emphasized that teaching was my chosen profession, and I wanted to keep improving and not get in a rut. I reminded them how important it was to be honest and provide me with accurate feedback. This is also a good time to remind them that peak performance is the ultimate goal and their evaluation is part of a personal improvement plan. Represented here is a list of the categories and a brief explanation as to why each was included.

Category	Explanation
1. Knowledge of subject	A knowledge base is essential for success.
2. Clearness of presentation	Students must comprehend in order to learn.
3. Fairness (impartial treatment of students)	Do the students view me as having favorites?
4. Control (orderly, but relaxed and friendly)	Does the proper classroom climate exist?
5. Success in stimulating an interest in history	Is the teacher a motivator?
6. Personal enthusiasm and joy in teaching	Is my attitude positive and contagious?
7. Attitude toward student ideas (Do I encourage and respect student opinion?)	Is the teacher open minded?
8. Sense of humor	Learning is enhanced when humor is present.
9. Assignments (challenging but fair)	Are they being overworked or under worked?
10. Appearance (grooming and dress)	I wanted to be perceived as a professional.
11. Self-control	Do I become agitated or fly off the handle?
12. Effectiveness (overall teaching success)	This is really what it is all about.

Checking these categories from poor to excellent took just a few minutes. The students were allowed to take as much time as needed to complete the five open-ended questions. Two to three lines were provided for writing. They took about ten minutes.

A. Describe your attitude toward history class:
B. What parts of the class did you enjoy most?
C. What parts of the class did you enjoy least?
D. What suggestions do you have to make history class more interesting?
E. Evaluate Mr. Collar's grading system: (Circle one)   Too easy   Fair   Too difficult
E. Other comments:

Student Cooperation

I told the students that since we had been together for almost an entire school year, they knew more about my teaching than anyone else. They were encouraged to take it seriously since every one would be read and then compiled. Students were asked to not sign their names and no attempt would be made to determine their identity. I explained if they just wrote something like, "I hated the class," it wouldn't help. They must explain why they hated the class.

The form was used most of the years that I taught. The students took it very seriously, and it was my most valuable resource for restructuring the class and adjusting my teaching style. Over the years I had several classes (as most of us do) that never demonstrated the maturity necessary to be trusted to do an honest assessment. Students in those classes asked when they would get to complete the evaluation. I explained why they would not.

Hot Tip! *It can be very beneficial to have students complete an evaluation form following a new activity or change in teaching strategy. The most important thing is to keep the lines of communication open and to realize some students will find fault with everything.*

Keeping in mind the characteristics of peak performers, the student evaluation experience certainly provides the teacher with the opportunity to "accept feedback and self-correct." Some type of reaction from the students can be gleaned at every grade level. It is up to the teacher to determine how this may most effectively be accomplished.

Positive Application

Before leaving this topic I want to look at how the results of the evaluation influenced my approach to teaching. After receiving the completed surveys, I read them carefully and tabulated the results. The most important thing was to look for trends where over ten per cent of the students were saying similar things. At the same time, an isolated comment was usually ignored. By compiling the results and looking for common remarks, early in my teaching career I was able to identify several categories that were in need of attention. Another positive application was the affirmation that many students were pleased with much of the class, and a number of them even wrote about what they liked in considerable detail.

Problems Revealed

When I was a young teacher, the student comments revealed several glaring weaknesses. They ranked me below average in items two, three and eleven. Numerous references were made that indicated I favored some students, was too strict, and would lose self-control. Comments pointed out, "Football players were favored," and "Students could be corrected without being put down." Students were bothered when I raised my voice and intimidated classmates. My first impulse was to rationalize my way out of these accusations and conclude that my actions were necessary at the time. However, after looking at the total results I realized many of the students with criticisms were complimentary in other categories. Finally I reached the conclusion that I needed to work on my methods of dealing with student disturbances and overall self-control.

> **Hot Tip!** *As I gained more experience I realized it was best to not talk about the sport I coached in the classroom. Too many students got the impression that I favored students who participated in that sport. I believe this is true about all activities. Support student participation in general, but be careful about promoting the activity you coach or advise.*

I made a pledge to keep football talk on the field and be particularly cognizant about the perception that " athletes were being favored."

Build on Your Strengths

Just as my shortcomings were revealed, I also saw positive ratings in knowledge, interest, enthusiasm and overall effectiveness. One of the most difficult things for an educator is determining whether or not students are grasping what is being taught, whether their minds are being stimulated and if they are enjoying learning. Tests and administrative observations can do some of this, but the students have the most insight. Students felt they benefited most when they actively participated in the learning process. Brief, (15-20 minute) dynamic lectures incorporating humor and stories were well received, but anything longer was considered a turn off. Because of the teacher evaluation form completed by students and devotion to the principles of peak performance, I know I improved as an educator. I ended my career a much better teacher than I began.

Peak Performance in all Activities

In his book *Seven Habits of Highly Effective People,* Stephen Covey stresses to "Be Proactive" and to "Begin with the End in Mind." Regardless of the activity a person must focus on the desired result. Remember that, "Teaching is coaching and coaching is teaching." The same peak performance principles so important in the classroom also apply in extracurricular activities. Consider your favorite school activity, and notice how this checklist - with an emphasis on mental preparation - is universally applicable. I've used this activity at numerous leadership and peak performance workshops for students. It is reproduced in the appendix on page 197.

The Mental Game: Training Your Mind for Peak Performance

To maximize your performance in any activity you must win the mental game. Rank yourself from 1 (low) to 5 (high) in each of the qualities below to determine your strengths and areas for improvement.

_____ 1. **Peak Performers Set Goals.** They have the ability to break their dreams down into small manageable parts and are able to work on them on a daily, weekly and monthly basis. Peak performers have precise objectives in mind and always keep their eyes on the prize.

_____ 2. **Peak Performers Practice Mental Rehearsal.** Mental rehearsal is often called the "master skill" because the development of many other skills depends on the ability of the individual to picture being successful at the desired task. Mental rehearsal means focusing on a goal to the point where the individual actually practices the activity in his or her mind. Research has determined the mind does not distinguish between real and imagined experiences.

_____ 3. **Peak Performers Practice With A Purpose.** Every practice session is viewed as an opportunity for personal improvement. Peak performers truly believe positive preparation and practice means perfect performance. They always practice with a purpose and never just to get it over.

_____ 4. **Peak Performers Strive For Excellence.** They believe they are capable of bettering their previous performance. Peak performers are capable of evaluating their accomplishments and determining how they can improve. As they push themselves to new levels they have the ability to relax and stay "in the zone."

_____ 5. **Peak Performers Are Confident.** They have the ability to rise above fear, worry, doubt and anger, and concentrate on controlling the emotions that will help them accomplish their task. They thrive on pressure situations because through the practice of mental rehearsal they have been there before.

_____ 6. **Peak Performers Take Educated Risks.** This means they are not being foolhardy or reckless, but accept the challenge and possibility of failure that is necessary for achievement to take place. They focus on success and know that in order to rise to their full potential, perseverance is essential.

_____ 7. **Peak Performers Are Team Players.** They are unselfish in team situations and are willing to play a lesser role to bring out the best in the team. When working with others peak performers demand the same type of commitment from team members and will encourage others to elevate their level of achievement. In the ideal team setting peak performers give support to others and receive it themselves.

_____ 8. **Peak Performers Focus On The Present.** Whether in sports, music or drama they have the ability to learn from, but rise above past mistakes and concentrate on the task at hand. While they tend to be perfectionists they are tolerant of error to the point where they will not allow previous flaws or setbacks to hinder future performance.

_____ 9. **Peak Performers Are Positive Thinkers.** They see what can be done and communicate in a manner that conveys belief. Peak Performers understand that thoughts control feelings, feelings control actions and actions become habits that influence attitudes and determine behavior. True believers control their minds to think constructive thoughts and visualize success.

_____ **10. Peak Performers Have Little Need For Outside Praise Or Recognition.** Since they are internally motivated and driven by the desire to excel, peak performers often give credit to others. Of course they appreciate a pat on the back, but they derive a great deal of satisfaction and fulfillment from their accomplishments.

Let's reflect on Conklin's quote from the beginning of the chapter, *"To the degree you give others what they need, they will give you what you need."* When this statement is applied to relationships in our daily life, we become much more action oriented. Peak performers treat others in a manner that brings out their best.

- When the principal gives praise and recognition, the teacher will put forth extra effort.
- When the teacher provides students with opportunities to demonstrate responsibility, they become more responsible.
- When the teacher is excited about teaching, the students are more enthused about learning.
- When the teacher shows care and concern for other educators, they demonstrate care and concern in return.
- When parents express confidence in their children's ability, the children improve their performance.
- When the coach provides the team with consistent, positive leadership, the team responds with extra effort and improved unity.
- When the husband treats his wife with more affection, she becomes more affectionate.

It Works!

That's the way it works. *You help provide others with what they need and they in turn do what they can for you.* After sharing this principle with others, criticisms have surfaced. Most common are the claims of "manipulation" and unreasonable expectations. That simply is not true. You don't do things for others because you expect reciprocation; you do it because it is the right thing to do. On occasion the person or group may be too immature to accept the show of confidence and respect, but in the long run it is an excellent practice to follow in assisting others to rise to the level you expect of them. The peak performer is an insightful educator who has the confidence and skills to monitor the response and adjust in the appropriate manner.

Persistence

On occasion I will be asked to speak at a school where the students have a "terrible attitude" or where the sports teams have experienced little success. Often when speaking with the coach or coaches I discover they don't believe in the ability of their students to compete with other schools in the conference. The peak performer doesn't complain; he or she takes action. During the early years we had a similar problem at Seymour.

Peak performers are willing to take risks. Even though I didn't realize it at the time, our summer in Seymour prior to the first football season was full of risk. Since the team was usually short of players I decided to get a list of all boys from grades nine through twelve who were potential football players. I then obtained a district map and spent a couple weeks speaking with parents attempting to convince them to encourage their sons to participate in football. I assumed parents would want their children to participate because of the many benefits involved. In my journey around the district I was met with much resistance and it was painful. Risking rejection and blows to my self-esteem, I persisted in spite of comments such as these:

"Why should he waste his time with football?"

"Seymour just can't compete with the city schools!"

"How are you going to make a difference?"

It was a real learning experience to hear all the excuses why Seymour would never be able to field a winning team. Without belief and persistence I would have given up. A lot of self-doubt entered in and at times I questioned whether our family should stay in Seymour. Fortunately a number of positive people in the community and several at school encouraged me to persevere.

The Perils of Recruiting

Imagine the impression when the new football coach drove into the farmer's driveway and several yelping and growling dogs were jumping on the car. Invariably someone came out on the porch and yelled, "It's OK they won't bite." Having been bitten several times as a child, I never got out of the car until the dogs were secured. In fact, a few years later I gave a student a ride home from a powerlifting meet and as we entered the driveway he cautioned me to not stop. He said, "Just slow down and I will jump out." When I asked why he replied, "Our dog likes to chew on tires and if you stop he will bite a hole in the tire." It was then that I realized how wise I was a couple years earlier to not play the role of the macho football coach and subject myself to those curious canines.

It's All About Teamwork

Whether you are coaching, teaching, or advising a club or organization, find the persistence and courage to stand up for what you believe in. If you don't believe, the students won't believe. But, be sure to exercise good judgment and consider the consequences of moving too fast! Identify people who feel similar to you and get them onboard. It is all about teamwork! Use the "Peak Performance Appraisal" and "Mental Game" activities to assist you and your students in performing at full potential.

"There is little difference in people, but that little difference makes a big difference. The little difference is attitude. The big difference is whether it is positive or negative."
W. Clement Stone

A Look Back - Peak Performance in Action

Ultimately students will enter the world of work. Part of the purpose of the educational system is to help young people discover their gifts so they take up a rewarding career. On occasion when I speak, someone from the audience will approach me and say he or she was a former student of mine. It is fun to follow up and determine what they remember most from history class. Invariably

"If you have knowledge, let others light their candles in it."
Margaret Fuller

the response has something to do with the type of work they are currently doing. Here are a few examples:

- *A major news anchor on television first appeared on classroom TV in a program for a history project.*

- *A graphic artist who received national recognition demonstrated his talents numerous times in history projects.*
- *Many former students who are teachers had the opportunity to lead the class or teach a particular concept during high school history class.*
- *An attorney played the role of a trial lawyer during a reenactment in history class.*
- *The personal qualities necessary to cooperate in a classroom setting are vital in the work place.*

The list could go on and on including examples of how quality educators provide students with real–life experiences that apply to their futures. One of the greatest rewards of teaching is to witness students performing at a high level doing something they enjoy.

 Since most people struggle when they are called upon to speak in public, I felt it was important to have everyone experience speaking into the microphone in the auditorium in front of a double class of students. Fortunately the teacher with whom I team taught American Studies shared my beliefs. Sometime in their life almost everyone will use a microphone to address a group of people. The probability of success is much greater after having a previous speaking experience. We told the students, "The microphone is your friend, and it is there to help you. Use it!" The same thing may be said about math skills, reading, writing, personal finance, science, etc. Organize your class in a manner that helps teach life long lessons and provides your students with the opportunity to experience personal growth on the way to peak performance.

Hot Tip! *For a quick self-evaluation complete the Teacher's Semester Exam on page 203 in the appendix. Coaches and advisors will find the exercise on page 188 to be meaningful.*

My Personal Commitment to Peak Performance
(Check the items that apply to you.)

☐ *I accept the fact that I have the ability to improve and perform at a higher level.*

☐ *I periodically review the success formula and implement it in my classroom.*

☐ *I make the commitment to be an excellent role model for students.*

☐ *I understand the characteristics of peak performers.*

☐ *I have devised a method to obtain meaningful feedback from my students.*

☐ *I engage in self-evaluation and use the peak performance principles for improvement.*

☐ *I build on my strengths to improve on my weaknesses.*

☐ *I comprehend the "Mental Game" and train my mind for peak performance.*

☐ *I have launched a personal program for peak performance.*

☐ *I am persistent in everything I do.*

The Art of Classroom Leadership

Chapter 2

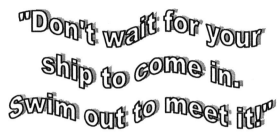

Captain your own ship!

➢ **"Don't judge each day by the harvest you reap, but by the seeds you plant."**
    Robert Louis Stevenson

➢ **"Most of us end up with no more than five or six people who remember us. Teachers have thousands of people who remember them for the rest of their lives."**
    Andy Rooney

➢ **"I would be disappointed if I were remembered as a runner because I feel that my contribution to the youth of America has far exceeded the woman who was the Olympic champion."**
    Wilma Rudolph

Objectives
- To define leadership
- To explain proven strategies for effective classroom leadership
- To provide methods for leadership development
- To identify what great leaders have said about leadership

The Art of Classroom Leadership

"A leader is one who knows the way, goes the way, and shows the way."
John C. Maxwell

A discussion of leadership with educators implies a discussion of the school's administration and how decisions are made. In reality every person in the school must possess some leadership ability. Too many people are willing to follow traditional beliefs and standards without questioning why the policy exists. However, "Getting along by going along," is no longer acceptable. Modern leadership thinking invokes the principle that people support what they create. All teachers must accept the challenge of leadership and be positive role models for students in and out of the classroom.

Leadership is everyone's responsibility. It is the behavior each of us exhibits when we take responsibility for our actions and their consequences. It is the voice within us that calls out and says, "Take charge!" Most important, it's what we do to make a positive difference in our lives and the lives of others.

"I'm not a leader. I'm better at following orders."

"It's not my problem. There is nothing I can do about it."

"Leaders are born, not made."

"I just do what I'm told."

Have you ever heard these? Have you said any of them yourself? You're not alone. It seems as if everyone has something to say about leadership – even if what they're saying is based on misunderstanding and misconception.

Sometimes we accept ideas as facts and let them rule our hearts and behaviors without taking the time to really think about them. This is unfortunate and may lead to the inappropriate application of leadership principles. A true leader brings out the best in others. A principal inspires colleagues, teachers, students, paraprofessionals and support personnel. An effective teacher inspires colleagues, the principal, students, paraprofessionals and support staff.

What is Leadership?

Literally hundreds of books have been written about leadership, and each offers its own definition. A personal favorite is Max DePree's explanation in his highly regarded book *Leadership Is An Art*. Leadership, DePree says, is "Liberating people to do what is required of them in the most effective and humane way possible." Thus, the leader is the "servant" of his followers in that he or she removes the obstacles that prevent them from doing their jobs. In short, the true leader enables his or her followers to realize their full potential. Based on this definition, an administrator should liberate teachers so they may utilize their personal gifts to maximize their potential in leading students.

Teachers in turn will provide unique opportunities for students to excel by challenging them to transcend previous levels of accomplishment. Through motivation and inspiration, expectations will be raised until the bar is set at a new height for each student. This results in a win, win, for all school personnel and students.

- ☑ *Without leadership, we are lost.*
- ☑ *Leaders are made not born.*
- ☑ *Leadership skill can be developed.*
- ☑ *Leadership is often the difference between success and failure.*
- ☑ *Leadership is everyone's responsibility.*

Why do I need to be a leader?

- What's more important than teaching others so they (and you) will be more successful in empowering all learners to succeed in their world?
- What's more important than following through on your commitment to faculty, staff, and students to provide each learner with the best education possible?
- What's more important than setting a good example for others? This includes administration, faculty, staff, students and parents?
- It's fun and important to be a positive leader!

What makes a good leader?

In order to best understand effective, ethical leadership it is valuable to examine the lives of great leaders and analyze the characteristics they possess. One central theme is they are all skilled at making the lives of those around them better. Honesty and integrity are not negotiable; they are the foundation of positive leadership. In order to lead someone we must first earn his or her trust. In any relationship people will ask three questions:

- ❖ Do you care about me?
- ❖ Can I trust you?
- ❖ Can I count on you?

> **Honesty and Integrity are not negotiable!**

This is especially true in the field of education where teachers have the tremendous responsibility of interacting with young people for the entire school year. During these formative years, teachers often have a significant amount of influence on the character and personality development of their students. We must have a high regard for trust and do everything possible to maintain impeccable professional standards.

"It is not fair to ask of others what you are not willing to do yourself."
Eleanor Roosevelt

"The price of greatness is responsibility."
Winston Churchill

"Example is leadership."
Albert Schweitzer

"If there is no struggle, there is no progress."
Fredrick Douglass

"I don't think much of a man who is not wiser today than he was yesterday"
Abraham Lincoln

Who is the best example of leadership in action?

Of all the impressive leaders in history, many could argue that Abraham Lincoln personifies the concept of leadership. In his book *Lincoln on Leadership*, Donald Phillips describes Lincoln as the ideal leader.

> "He was innovative at a time when the age of discoveries and inventions was just beginning. He was compassionate and caring yet, when necessary, could put his foot down firmly and be decisive beyond question. He was patient, persistent, consistent, and persuasive rather than dictatorial. But, without a doubt, the foundation of Abraham Lincoln's leadership style was an unshakable commitment to the rights of the individual."

Leadership is essential in all educational positions. The characteristics exhibited by Lincoln in keeping the nation together during tumultuous times are applicable to providing effective classroom leadership. To understand and apply these techniques, it is necessary to take a closer look at the man who demonstrated the application of these principles with positive results. Phillips identified fifteen strategies utilized by Lincoln to maintain stability during challenging times.

Lincoln on Leadership: Fifteen Proven Strategies For Effective Leadership (Based on the book *Lincoln On Leadership* by Donald Phillips)

1. Get out of the office and circulate among the troops.
❖ Lincoln spent 75% of his time meeting with people.
Educational application – Demonstrate interest in students outside the classroom.

2. Build strong alliances.
❖ "Á house divided against itself cannot stand."
Educational application – Maintain a great working relationship with your colleagues.

> "Upon the subject of education . . . I can only say that I view it as the most important subject which we as a people may be engaged in."
>
> *Abraham Lincoln*

3. Persuade rather than coerce.
❖ Lincoln knew the value of making requests as opposed to issuing orders.
Educational application – Continually work toward developing excellent communication skills.

4. Honesty and integrity are the best policies.
> ❖ "Honest Abe." Divorced from ethics, leadership is reduced to management.
>
> *Educational application – Always maintain your professionalism.*

> "*You may fool all of the people some of the time; you can even fool some of the people all of the time; but you can't fool all of the people all the time.*"
> *A. Lincoln*

5. Never act out of vengeance or spite.
> ❖ "With malice toward none; with charity for all."
>
> *Educational application – Pardon mistakes and begin each day with a fresh outlook.*

6. Have the courage to handle unjust criticism.
> ❖ "Grace under pressure" defines courage. Lincoln stayed focused on success.
>
> *Educational application – Have a plan to deal with criticism.*

7. Be a master of paradox.
> ❖ He was consistent yet flexible, compassionate yet tough.
>
> *Educational application – Demand and earn respect while being sensitive to student needs.*

8. Exercise a strong hand; be decisive.
> ❖ Lincoln had the ability to make tough decisions.
>
> *Educational application – Take personal responsibility for your classroom decisions.*

9. Lead by being led.
> ❖ When a subordinate did a good job, Lincoln praised and rewarded the individual.
>
> *Educational application – Give credit to students and colleagues to recognize excellence.*

10. Set goals and be results-oriented.
> ❖ Leaders in general are self-starting and change oriented.
>
> *Educational application – Goals will help motivate your students and focus their talents.*

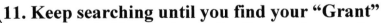

11. Keep searching until you find your "Grant"
> ❖ Lincoln chose subordinates who craved responsibility and took risks.
>
> *Educational application – Identify classroom leaders and utilize their skills.*

12. Encourage innovation.
> ❖ Genuine leaders are not only instruments of change, but catalysts for change.
>
> *Educational application – Constantly be in search of the most effective ways to educate.*

13. Master the art of public speaking.
> ❖ Lincoln was a speaker who had the capacity to raise the emotions of his audience.
>
> *Educational application – Refine your communication skills to reach all learners.*

14. Influence people through conversation and storytelling.
> ❖ Lincoln is regarded to be the best humorist of all Presidents.
>
> *Educational application – Research indicates humor aids learning retention and improves classroom climate.*

15. Preach a vision and continually reaffirm it.

❖ Lincoln kept reaffirming his vision to maintain his belief and enthusiasm.
Educational application – Establish classroom goals and continually work to achieve them.

What happens when leadership is absent?

When there is no classroom leadership...

☑ Nobody listens. Nobody pays attention. Students stop doing quality work.
☑ Teamwork breaks down.
☑ Classroom management disintegrates.
☑ Students pick on each other.
☑ Student and parents become unhappy.
☑ Teaching becomes hard work.
☑ Learning is minimized.
☑ Teacher frustration is common.

The teacher's commitment to effective leadership is tested every day. We must be sensitive and understanding, yet firm when necessary. We must be organized and efficient, yet flexible and patient. We must be creative and innovative, yet standards oriented. We must master the subjects we teach, yet realize each student is unique and will require individual attention. Classroom leaders are life long learners who practice the five "A's" of leadership.

The five "A's" of Classroom Leadership
(Used with permission from Robert Hammond, Dist. Supt. Sycamore, IL)

Approachable – Listen to what others have to say. Make yourself accessible to students and parents and invite them to discuss what is on their mind.

Accepting – Keep an open mind. Great ideas may come from everyone – students, secretaries, parents, teachers and administrators.

Acknowledging – Recognize the contributions of others. Give praise when appropriate and thank others for their cooperation.

Accountable – Be responsible for yourself and your students.

Adaptable – Change is a challenge. Constantly reassess your classroom management procedure and your teaching methods.

Always: *Believe in yourself and your ability to influence students!*

What ineffective leaders have to say . . .

"Because I said so!"

"Of course I want you to take risks. Just don't make any mistakes!"

"Don't blame me. It wasn't my idea."

"If I wanted your opinion, I would have asked for it."

"Can't you do anything right?"

"It's my way or the highway!"

"I don't make the decisions, I just follow orders."

"Why can't you be like everyone else?"

"Just shut up and listen."

"Maybe I said that yesterday, but this is today."

If you have the urge to say any of these ----- Fight the Feeling!

Classroom leadership and classroom management

Classroom leadership means setting a positive example for students and influencing them to cooperate to build the best possible conditions for learning. Management is an organizational style in which the teacher determines classroom behavior and the students follow policy or suffer the consequences. Leaders bring out the best in their students by gaining trust through effective communication and mutual respect. The master teachers possess the skills of leadership and management and know when to employ each. Management skills are much easier to learn and are often associated with keeping order. Leadership skills take time to develop and are gained through experience. Much has been written about leadership styles ranging from teacher-centered to student centered. A teacher is most effective as a leader when he or she has the ability to adjust leadership style to best fit the situation.

How do you measure up as a leader?

President Kennedy said, "Leadership and learning are indispensable to each other." In discussions with teachers about their leadership roles I often hear the comment, "I just follow orders." This dodge of responsibility excludes input from those who have the most interaction with students. Teachers must take an active role in school decision-making and then support established policies by the way their classrooms are organized. The following check list provides educators with the opportunity to determine their capacity for leadership. It is also in the appendix on page 186.

Determine Your Leadership Potential

Common Characteristics of Leaders - Bill Collar "All The Way With PMA!"

> **Instructions:** Respond to each item by placing an (X) in the space that best expresses how the statement describes you. If the statement is not like you at all, check space number one. If it fits perfectly, check space five. The spaces in between allow you to indicate various degrees of fit. If you are torn between feeling it does or does not apply, check space number three, the halfway mark.

Unlike Me   **Like Me**

1   2   3   4   5

___ ___ ___ ___ ___   **1. Goals** - I am a goal setter. I have a strong sense of purpose and know where I am going with my life. I have written goals.

___ ___ ___ ___ ___   **2. Positive Mental Attitude** - I possess a high degree of confidence and self-worth. I approach every new day with positive expectancy.

___ ___ ___ ___ ___   **3. Persistence** - I have the ability to bounce back from failure. I view failure as a learning experience rather than a setback.

___ ___ ___ ___ ___   **4. Risk Taker** - I am willing to attempt new tasks and welcome a positive challenge even if I am not certain of success.

___ ___ ___ ___ ___   **5. Decision Maker** - I understand the decision-making process. Making decisions usually comes easy for me.

___ ___ ___ ___ ___   **6. Courage** - I am able to take a firm stand even when my position is not real popular. I am in charge of my life.

___ ___ ___ ___ ___   **7. Seek New Learning** - I find it rewarding to acquire new skills and information. I plan to be a life-long learner.

___ ___ ___ ___ ___   **8. Enthusiasm** - I get excited about projects I believe in and possess a great deal of energy to complete them.

___ ___ ___ ___ ___   **9. Focus On Success** - I can accept constructive criticism and value the opinions of people I respect.

___ ___ ___ ___ ___   **10. Seek To Serve Others** - I am able to work with other people and find teamwork enjoyable.

___ ___ ___ ___ ___   **11. Sense of Humor** - I realize the importance of humor and am able to laugh at myself.

___ ___ ___ ___ ___   **12. Integrity** - I take pride in being truthful and in keeping my word.

___ ___ ___ ___ ___   **13. Communication** – I am effective in expressing my thoughts to others in a clear, concise manner. I am an active listener and show interest in what is said.

___ ___ ___ ___ ___   **14. Initiative** – I am a self-starter.

_____ -----My Score

Scoring: Add up your total points to determine how prepared you are to be a positive leader. The following scale will give you some idea of your leadership potential at this time.

60 – 70 Outstanding leadership potential! You are ready to take on major tasks.

50 – 59 An impressive score! You possess the key characteristics of leadership.

40 – 49 Improve in several categories and you will become an excellent leader!

30 – 39 Much potential exists. Keep working on a self-improvement plan.

Below 29 – It is up to you to alter your attitude and lifestyle to develop more leadership ability.

How were these characteristics determined?

During my 35-year career, I noticed significant leaders throughout history shared certain common characteristics. These 14 appeared most often. While it would be the exception for any leader to be highly skilled in all categories, the ideal person, such as Lincoln, ranks high in most. Leadership is a learned skill and can be refined through striving to acquire the characteristics possessed by the greatest leaders in history. However, as Mayor Giuliani stated in his book *Leadership,* a degree of altruistic motivation must exist in order for positive leadership to take place.

> *"Good people act from a combination of altruism and self-interest. The altruistic part comes from the feeling that you are helping people, that your talents are being used to do good. There's an exhilaration in doing something important, which other people pay attention to and respect."*
> *Rudolph W. Giuliani*

Consider these explanations of the leadership characteristics:

Goals – Advance planning provides us with purpose and direction. Ben Franklin said, "Going through life without a goal is like shooting without a target." What would have happened to the space program if President Kennedy hadn't challenged our nation to "Put a man on the moon by the end of the decade?" Research says less than three per cent of adults actually find the time to make written goals. Putting a goal in writing and establishing a deadline for completion cause a person to take action.

Positive Mental Attitude – It is absolutely essential to believe in yourself and maintain a positive attitude. If you don't believe in yourself, who will? When Mac Arthur left the Philippines in 1942 he said, "I shall return." What if he had said, "I'll try to return"? Positive, affirmative language helps build belief; belief is the foundation to motivation.

Persistence – The greatest people in history are those who have failed most often. People are not measured by how seldom they fail, but by how often they rise again after failure. Susan B. Anthony, after working 50 years to get women the right to vote, on her deathbed, said to the women gathered around her, "Failure is impossible. The struggle must continue." What great things we can accomplish when we truly believe failure is impossible.

Risk Taker – Every time we do something that we are not certain we will succeed at doing, we experience personal growth. It is easy to get in a rut in the classroom and do things the way we have always done them. If we do what we have always done, we will get what we have always gotten. Make an effort to transcend previous levels of accomplishment. At a time when few newspapers hired women reporters, Edna Ferber accepted the challenge. Her words are worthy of consideration: "A closed mind is a dying mind."

Decision Maker – In order to get things done a person must make decisions. In your classroom you are the individual everyone is expecting to make correct choices. Elizabeth Cady Stanton made the decision to organize the first women's rights convention in 1848. At that time she called for the vote and equal opportunities for all women. An important part of decision-making is accepting personal responsibility for the action taken. As Stanton said, "Nothing strengthens the judgment and quickens the conscience like individual responsibility."

Courage – Without the courage to act on our beliefs, all other characteristics are meaningless. Courage may be defined as overcoming fear. Fear tends to paralyze a person and prevent one from taking action. The effective educator must have enough personal conviction and belief to take action when necessary. With one third of the nation ill clad, ill fed and ill housed, Franklin Roosevelt had the courage to say, "Our nation will endure as it has endured, it will revive and it will prosper… the only thing we have to fear is fear itself."

 Seek New Learning – "The most extraordinary thing about a really good teacher is that he or she transcends accepted educational methods." This statement by Margaret Mead remains true. What one learns after the start of teaching is what really counts. A true professional engages in a constant search for more knowledge, both in the subject area as well as in innovative educational practices. It is vital to take classes, attend workshops and join professional organizations.

Enthusiasm – When the teacher is excited about the content and has a zest for facilitating learning, the student will be enthused about learning. Attitudes are contagious, and the classroom climate is dictated by the passion exhibited by the instructor. Emerson said, "Nothing great was ever accomplished without enthusiasm." The art of teaching includes stimulating a joy in learning through creative expression and classroom interaction. Setting an enthusiastic example opens the door to educational excellence.

 Focus On Success – Through visualization of the end result, a person can be influenced to expect success. Helen Keller was deaf and blind, but with the assistance of Anne Sullivan she was recognized as deep thinker and social reformer. She refused to see barriers, only hurdles. Keller encouraged others to, "Keep your face to the sunshine and you cannot see the shadows. Life can be a daring adventure or nothing." Practice mental rehearsal to see yourself being successful.

Seek To Serve Others – This is a given in education. Most educators are in the field because of a desire to make a difference in the lives of youth. Teachers make the commitment to reach every student. The goal has <u>always</u> been to, "Leave no child behind." Booker T. Washington, a man who devoted his career to improving the quality of life for others declared, "The world cares very little about what a person knows. It's what the person does that counts."

 Sense Of Humor – When humor is added to the classroom, students pay better attention, remember more, and have more fun. Leaders throughout history utilized humor either to make a point or loosen up a tense situation. Lincoln was a skilled storyteller, Churchill a master of mirth, and Reagan was a competent comedian. When asked what was wrong with Soviet agriculture, Reagan replied, "Just four things, spring, summer, winter and fall."

Integrity – Classroom relationships are built on trust. Trust comes from maintaining a high degree of integrity. It takes a lifetime to build a reputation, one incident can destroy it. Professional educators are counted on to maintain confidentiality and be honest in their relationships with others. John Wooden, the legendary basketball coach at UCLA, established his Pyramid of Success to promote winning on and off the court. His philosophy may be summed up by his famous quote: "Be more concerned with your character than your reputation because your character is what you really are, while your reputation is merely what others think you are."

Communication – Even though he had to work hard to overcome stuttering and lisping problems, Winston Churchill is recognized as one of the best speakers of all time. When almost all of Europe had fallen to Nazi Germany, Churchill spoke with confidence: "We shall fight on the beaches, we shall fight on the landing grounds, we shall fight in the streets, we shall fight in the hills, we shall never surrender." Never surrender in the classroom; never give up on your ability to communicate with all students. Effective communication transforms classroom management to classroom leadership.

Initiative – Throughout her life Sandra Day O'Connor was a self-starter. In a field dominated by men, she rose to the highest level possible, that of Supreme Court Justice. Her work ethic is reflected in the statement, "I don't know that there are any short cuts to doing a good job." As a teacher you must have an indefatigable sense of drive.

Three of the most important words in leadership are Communicate – Communicate – and – Communicate!

"Kind words can be short and easy to speak, but their echoes are endless."
Mother Teresa.

Signs of a leader in trouble!

- ❑ **Lacks imagination.**
- ❑ **Has personal problems.**
- ❑ **Lacks organization.**
- ❑ **Loses composure.**
- ❑ **Unwilling to take risks.**
- ❑ **Is inflexible.**
- ❑ **Resists change.**

- ❑ **Has poor understanding of people.**
- ❑ **Is insecure.**
- ❑ **Is overly defensive.**
- ❑ **Is a chronic complainer.**
- ❑ **Loses temper.**
- ❑ **Has poor time management.**
- ❑ **Lacks teamwork skills.**

Excellent leaders understand basic human needs!

Paul "Bear" Bryant, the outstanding football coach at the University of Alabama, said there are five things winning team members need to know. These are also important for the classroom leader to understand about students.

*S*tudents must know what is expected of them. This will be clearly explained the first day of class.

*S*tudents must understand that each will be given the opportunity to be successful.

*S*tudents must be kept informed of their progress.

*S*tudents must be aware they will get assistance as needed.

*S*tudents must know they will be rewarded consistent with their performance.

When teachers accept the role of being a leader in the classroom, they influence their students to become more responsible for their performance. Leadership is influence, and the teacher is the role model. Just as a ball rebounds from the wall with the same force with which it was thrown, the attitude of the educator determines the attitude of the student. You get from students what you give to them. **Now is the time to accept the challenge of leadership and make a difference every day!**

> *"Leadership: The art of getting someone else to do something you want done because he wants to do it."*
> *Dwight D. Eisenhower*

A Look Back - Classroom Leadership in Action

Making U.S. History meaningful and maintaining student interest were major challenges. The most difficult thing to accept was when students would just memorize facts for tests without really comprehending the significance of historical events. This bothered me to the point where I completely reassessed the way I was teaching. After a few years, in order to pick up student interest, I decided to teach history in reverse chronological order. We started with a two-week unit on the future. By studying what the top futurists were saying the students felt history class had more significance. It was also a frustration when I taught the typical survey class of history, and had to rush through the last fifty years, which were the most interesting to students.

After modifying the sequential approach, it still bothered me that in American literature students were reading great works of literature, but not in coordination with when that period was being studied in history class. With cooperation from an innovative English teacher, we managed to combine the classes in a semi-block manner and coordinate the teaching of history and literature.

> *"Keep away from people who try to belittle your ambitions. Small people always do that, but the really great make you feel that you, too, can become great."*
> *Mark Twain*

It made much more sense to the students that when we were studying the 1920's in history they were reading *The Great Gatsby*, and when they were reading *The Grapes of*

26

Wrath, we were studying the 1930's. As teachers we weren't happy with traditional tests and moved toward performance activities. Students were provided with options from which to choose.

Keeping in mind multiple intelligences, a typical unit from the 1920's would include ten to fifteen groups of four performing on the stage. One group might act out a scene from *The Great Gatsby*, another dance the Charleston, another participate in a fashion show, and yet another play a musical selection or choose from a variety of other activities. It was exciting to see students use their creative talents in art, music, drama, speaking, writing and producing.

Through positive classroom leadership from the teachers, the students were provided with the freedom and flexibility to participate in history rather than just memorize it. Of course it takes teamwork and communication on behalf of the teachers. One must be receptive to the ideas of the other teacher and sensitive enough to realize all needs must be met. In our case synergy took place, and the both teachers benefited as well as the students.

💣 ***Hot Tip!*** *It takes awhile to see yourself as an effective leader. Even though you may have taught classes for years, perhaps you have relied on others to make the tough decisions. To help build your confidence as a leader, volunteer for tasks that are somewhat out of character for you. These may include chairing a committee or speaking in front of a group.*

My Personal Commitment to Positive Leadership
(Check the items that apply to you.)

☐ *I accept the responsibility of positive classroom leadership.*

☐ *I realize I have the ability to inspire others.*

☐ *I'm aware leadership can be developed and I work toward being a better leader daily.*

☐ *I study the lives of effective leaders to better understand the principles of leadership.*

☐ *I evaluate my leadership style and identify my strengths and areas for improvement.*

☐ *I approach each leadership role with the expectation of success.*

☐ *I maintain a persistent and determined attitude in spite of temporary setbacks.*

☐ *I inform students of my expectations to keep open clear lines of communication.*

☐ *I have a plan to sharpen my leadership skills.*

☐ *I provide students with the opportunity for leadership in the classroom.*

Clear and Concise Communication

Chapter 3

"Victory has many fathers; defeat is an orphan."
JFK

➤ "Communication is a skill that you can learn. It's like riding a bicycle or typing. If you're willing to work at it, you can rapidly improve the quality of every part of your life."

Brian Tracy

➤ "As I grow older, I pay less attention to what men say. I just watch what they do."

Andrew Carnegie

➤ "I think that education is power. Communicating with people is power. One of my main goals is to encourage people to empower themselves."

Oprah Winfrey

Objectives

- To explain the importance of communicating with students and parents
- To illustrate the value of positive self-talk
- To establish a system to follow for proactive parent conferences
- To emphasize the importance of good listening skills

Communication Begins With Listening

"When people talk, listen completely. Most people never listen."
Ernest Hemingway

When the word communication is used, many people think of speaking, but the true communicators know listening is extremely important. Have you ever known someone who is an excellent listener, someone you enjoy conversing with because he or she is an "active listener," responding with thoughtful nods and verbal confirmations so you know what you're saying is not only being heard, but also comprehended? My spouse, Holly, is a master of the art of listening. Unfortunately, I don't always reciprocate, but I'm working at improvement. Friends love to get together with Holly for breakfast, lunch, book group, shopping or a social outing because she is "so easy to talk with." I have witnessed her in action on numerous occasions and what they really mean is "she is such a good listener." Holly serves as a model of good listening.

> **Listening is a skill that must be worked on daily.**

Focus on the Speaker

Holly has a knack of focusing on what is being said and has all the proper body language-- forward lean, eye contact, inviting gestures and a warm smile. I once facetiously suggested she start a business, "Talk to Holly," and charge a fee for folks to stop by and share their thoughts with her. Perhaps what people find so inviting is her non-judgmental nature and her absolute confidentiality. Holly has the ability to listen with her eyes and her heart and is a master of empathy. Even though she no longer teaches school, she is extremely effective in her most important teacher role, that of a mother and grandmother. In happy, nurturing families, members communicate effectively and listen with interest to what others say. Holly has mastered the art of treating the speaker with respect and patience and will draw out the best in an individual. As educators, we must learn from those individuals who make us feel comfortable and strive to implement the techniques they demonstrate.

> **Listen with your eyes!**

Listening Skills

In the late 1960's and early 70's, I was the Assistant Director of Housing at UW-La Crosse. The Vietnam conflict was heating up, and it was a tumultuous time on college campuses. A movement was taking place in which students were not only protesting the war, but were demanding more freedom on campus and in the residence halls. Sometimes I refer to these four years as my term as "Assistant Director of Wildlife Management." The Director of Housing and the Assistant Dean of Men were individuals who possessed excellent communication skills. In many ways they were my mentors. To help keep the lid on the boiling pot of student unrest, they would hold "rap sessions" in the lower levels of the residence halls. These meetings were well attended by students, some who had little interest in school, but enjoyed the security of their 2-S deferment.

For the first dozen or so meetings, I was instructed to just observe and not say much. That was difficult for me to do, as I was shocked at the disrespect some of the students displayed toward people I admired. In fact I couldn't understand why the university officials didn't give the students a piece of their minds and establish serious consequences for continued disruptive behavior. Later I was told they were giving the students the opportunity to ventilate, and by keeping calm in the face

of an emotional outburst, they could control a potentially explosive situation. As I reflect from today's perspective, this experience demonstrated the art of listening as a key in effective communication. This made an impression on me and built a foundation that was helpful later in my teaching career.

Communication With Students

I've always felt it is important for people in any profession to understand what is expected of them to be successful. Early in my teaching career I was encouraged by an experienced educator to have clear and concise expectations for my students. With that in mind, I decided to develop a simple check system that could be distributed to all students during the first week of class. The time spent going over the list was well worth it. The form was printed on 4 x 5 card stock and I told the students to use it as a bookmark during the year.

The card was titled **"Twelve Keys to Success in U.S. History."** I told the students this was the formula for success and they should follow it as closely as possible. The card was also beneficial during parent conferences. If a student was experiencing difficulties, my reviewing the success formula with the parent was helpful.

Twelve Keys to Success in U.S. History

1. **PMA** – *Believe in your ability to learn.*
2. **Attendance** – *Always be in class on time.*
3. **Participate** – *Ask questions and volunteer for activities.*
4. **Take Notes** – *Write down essential facts.*
5. **Desire to Learn** – *Constantly be in search of more knowledge.*
6. **Homework** – *Find the time to complete all assignments.*
7. **Respect Others** – *Be a good listener and tolerate individual differences.*
8. **Follow Directions** – *Read instructions carefully.*
9. **Challenge Yourself** – *Work to your full potential.*
10. **Teamwork** – *Cooperate with others on group projects.*
11. **Stay Alert!** – *Eat healthy foods and get plenty of rest.*
12. **Have Fun!** – *Learn to laugh at yourself and with others.*

Follow these hints and you will do your best in U.S. History
----- Mr. Collar -----

Understanding these concepts is so important to success that I devoted an entire period to going over them in more detail. I quickly learned that the list was valueless if I passed it out and never referred to it again Periodically, I asked students how they were doing with the keys for success and we would get the card out and review it. Below is a look at the keys to success in greater detail. Keep in mind this is what was used with juniors. Different grade levels might require some adjustment.

- **Positive Mental Attitude (PMA) – Believe in Your Ability to Learn**

All success in class begins with belief and confidence. Some students expect to perform poorly and will make little effort because they either believe they don't like the subject, the teacher, or themselves. That presents a good time to discuss the value of different learning styles and various interests. Assure the students you are eager to know more about them and you are

> *"Personally, I'm always ready to learn, although I do not always like being taught."*
> *Winston Churchill*

excited to have them learn more about the subject. It is also beneficial to point out how the knowledge obtained in class will help them later on in life. I like to compare the classroom to the world of work and inform students of the research that has been done with regard to success in the workplace. When learning has meaning for them motivation is increased.

- **Attendance – Always be in Class on Time**

Stress the value of getting started on time and point out how important it is to accomplish as much as possible during each class period. Speak in an affirmative tone when stating "We will always start right after the tone. It is your responsibility to yourself, to the class and to the teacher, to be in the classroom when the tone sounds. We need your help on this." I would also state, "If you must be late, for some very good reason, just come in and sit down and pick up where the class is. You will not be asked where you have been. It is your responsibility to see me after class and explain the situation."

> *"Time is like money. Spend it wisely."*
> *Benjamin Franklin*

Usually students appreciate the trust and it works out well. If anyone has a problem handling the responsibility, speak with that person individually and appeal to his or her sense of decency and cooperation. Often this will work. If not, contacting the parent would be the next step. Very seldom was it necessary to contact the parents regarding a situation where the student failed to cooperate. I don't believe in sending the individual to the office since that indicates communication and trust have broken down. Other teachers may lock the door as the tone sounds. This sends the wrong message and simply creates problems for others. Of course, for my system to be effective, the teacher must be in the room, start class on time and be a good example.

- **Participate – Ask Questions and Volunteer for Activities**

All research indicates retention is enhanced when the learner participates in the learning process. Students must know this and realize the value of participation. As the teacher you must provide a non-threatening environment to guarantee a climate of mutual respect in the classroom. Accentuate the value of interaction with others and how important it is to develop interpersonal skills for success in most walks of life. Make it clear that it is all right to be nervous and concerned about speaking or performing in front of the class. Stress that it is perfectly normal, and you will assist them in preparing to demonstrate their knowledge to others.

- **Take Notes – Write Down Essential Facts**

By the time students become juniors, they should know how to take notes that will assist them in experiencing success on a test. However, this is sometimes an invalid assumption. I found some students thought taking notes meant outlining the book or writing down <u>everything</u> the teacher has on the board. During my second year of teaching, I shared a classroom with a math teacher. He had a habit of not erasing the board when he left the room. I was teaching ninth grade world history and started the class by pointing

> *Find the time to demonstrate how to take notes. This is important at all grade levels.*

to the board saying, "Make sure you get this down in your notebook. It will be on the test." As we proceeded with the class one student was diligently copying the math notes from the blackboard! That experience helped me realize the value of clear, concise, communication. Make sure you find the time to review the fundamentals of proper note taking, and be sure to periodically check for understanding.

- **Desire to Learn – Constantly be in Search of More Knowledge**

People learn better when information is put in the form of a metaphor, analogy or some type of story. I liked to share the story that the human brain is like a huge sponge and the fountain of knowledge is constantly dripping on the sponge. Knowledge will be soaked up, and when needed, simply squeeze the sponge and you will find the data necessary. I explained that at this time in a student's life, one really doesn't know what will be helpful in the future and what will not. It is valuable to build up an eclectic collection of knowledge since that will help provide one with the ability to make better choices. Now here is the rest of the story for the students – Be sure to take the cellophane wrapper off the sponge. In other words, come to class ready to learn. That is the responsibility of the student. I also liked to inform the students that taxpayers invest an average of $50.00 to $60.00 a day per person for their education.

- **Homework – Find the Time to Complete All Assignments**

In recent years some students and parents are under the impression that homework is an imposition on their time and expect that all assignments should be completed at school. This is particularly true at the high school level where jobs are often considered to be more important than schoolwork. It is difficult to comprehend how

> *Their number one job is to do their best in school.*

people feel test scores must improve, but homework should be reduced. Take the time to explain to the students that their number one job is to do their best in school. Teachers must control the amount of homework and make sure it relates to the learning standards being addressed and is not just busy work. Communication between teachers helps guarantee that students won't be burdened with assignments in all classes. Consider providing flexibility with deadlines and inform students several days in advance when major projects are due.

- **Respect Others – Be a Good Listener and Tolerate Individual Differences.**

Research indicates the average person speaks at a rate of 125 words per minute, but can listen to over 500 words a minute. Share these statistics with your class, and stress to them how important it is to focus on what a speaker is saying. This tells the speaker they are interested in what the speaker has to say and helps establish the proper classroom climate for the free exchange of ideas. Review key listening techniques such as patience, eye contact, body language, respect, and asking follow up questions. Encourage class members to withhold judgment and avoid making assumptions about what the other person is going to say. Point out the value of reacting to ideas and not to the person speaking. The difference between hearing and listening is similar to that of a light bulb and a laser beam. They both are light, but one is highly diffused while the other is intense and focused. Focus on the speaker's message. Be a laser beam!

- **Follow Directions – Read Instructions Carefully**

    Many of us remember the teacher who passed out an assignment with lengthy written directions, with the last one being, "Don't complete this assignment. It is a test of your ability to follow directions." The problem of students not following instructions can be addressed properly without the embarrassment of classroom ridicule. Use real life examples to stress the value of following directions. Explain to the students you will make the directions as clear as possible and always check for understanding before they begin a task. Perhaps, ask a student to repeat the directions in his or her own words. This is a good time to impress upon the class that you want them to experience success, and part of preparing to be successful is to understand what is expected on the assignment.

- **Challenge Yourself – Work to Your Full Potential**

    As students mature, they tend to categorize themselves based on previous experiences. Emphasize to the students you are concerned about them setting their goals high and then working to achieve those goals. In many ways life is a self-fulfilling prophecy, and we get what we expect. Encourage the members of your class to glance at the past, but to focus on the future. For years social scientists have told us that most people use less than 25% of their potential. By establishing

    > *"Nobody becomes great without self-doubt. But you must not let it consume you."*
    > *John McKay*

    goals and developing plans to achieve them, people are capable surpassing previous levels of achievement. Students cut themselves short when they allow self-imposed limitations to bottle up their potential.

- **Teamwork – Cooperate With Others on Group Projects**

    In your discussion on the value of teamwork, emphasize the research done on why people are fired from their jobs. Eighty-five per cent of people released are fired not because they lack the skill to complete the task, but because they had difficulty working with others! Some excellent students would rather work alone because they feel it enhances their chance of success. Explain the concept of synergy and multiple intelligences. Students must understand how group work can benefit everyone. To influence the students to believe in teamwork, the teacher must make adjustments in assessment to reward the individuals who are most responsible for the success of the group.

- **Stay Alert – Eat Healthy Foods and Get Plenty of Rest**

    The importance of physical energy and mental alertness is obvious to athletes, combat soldiers, and peak performers in any profession. Yet students come to school without eating breakfast and are sleep deprived. This issue must be addressed. Make sure students understand what is expected of them in your classroom. Sitting with the head down on the desk is unacceptable and won't be tolerated. Encourage everyone to eat breakfast and drink plenty of water

    > *"To keep a lamp burning we have to keep putting oil in it."*
    > *Mother Teresa*

throughout the day. Stress how certain foods tend to help keep us more alert and how foods rich in white sugar lead to lethargy. Other than eating and breathing, sleeping is the most important source of recovery in our lives. Students require eight to nine hours of sleep to be ready for a day of learning.

Physical exercise helps stimulate the body and mind and assist in learning retention. Numerous studies indicate a positive relationship between exercise and the ability to stay alert and concentrate. Peak performance requires us to be physically energized, emotionally stable, mentally focused, and confident in our ability to learn.

- **Have Fun – Learn to Laugh at Yourself and With Others**

Establish plain and succinct guidelines for classroom humor. Be certain students understand what is considered to be appropriate humor for the classroom. At times humorous incidents will take place, and students must feel confident that the class is laughing with them and not at them. The best way to make this clear is for the teacher to be a positive role model. Explain that sarcasm, insults, and finding fault with others is not humor because they are at the expense of another person. Here is a good rule to follow: Anything that hurts someone's feelings is inappropriate. Show the students that you enjoy humor. Have the courage to look silly, sing, dance, or make a comment or two to get the students attention or anchor in a key concept. Also be sure to explain the importance of getting back on task after a humor break. Your physical position in the room can help achieve this. Students will come to understand when you are in certain parts of your room a clear message is being conveyed. For example, students knew when I stood behind the podium and raised my hand they were expected to listen. Chapter 9 examines the use of humor in the classroom.

═══════════════

💣 Hot Tip! *The note card explaining the twelve tips for success served as an effective reminder for the students. Additional visual aids may be posted throughout the room. My classroom was filled with diagrams, charts and illustrations reinforcing the keys for success. Make sure your policies are grade level appropriate. You know what is fitting for your students. For example: Writing names on the board, as a form of classroom management, just doesn't work at the high school level.*

Say What You Mean

While it is important for students to understand what is expected of them, teachers can assist in promoting comprehension through using effective communication techniques. When President Reagan met with Gorbachev he said, "Tear down this wall." He used clear, concise communication to make his point. In 1933 when FDR spoke with the American people in the depth of the Depression he said, "Our nation will endure as it has endured, it will revive and it will prosper…" Both of these statements are examples of positive, affirmative language and represent power statements. What if Reagan would have asked, "What do you think we should do about this wall?" or if FDR would have remarked, "Things look extremely bleak". A slight change in expression can have a dramatic change in meaning. When dealing with students in a situation where you must take control, go

> *"Speak properly, and in as few words as you can, but always plainly; for the goal of speech is not ostentation, but to be understood."*
> *William Penn*

with the power phrase.

At other times you will find it valuable to soften your language. While power phrases are clear, concise, to the point, and targeted at some desired action, phrases that solicit cooperation without an implication of power should be put in the form of a question or request. "I need your help on this," or "Could you help me with this?" are both ways to get cooperation without sounding bossy. It is human nature to respond more positively when one is requested to take action as opposed to being ordered.

Positive Language

It is difficult to motivate someone by using negative language. Always use language that expresses the desired result. In the classroom instead of saying, "Don't copy," the effective teacher says, "Do your own work." Substitute "Could I have your attention please" for "Nobody is paying attention." While this may seem obvious, in many years of working with student teachers, I saw few demonstrate the mastery of positive language.

Negative Statements	Positive Statements
Don't use drugs.	Make good choices.
Don't waste your time.	Make good use of your time.
It's too loud in here.	Quiet down please.
I can't hear you.	Please project your voice.
Don't put your head down on your desk.	Please sit up and pay attention.
Don't lose this paper.	Put this somewhere where it will be safe.

Coaching/Teaching for Success

Effective communication in coaching is a must. Before realizing how improper language can negatively influence an outcome, I often violated that principle. During a critical situation in a football game I called timeout and went into the huddle to set up the winning pass play. After making sure everyone understood his responsibility, I told the quarterback, "Remember it is third down. Don't throw an interception." As the play developed, the receiver  was open, but the quarterback threw it to the opposing linebacker. The last words he had heard me say were, "Throw an interception." Later in my career I learned to say, "Make good decisions" or "Hit the open man."

Positive language makes a tremendous difference especially when the same terminology is used in practice as in the game. Many times during the course of my career we would call a time out and I would say, " Here is what we are going to do" in a positive, affirmative manner, and often that outcome would be the result. Whether you are in the classroom, on the court, the track, the pool, or the field, always express an idea in language that presents a mental picture of the desired outcome. During 25 years as a shot put and discus coach, I often heard opposing coaches say to their throwers, "You're stepping in the bucket," or "You're not following through." Explain to student/athletes what they <u>should</u> be doing, not what they shouldn't be doing. It doesn't make sense to introduce or reinforce negative actions.

 Hot Tip! *The defensive checklist on page 212 is an example of using positive language in coaching.*

Negative Language	Positive Language
Don't drop your head.	Keep your head up.
Don't fumble.	Hang on to the ball.
Don't pull your head away.	See the bat hit the ball.
Don't get overextended.	Keep your feet under you.
Don't run the first lap too fast.	Pace yourself and finish strong.

The Elephant

Think of an elephant, and visualize it in your mind. When you concentrate hard enough, you can actually activate the senses of touch and smell, in particular if you have had the opportunity to touch an elephant. You can feel the rough, pocked hide with stiff bristles and a course texture. The smell of manure may permeate the air, and you can see the sensitive trunk searching the area for morsels of food. The degree to which you have experienced this will determine the detail of your visual image. But wait! Even if you have never seen a live elephant, I guarantee you are visualizing a gray one. Why? Because all the pictures and television images you have seen of elephants are gray. No way would you think of a pink elephant. But what if the second sentence in this paragraph said, "Don't think of a pink elephant." What color would your elephant be? At least for a few seconds, you would see a pink elephant, because that thought was introduced. This is an excellent example to use with students to emphasize the importance of positive self-talk.

Self-Talk

In our communication, we actually talk to ourselves more than anyone else. We are constantly influencing our actions through how we program our sub-conscious mind. Everyday we make a choice as to what type of day we are going to have. Basic psychology tells us we are moved by our dominant thoughts. Be an "I can, I shall and I will" type of person as opposed to an "Ifa, woulda, coulda, shoulda and yeah but" individual. Check page 209 for more on self-talk.

Thoughts ➡ Feelings ➡ Actions ➡ Habits ➡ Attitudes = Behavior!

Influencing Others

It is not enough to just use affirmative language. All educators must make it a point to encourage their students to express themselves in a proactive way. Often when faced with a challenging task, students will respond by saying, "I can't do this." That is a teachable moment. Explain to the student "I can't" means "I can not do this - **ever.**" Correct them to say, "I'm having difficulty," and that means with some guidance they can work their way through the task.

"Try" is another weak word. Don't allow students to use it. Too often when we "try" something, we are already convinced we won't be able to accomplish it. People are not interested in what you are going to try to do. They are more concerned about what you will do. Encouraging a student to do his or her best is much more positive than instructing them "to try."

Building Positive Communication

Eliminate These Phrases	Use These Phrases
I Can't	→ I Can
If	→ I Will
I'll Try	→ I Will Do My Best
I Don't Have The Time	→ I Will Find The Time
I'm Afraid Of	→ I'm Confident

General Douglas MacArthur

Meaningful stories are excellent ways to anchor learning. To highlight the importance of the use of positive language, remind students of General MacArthur's comment when he was forced to leave the Philippines in 1942. In spite of the fact that the Japanese had conquered most of the Pacific, MacArthur left on a positive note proclaiming, "I shall return." What if he had said, "I'll try to return"? His statement certainly loses its impact and meaning with the use of the soft word "try." Make it a point to speak with the end result in mind, and influence your students to do the same.

Be a Positive Role Model

Your actions are your most important tools of communication. Teach who you are first, then what you know. The old saying "Practice what you preach" certainly applies. We are constantly giving students messages through our actions. These actions must be consistent with our expectations of the students. Nothing communicates more eloquently who you are than what you do. When you

> *Nothing communicates more eloquently who you are than what you do.*

show interest in what a student is saying you are affirming that you care about that person as an individual and you demonstrate to them that they are more than just a name in your classroom. Likewise, if you are not in your classroom when the bell rings, you are communicating to students that being on time is not important.

Communicating With Parents

At all grade levels, it is important to know about the student's family and environment. Often young people who experience difficulty conforming to classroom guidelines also have adjustment problems at home. An information card filled out during the first week of class and kept on file provided me with basic facts about the student. Parent conferences are helpful, but sometimes the parents you wish to speak with the most don't attend conferences. Having students write about whether or not they want their own children to grow up in the same situation as they have is an excellent way to learn about their lives. Early in the school year I would take a drive around the district to acquaint myself with where students lived. Students were impressed when I could relate what part of the district they came from. Also, having all the addresses, phone numbers and e-mail addresses on the information card, saved time when I needed to contact the parents.

Teaching juniors was rewarding for many reasons, but seeing the maturation that took place in the nine months they were in the classroom was extremely gratifying. Most of the time when a concern was evident, communication directly with the student was effective since most students were capable of correcting the situation. As stated earlier, contacting parents instead of the student for minor reasons breaks down the trusting student-teacher relationship that is so difficult to establish. The student and I usually managed to work things out. At the lower grades, things are different, and parental involvement may be required much sooner.

Be sure to find the time to communicate with parents when things are going well. Parents will appreciate it and the students will be impressed. I always sent out more letters of commendation than insufficient progress reports. This is a great motivational technique. Seldom did a student slack off because the parent had been informed that he or

> *Communicate with parents about positive experiences.*

she was making good progress. I devoted one or two nights every semester to making positive calls to the parents of students who were doing quality work. With the Internet and e-mail, communication has become more expedient. Take advantage of the opportunity to keep in touch with the parents of your students. They will appreciate it, and the time you invest will pay dividends!

Disagreements

Dr. Phil McGraw has gained national recognition by helping people resolve their conflicts with others. He encourages people to consider the price of being right all the time. When you disagree with someone, do it in a manner that doesn't exacerbate the situation. If you are convinced your position is right, still take the time to listen and consider the other person's point of view. Remember Stephen Covey's philosophy of "win – win." Find a way to work things out in a manner acceptable to both parties. How you react and the type of language you use will play a huge role in either creating understanding or building a wall of permanent disagreement and inability to compromise. Instead of saying, "You're wrong or I disagree" consider:

- That's one perspective; I see it a little differently....

- That may be, but what makes sense to me....

- I think I understand what you are saying; can you elaborate on that for me?

- It looks like we are in agreement on a couple things, but....

Comments such as these give credit to the other person's point of view and are less likely to be offensive.

Show Appreciation and Give Credit to Others

One of the best ways to influence others is to show appreciation for their cooperation or assistance. Periodically when everyone in the classroom is cooperating, pause and tell the class, "I like the way everyone is paying attention," or "It is terrific to see everyone participating." A fundamental axiom of effective teaching is to reinforce the behavior you want repeated. We all learned this, but it is easy to get immersed in the subject matter and neglect the essential motivational devices. Also, anytime you are recognized for achievement, be sure to give credit to others who assisted you in accomplishing

the task. Just as an uncooperative group of students can be a real challenge, a cooperative class or team can rise to levels beyond the expectations of others.

Parent Conferences

I remember vividly my first year of teaching and how nervous I was about meeting with parents. The word around the lounge was, "Don't do what Mr. Arnoldson did last year." He confronted a parent and told him that his son was the worst student he ever had in his years of teaching. An argument ensued which led to shouting and pushing and culminated with the parent delivering a knockout blow to the chin. Obviously a teacher, who is a trained professional, must have a plan to make sure such a hostile atmosphere never develops!

> ●*Hot Tip!* *It can be embarrassing when parents stop by during conferences and you just don't recognize them or you have forgotten their names. Usually you can determine who they are by asking, "Do you have the report card with you?" Most often they will give you the card and you can check the name.*

Parent conferences provide the teacher with an opportunity to obtain more insight into the life of the student. As all experienced teachers know, unfortunately some of the parents you need to speak with the most don't attend. This can be especially true at the junior and senior level where some of the parents have the attitude that they have done everything possible up to this point and they no longer have a great deal of influence on their son or daughter. At the same time teachers must stay positive and look forward to conferences with optimism. Here are a few tips that can help make the parent conference a rewarding experience.

Conference Tips

1. **Be Prepared** – Make sure you have gathered all the background information about the student. This means knowing more than just test scores and how the student is doing in your class. This is where a student profile card filled out during the first week of class will come in handy.

2. **Look and Act Professional** – You have only one chance to make a good first impression. Dress for success and greet the parents with a warm smile and friendly handshake. Get a good night's sleep, and be prepared to be as sharp during the last conference as you are for the first.

3. **Start with a Conversation** – By discussing a topic or two of mutual interest, you will relax the parents and yourself. Your time is important, but don't act rushed. Take the time to establish a common foundation and demonstrate your communication skills. Think how much you value your doctor or dentist who take the time to show interest in you and your family.

4. **Reach Out by Asking Questions** – I always liked to start the discussion by inquiring how the student feels about school, the class, activities or a related topic. By providing the parent with the opportunity to speak, the teacher has a chance to determine the attitude of the parent.

5. **Be an Active Listener** - Focus on what is being said. Show interest, respect, and consideration for every comment made. Remember the keys to active listening: eye contact, lean forward, nod, verbal affirmations, etc. When the parent realizes you value his or her comments, he or she will be more willing to ask the difficult questions and listen more attentively when you speak.

6. **Discuss Relationships and Social Adjustment** – While teachers at the elementary and middle school levels elaborate on these items, too often high school teachers go directly to academic performance. A computer printout showing all assignments and test scores is valuable, but it always impresses parents when the teacher shares thoughts about teamwork, behavior, communication, and emotional maturity.

7. **Be Organized** - This includes showing some examples of the child's work and samples of the activities you do to promote higher level thinking. It is impressive when you share several of your most creative projects with the parents. Have folders on each student so you can refer to them when needed. It is embarrassing to be looking for something and being unable to find it. This has happened to me, and it is painful.

8. **Have a Plan for Improvement** – Be proactive in your conference. As Covey says, "Begin with the end in mind." Know what you want to accomplish and remember you are looking for a "Win – Win." When student performance is in need of improvement, lay out a plan for success. This is where the previously described 12-step card is invaluable. Go over it step by step with the parents. This works well when the student is present, and he or she can participate in formulating the personal improvement plan.

9. **Maintain high Values** – I always had high expectations for my students and did my best to challenge them. During several conferences, I had parents confront me by saying, "Our daughter has all A's, but a B in your class. What is wrong?" Some even accused me of being the problem! It is best to stay calm and point out what has to be done to earn an A. Always remain positive, stress what the student is doing right, and lay out a plan for success.

10. **Finish on a Positive Note** – Regardless of previous performance, emphasize that what transpires from this point on is what is most important. Briefly review the points of agreement and stress the importance of working together. Focus on the future and conclude with a smile and a friendly handshake.

The parent-teacher conference is an excellent opportunity to gain a better understanding of the student and then more effectively meet his or her needs on a daily basis. Much of the value is determined by your degree of preparation. Success is what happens when preparation meets opportunity. This is your opportunity to make a difference.

> *Success is what happens when preparation meets opportunity.*

Seven Keys To Effective Listening

➤ **Concentrate on the Speaker.** People have a tendency to formulate a reply when another person is speaking. The speaker who notices a lack of focus and eye contact can usually detect this. Carefully consider what is being said, and use your active listening techniques to verify your attention.

➤ **Use Positive Body Language.** Be active as you lean forward and occasionally nod or use facial expressions to confirm you are listening carefully to the speaker.

➤ **Pause Before Replying.** By pausing you guarantee that you will not interrupt the speaker. You also demonstrate to the other person that you are pondering what he or she said. The intelligent conversationalist is patient and understanding and is aware of the power of non-verbal communication.

➤ **Use Names.** Periodically throughout the communication process use the name of the person. This assures the speaker you are interested in what he or she has to say. When you have the opportunity to speak with a group and questions are asked, when possible, say the name of the questioner when you respond.

➤ **Ask Follow-up Questions.** There is no better way for you to affirm your interest than asking a question related to what has been said. You might call for clarification such as, "Could you elaborate more on that?" or "Why do you feel that way?" Another effective technique is to ask for an example.

➤ **Sum Up What Has Been Stated.** By paraphrasing the speaker's words, you confirm that you have listened. You can structure questions in hundreds of different ways, but hitchhiking on a previously expressed idea will build rapport and keep the discussion moving.

➤ **Build Trust.** The more you listen to another person, the more you build trust and understanding. Through expressing a positive regard for what has been said, you are being non-judgmental and inviting others to freely contribute their thoughts.

Keep in mind the little poem by Rudyard Kipling: "I had six honest serving men – they taught me all I knew: Their names were Where and What and When – and Why and How and Who." The use of these words as sentence starters requires the person answering to respond in a manner that will enhance the discussion rather than with a simple yes or no. When you ask open-ended questions in a conversation, and then listen patiently and attentively to the answers, the likelihood of your getting your point across is far greater than it would be if you just continued to talk.

> *"I had six honest serving men,*
> *they taught me all I knew:*
> *Their names were Where*
> *and What and When ,*
> *and Why and How and Who."*
> *Rudyard Kipling*

Think Before You Speak

Recently, I had some minor surgery, (if there is such a thing as "minor surgery!") A young nurse, possibly still in training, said to my wife, "I'm going to take your husband into the prep room to get him ready for surgery. Then I will come out and get you and you can come in and kiss him good bye." I said, "Wait minute. That sounds awful fatalistic! Could you restate that?" Obviously, considering the situation, she used a poor choice of words. I've done the same thing with students many times. The lesson is to always consider the situation and choose your words carefully.

The Three C's

Remember the three C's of effective communication. The first C refers to **clearly** speaking directly to the subject. It can be very frustrating attempting to communicate with someone who speaks around an issue but doesn't get to the point.

The second C is related to the first. Why would one use complicated terminology when common more **concise** words would get the job done? Speak to communicate and not to impress.

The third C conveys a feeling of consideration for the welfare of the speaker. We have all heard the statement, "Students don't **care** how much you know until they know how much you care." When you really care about someone, you are cautious to communicate in a manner that preserves his or her dignity and demonstrates respect for the person's views.

Research indicates up to 85% of communication is non-verbal. Make sure your body language and tone of your voice are consistent with the meaning of what you are saying. In his book, *The Seven Habits of Highly Effective People,* Stephan Covey recommends that you "Seek first to understand, then to be understood." He points out that most of us are so busy trying to get people to understand us that we spend very little time trying to understand them. Always take time to listen to others and demonstrate interest in their views.

> *"No man has ever listened himself out of a job."*
> Calvin Coolidge

Consciously work on improving your communication stills. Volunteer to speak at a faculty meeting, share your unique programs with community organizations and actually look for opportunities to speak in front of a group.

A Look Back - Every Day is "Fire Prevention" Day

Sometimes we learn more from a negative experience than a positive one. Late in my teaching career, when I should have known better, I had what could have been a terrible experience. It was in my alternative history class where all of the students had some special needs. I team taught the class with a special education teacher. We usually had between 15 to 20 students and it was a challenge.

Many of the students hadn't experienced much success in school and lacked motivation. My partner and I did everything we could to keep their interest and still teach the basics. These are the type of students who will always have trouble demonstrating proficiency on tests. People who haven't been there just don't understand. Many of these juniors were reading at the third or fourth grade level.

> *"The buck stops here."*
> Harry S. Truman

In doing my best to keep a discussion going and to involve one of the quieter students, I got down on one knee and said, "How do you feel about that, John?" It was an easy question, but he refused to speak. Then I got right in front of him and dramatically said, "Look you've got over 17 billion brain cells and I'm asking you to agitate just one of them. Can you do that for me?" He replied, "Get out of my face or I'll shit all over your bald head!" The class was silent, and all the students were watching me and thinking, "What will Collar do now?"

Realizing I caused the situation by putting John in a defensive position, I paused, stepped back, and said, "Defecate, that's the word you want to use. It means the same, but is a much better word." The class laughed, John relaxed and I explained that I shouldn't have gotten in his face. We went on with the class and I talked things over with John at the end of class.

Always remember that you are the professional. You have the well-developed problem solving skills. If I had sent John to the office or chastised him severely, I would have started a "fire." Reacting the way I did prevented the "fire" from breaking out. Everyday is fire prevention day!

Hot Tip! *Sometimes it is difficult to determine if students are catching on to the lesson. Immediate feedback is valuable. Various techniques can be used to communicate with your students. Perhaps you have your favorites. I used a simple "Thumbs up" for students who understood the lesson. "Thumbs down," meant those students were confused. If the thumb was turned sideways, the student was undecided. I could get a quick read on the class by saying, "Thumbs."*

My Personal Commitment to Clear, Concise, Communication
(Check the items that apply to you.)

☐ *I focus on what people say, and I am an active listener.*

☐ *I always find the time to listen intently to my students.*

☐ *I listen with my eyes in addition to my ears.*

☐ *I have clearly defined guidelines for success in my classroom.*

☐ *I communicate in positive language, with the desired end result in mind.*

☐ *I relate to colleagues and parents in a constructive manner.*

☐ *I show appreciation and give credit to others when appropriate.*

☐ *I am always prepared for, and look forward to parent conferences.*

☐ *I seek first to understand others, and then to be understood.*

☐ *I welcome the opportunity to share my message with others.*

Tools for Success: Imagination, Visualization, and Affirmation

Chapter 4

> "Imagination is more important than knowledge."
> *Albert Einstein*

> "The future belongs to those who believe in the beauty of their dreams."
> *Eleanor Roosevelt*

> "You see things and you say, 'Why?' But I dream things that never were and say, Why not?"
> *George Bernard Shaw*

Objectives

- To encourage educators to reflect on the early years of child development
- To summarize the steps necessary to practice effective visualization
- To demonstrate how affirmations assist in building self-confidence
- To point out the value of imagination, creativity, visualization and affirmation

Tools for Success: Imagination, Visualization and Affirmation

"Go confidently in the direction of your dreams. Live the life you have imagined."
Henry David Thoreau

In their book, ***Einstein Never Used Flash Cards***, child psychologists, Kathy Hirsh-Pasek and Roberta Golinkoff praise the benefits of play. The authors emphasize how important it is for pre-school children to engage in unstructured activities that stimulate the imagination. With the current emphasis on testing and standards, educators must remember the value of play in kindling the imagination and igniting the fire of creativity. Roger von Oech's book, ***A Whack On The Side Of The Head***, stresses the importance of opening mental locks to become more creative. He states that creativity is important in the business world and that it is a valuable aid in problem solving. Both skills, imagination, the ability to form a mental image not present to the senses, and creativity, producing through the application of imagination, are essential in teaching.

The next step is visualization or mental imagery. I prefer to perceive this process as forming a mental picture of success before it happens. Using the five senses of sight, sound, smell, taste and touch, the person forms a vivid and detailed image of successfully completing the upcoming task. An individual cannot effectively apply the tool

> **"Our aspirations are our possibilities."**
> *Robert Browning*

of visualization without setting the imagination free and believing in the concept of creativity. Because of this, the first part of the chapter will lay the foundation for visualization with reference to imagination and creativity.

The last part of the chapter demonstrates how affirmations may be used to strengthen the visualization experience. By combining visualization with affirmation, the individual becomes more self-confident.   Greater self-confidence provides a person with the necessary tools to win the mental game as described in Chapter One.

All of us have many opportunities to use our imaginations and develop our creative skills. During my preteen years, my older brother Larry and I would play some type of baseball everyday. At times we just played catch, but most often one of us would throw the ball up and hit fly balls and the other would field. The game became more complex as we counted outs, hits, runs, and kept score as if it was a regular game. To increase the level of interest he would stand for one major league team and I would represent another.

As we played our backyard game, hitting fly balls and chasing them, calling out the names of players and broadcasting the game to the fans, our imaginations blossomed like spring flowers. Being a fan of the St. Louis Cardinals it wasn't long before I

> **"Far away there in the sunshine are my highest aspirations. I may not reach them, but I can look up see their beauty, believe in them and follow where they lead."**
> *Louisa May Alcott*

began to imitate Stan Musial's peek-a-boo batting style. It didn't stop there. When we picked sides and played in the neighbor's field, kids would pick out certain players to proudly imitate.

During the cold Wisconsin winter, our imaginations heated up as the games now moved indoors with our extensive collection of baseball cards strategically placed on the basement floor to represent players at each position.   The grandstand consisted of cigar boxes or other items surrounding the field representing the ballpark. A pencil replaced the bat, and a die represented the ball. Everything was the same except we now took turns representing various players hitting the die. If the "ball" hit any of the cards, it was an out. Our active imaginations took over, and when a power hitter such as Musial came to bat we swung the bat (pencil) harder with a blast out of the park often being the result. The weaker hitters usually struck out or grounded out. We took turns announcing and usually managed to agree on the rules of the game. Everyone knew we were using our imaginations, but the concepts of visualization and affirmation were foreign to us.

The Toy Room

When observing small children at play, it is fun to see how they use their imaginations. For years my wife has collected old Fisher-Price toys. She has them displayed on shelves in the "toy room." The most expensive collectibles are on the top shelves and out of reach of the grandchildren. On the lower shelves, she stores the less expensive toys and these are fair game for the kids. These consist of all the little people and their habitats. Some of the favorites include the barn, gas station, airport, castle, A-frame, circus, Sesame Street House and school. The toys are not animated and use no batteries, but capture the attention of the two to seven year olds for hours.

The "Toy Room"

Effective Teaching

As a guest in my granddaughter's kindergarten class, I noticed a wide variety of materials designed to maintain student attention and set their imaginations free. This seems to be  the case throughout the primary grades. When students move into middle school and later high school, the intensity of the learning tends to increase and the "play" usually decreases. Too often, pressured by the demands of testing and the desire to "finish the book," the educational experience becomes one in which the teacher is the "sage on the stage" and the student becomes an inactive listener. This isn't always the case, but because of increased demands to "cover the subject," teachers are pressured to resort to the lecture method. There is a big difference between what is taught and what is learned. With an increased emphasis on standards and benchmarks, one must remember it is more effective to teach the critical attributes of each discipline through student involvement activities. However, always keep in mind that setting higher standards is not the key to improving education. The real key is more effective teaching! It is the responsibility of each teacher not to cave in to the pressures of testing and just start "data dumping."

> *Setting higher standards is not the key to improving education. The real key is more effective teaching!*

A Sense of Wonderment

It is possible to create a sense of wonderment in students and tap into their imaginations and creative skills through employing unique and challenging methodologies. The greatest classroom resources at any grade level are the curious and engaging minds seated in the desks. After I presented at a teacher development workshop, a participant gave me a copy of an article titled "Imagination." Even though it deals with the primary grades, it caused me to reevaluate how I was teaching history to juniors.

Imagination

By Mary Schramm from the book *"Gifts of Grace"*

Once a little boy went to school.
He was quite a little boy.
And it was quite a big school.
But when the little boy
Found that he could go to his room
By walking right in from the door outside,
He was happy,
And the school did not seem
Quite so big anymore.

One morning,
When the little boy had been in school a while,
The teacher said:
"Today we are going to make a picture."
"Good!" Thought the little boy.
He liked to make pictures.
He could make all kinds:
Lions and tigers,
Chickens and cows,
Trains and boats –
And he took out his box of crayons,
And began to draw.

But the teacher said" "Wait!"
It is not time to begin."
And she waited until everyone looked ready.

"Now," said the teacher,
"We are going to make flowers."
"Good!" thought the little boy.
He liked to make flowers.
And he began to make beautiful ones.
With his pink and orange and blue crayons.

But the teacher said, "Wait!"
And I will show you how."
And it was red with a green stem.
"There," said the teacher.
Now you may begin."

The little boy looked at the teacher's flower.
Then he looked at his own flower.
He liked his own flower better than the teacher's.
But he did not say this.
He just turned his paper over
And made a flower like the teacher's.
It was red, with a green stem.

And pretty soon
The little boy learned to wait,

And to watch,
And to make things just like the teacher.
And pretty soon
He didn't make things of his own anymore.

Then it happened.
The little boy and his family
Moved to another house
In another city.
And the little boy
Had to go to another school.

This school was even bigger
Than the other one.
And there was no door from the outside
Into his room.
He had to go up some big steps,
And walk down a long hall
To get to his room.

And on the very first day
He was there,
The teacher said:
"Today we are going to make a picture."
"Good!" Thought the little boy.
And he waited for the teacher
To tell him what to do.
But the teacher didn't say anything.
She just walked around the room.

And when she came to the little boy
She said, "Don't you want to make a picture?"
"Yes," said the little boy.
"What are we going to make?"

"I don't know until you make it."
Said the teacher.
"How shall I make it? Asked the little boy.
"Why, anyway you like." Said the teacher.
"And any color?" asked the little boy.
"Any color." Said the teacher.

"If everyone made the same picture,
And used the same colors,
How would I know who made what,
And which was which?"

"I don't know," said the little boy.
And he began to make a red flower.
With a green stem.

The Rest of the Story

Several years later the story of the red flower with a green stem became much more meaningful. Our youngest daughter, who was in the early primary grades, was assigned a homework project to draw her favorite animal. Sarah always was fascinated with turtles and decided to make that her choice. We browsed through an encyclopedia and found a colored page  with pictures of about a dozen turtles from all over the world. She went to her room to design her masterpiece. Some time later she emerged grinning like the cat that caught the canary. When she revealed her creation, it was an outrageous looking creature. It was multicolored with claws on two feet and flippers on the others. The shell was flat in the front and rounded in the back with a head that appeared too large to seek the safety of the armor-like back.

Fighting to hold back a chuckle, I exclaimed, "That is quite an interesting looking turtle," and proceeded to question its configuration. For every question, the little artist had a reasonable answer. "You see dad, some turtles live in the forest and some in the ocean. That's the reason for the claws and flippers." I was amazed how she incorporated at least one feature from each of the turtles displayed to come up with her "eclectic turtle"

Disappointment

Proud as could be, she took her creation to school the next morning. When I returned home that evening, my wife said, "You better have a talk with Sarah." She appeared with her chin on her chest, and fighting back tears mumbled, "Dad, I have to draw my turtle over." I asked, "Why? What's wrong?" She replied, "My teacher said, "That isn't what a turtle looks like!" I inquired if the teacher asked her why the turtle had all the different parts. Deeply disappointed, she responded, "No. I just have to do it over."

> *"Every child is an artist. The problem is how to remain an artist after he grows up."*
> *Roger von Oech*

Creativity

One of the greatest gifts all children have is the ability to use their imaginations, the capacity to form mental images and to use their skills to make the image come to life. This is  known as creativity. To solve tomorrow's problems, people must transcend today's thinking. The problem solvers of tomorrow are in our classrooms; it is our responsibility to help them give their dreams wings. We must not allow our children to enter kindergarten as question marks and graduate from high school as periods.

Honest Abe

Recently one of our grandchildren was given the homework assignment of designing a disguise for a Thanksgiving turkey. All of the children in kindergarten would then have their creative turkeys displayed in the hallway. After much deliberation, Justin decided his turkey would be dressed like Abraham Lincoln. His mother agreed it was an excellent idea, and sure enough when we visited school, there were numerous turkeys exhibited on the wall. There were turkeys with ears like rabbits, people riding them like horses, Jack-O-Lanterns, a Santa Claus and one all dressed in black wearing a stovepipe hat and a black beard. Justin was beaming from ear to ear as he said, "Which one do you think is mine?" Standing behind him just as proud as a peacock was a kindergarten teacher – his mother Sarah. Yes, the same Sarah who years earlier created the eclectic turtle.

A Whack

In the early 1980's, Roger von Oech, a creative thinking consultant in the Silicon Valley in California, authored a book titled, *A Whack On The Side Of The Head – How To Unlock Your Mind For Innovation.* It is the best book I have read in the field of creative thinking and opening mental locks. von Oech encourages his readers to break stereotypes, learn from failure, have fun at work, look for more than one right answer and believe in their ability to be creative. His research determined that the major difference between creative people and less creative people was the way they viewed themselves.

A Kick

Several years later von Oech followed up with another must read for dynamic educators, *A Kick In The Seat Of The Pants – Using Your Explorer, Artist, Judge, & Warrior To Be More Creative.* He implores the reader to find the time to break away from doing things the way they have always been done.

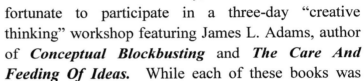

He encourages each person to utilize his or her unique talents to destroy mental blocks. During my exploration into the world of creativity, I was

> *"When I examine myself and my methods of thought, I come close to the conclusion that the gift of fantasy has meant more to me than my talent for absorbing positive knowledge."*
> *Albert Einstein*

fortunate to participate in a three-day "creative thinking" workshop featuring James L. Adams, author of *Conceptual Blockbusting* and *The Care And Feeding Of Ideas.* While each of these books was popular in the business and sales fields, they have tremendous application in education. After all, we are in the business of sales and often our customers must be convinced that they need our product.

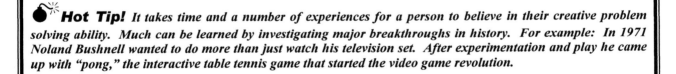

Hot Tip! *It takes time and a number of experiences for a person to believe in their creative problem solving ability. Much can be learned by investigating major breakthroughs in history. For example: In 1971 Noland Bushnell wanted to do more than just watch his television set. After experimentation and play he came up with "pong," the interactive table tennis game that started the video game revolution.*

Creative Problem Solving

One of the greatest gifts teachers can pass on and nurture in their students is the ability to problem solve. A concern associated with high stakes testing is the tendency to teach toward the test through focusing on facts, figures and formulas. Certainly, fundamentals are important, but real learning takes place when students are encouraged to utilize life skills and apply them in the classroom.

After reading a number of books and going to several workshops, I decided part of my responsibility as a teacher was to educate students to open up their minds and use their imaginations for creative problem solving. During the first week of class my students participated in a number of activities challenging them to think beyond the obvious. Simple brainteasers such as the following helped demonstrate the value of "Blue Sky" thinking and the worth of working in teams.

1. WEAR LONG	2. CYCLE CYCLE CYCLE	3. IKD	4. G. I. CCCCC CCCC
5. MIND MATTER	6. R ROADS A D S	7. LE VEL	8. DICE DICE
9. 0 BS MS PHD	10. KNEE LIGHTS	11. T O U C H	12. ROSIE
13. MAN BOARD	14. GESG	15. 1111 111111 00000 0000	16. YOU J U S T ME
17. FRIENDS FRIENDS STANDING MISS	18. CHAIR	19. ECNALG	20. R/E/A/D

1. M. + M. + N.H. + V. + C. + R.I. = N.E.
2. "1B. in the H. = 2 in the B."
3. 8D. − 24H. = 1W.
4. 3P. = 6
5. H.H. & M.H. at 12 = N. or M.
6. 4J. + 4Q. + 4K. = All the F.C.
7. S. & M. & T. & W. & T. & F. & S. are D. of W.
8. A. + N. + A.F. + M.C. + C.G. = A.F.
9. T. = L.S. State
10. 23Y. − 3Y. = 2D.
11. E. − 8 = Z.
12. Y. + 2D. = T.
13. C. + 6D. = N.Y.E.
14. Y. − S. − S. − A. = W.
15. A. & E. were in the G. of E.
16. My F.L. and South P. are both M.C.
17. "N.N. = G.N."
18. N. + P. + S.M. = S. of C.
19. 1 + 6Z. = 1M.
20. "R. = R. = R."
21. A.L. & J.G. & W.M. & J.K. were all A.
22. N. + V. + P. + A. + A. + C. + P. + I. = P. of S.
23. S. + H. of R. = U.S.C.

Unscramble or interpret the hidden phrase.   *What phrases are abbreviated here?*
(Solutions are in the appendix on page 207)

These two samples are representative of the type of projects the junior students faced during the course of the year. The teacher can use his or her imagination to develop different activities to go with each puzzle. To teach the value of working in groups, the puzzles were assigned individually. Then as the frustration level grew, students were encouraged to get into groups of four or five, and it became obvious to them how much quicker solutions were reached. Another effective technique is to take the more difficult of the two, and brainstorm solutions, consequently guiding the class through a creative problem solving experience.

A critic could say, "Why teach creative thinking when it really can't be tested nor is it one of the standards in my particular discipline?" The answer is clear. By helping a student consider information in different ways, the individual expands his or her problem solving ability and becomes more capable of relating to others. Communication skills are enhanced as creativity is expanded.

Visualization Is Applied Imagination

Let's return to that backyard baseball example. Now I realize as I adopted Musial's batting style, I could actually see, hear, feel and touch "Stan the Man." It didn't take much effort to smell the pungent odor of hot dogs liberally laced with yellow mustard.

Fortunately my high school baseball coach emphasized the value of "seeing success" and positive self-talk. While sports served as my introduction to visualization and affirmation, I became a true believer during my early teaching years. It was at this time that I was introduced to cassette learning and began to listen to tapes by Napoleon Hill, Earl Nightingale, Dennis Waitley, Charles Garfield, Zig Ziglar and Brian Tracey. Since these top motivational speakers all proclaimed that "seeing is believing," and "the body can only achieve what the mind can perceive," it seemed this was something I should be using in my teaching and coaching to help students reach their maximum potential.

> **"The body can only achieve what the mind can perceive."**

A colleague passed on a copy of ***Think and Grow Rich*** by Napoleon Hill, and then I picked up ***Psycho-cybernetics*** by Maxwell Maltz and became convinced that practicing visualization and affirmation was essential to winning the inner game. What follows is a concise summary of the critical attributes of both. These worked for me and many of the young people I have had the opportunity to teach and coach.

The Art of Visualization

Visualization is a powerful tool that will help you reach your desired goal. For this process to be effective, immerse yourself actively into what you are seeing in your mind's eye. Through mental rehearsal you must see, feel and sense yourself participating in what is being visualized. This process is equally effective with you and with your students. You must take the time to teach it to them. Use your judgment to make age-appropriate adjustments.

When and Where to Practice Visualization – The best time is prior to sleep or at a time when you are able to focus on the task and block out all distractions. Find a quiet environment where you will be uninterrupted for 3-5 minutes.

1. **Relax** – Allow yourself to become completely relaxed. Sit or recline comfortably, close your eyes and take a few slow, deep breaths. Feel yourself relax from the tips of your toes to the top of your head.

2. **Focus on a Stress Free State** – Put your major concerns behind you and strive to "think black." In other words clear your mind so you may concentrate on the desired result.

3. **Visualize Your Goal** – Begin filling your cleared mind with positive images of the goal you desire. Vividly see yourself completing the task on which you are focusing.

4. **Be Specific and Detailed** – Make these images as vivid and detailed as possible. Picture body movements and conversations, rehearse how you will look, feel, act, and talk. Realism provides credibility to the experience. Each time you visualize make an effort to fill in more details, employing as many senses as possible.

5. **Concentrate on One Vision** – See yourself in successful situations. Be in control of the environment and the people around you. Concentrate on a specific vision to intensify the influence of that particular image. Eliminate distractions. If you are preparing to make a presentation, actually see yourself in front of the group, and review step by step the critical attributes of your speech. I like to arrive at the program site at least an hour early. Then review my speech in the empty room, visualizing the chairs filled with people.

6. **Use Positive Affirmations** – After you have engaged in the sharpest imagery possible for several minutes, tell yourself you deserve the best in life, and the scene you have pictured will become a part of your existence. Repeat these thoughts over and over.

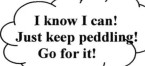

I know I can! Just keep peddling! Go for it!

7. **Reflection** – Take the time to review your visualization experience. You may find it meaningful to keep a log of your successes and setbacks. For visualization to be most effective, you must believe in it and practice it daily.

Hot Tip! *It takes awhile to effectively practice visualization. Stay with it and you will find your confidence will get a big boost! A person can pick up entire books written about visualization. To me they seem more complex than necessary. The procedure previously described worked for me!*

Visualization Can Change Your Life

You can use the powerful tool of visualization to build an image of the person you wish to become. The law of attraction will pull you in the direction of your dominant thoughts. When you form a clear mental picture of what you want to be, or accomplish, or how you wish to influence others, then you become enthusiastic about it and are more likely to take action. With renewed belief, you are more likely to challenge yourself to transcend previous levels of achievement. Simply stated, visualization helps build belief and confidence.

Visualization and Sports

I first witnessed applied visualization in my mid twenties while coaching football at UW-Lacrosse. Roger Harring, the highly successful head coach, put the players through a routine that included visualizing the perfect tackle. He would have them lie prone on the ground and close their eyes while he would talk them through the proper technique. Shortly after this experience, I read an article about a study that was done with shooting free throws and visualization. One group just practiced shooting, another mentally rehearsed the proper technique and then shot. The second group far out performed the first.

The Mental Game

Many outstanding athletes and sports psychologists talk about the value of winning the "mental game." Not everyone has the natural ability to practice effective visualization. It is a learned skill and it is a key step in performing tasks more efficiently.

Being a random and intuitive thinker, I made structured unit plans for my classes, but sketchy lesson plans permitted flexibility in the daily activity. Since I had comprehensively visualized the daily outcome, the class would naturally be pulled in the desired direction. Through practicing the art of visualization I was able to rehearse and troubleshoot problems before they took place.

It is possible the school principal may be a concrete and sequential thinker. When a lack of tolerance for different teaching styles exists, this can lead to conflict. A typical example might be an art teacher who is confronted for having a "messy room." The creative nature of the class and the teaching style of the teacher will influence the learning environment. Teachers are expected to recognize individual differences in students and teach to their strengths, but often teachers are expected to conform to rigid standards. Set your imagination free, that is what makes your classroom unique. Have a mental picture of the desired result and visualize your way to success.

Affirmations

To whom do you speak the most? The most common answers are, "my spouse," "my friends," or "my parents." Upon closer investigation, the best answer is "myself." We are constantly giving ourselves messages. Too often we have a tendency to dwell on negative thoughts such as, "Why me?" "I can't," "I don't have the time," or some other phrase that contributes to self-doubt. It is important to program

> *"Imagination sets the goal 'picture' which our automatic mechanism works on. We act, or fail to act, not because of 'will', as is so commonly believed, but because of imagination."*
> *Maxwell Maltz*

your mind with positive thoughts. These thoughts must be, "I can, I shall or I will." Maxwell Maltz in his landmark book ***Psycho-cybernetics*** refers to this as the "Success Mechanism Within You." When thinking this way, your sub-conscious mind automatically functions in a positive manner and influences you to act in a manner that drives you in the direction of your dreams.

Building Self-Confidence

Affirmations are essential tools in building self-confidence and following up on a goal setting plan. An affirmation is simply the act of expressing your belief in the truth of a particular statement. They are sometimes known as self-motivators, self-talk, or autosuggestion. The most effective affirmations are those based on goals. They help you overcome obstacles and build determination and self-confidence. The following tips will assist you in creating effective ways to affirm your goal plan.

> *Hot Tip! We all use affirmations. The key is to control your thinking, visual keys and self-talk so the affirmations are positive.*

I Can.
I Shall.
I Will.

Tips for Positive Affirmations

1. **We all talk to ourselves.** These messages may be good or bad. To achieve your goals it is essential to overwhelm negative messages with positive self-talk. To demonstrate the value of positive self-talk do this simple exercise. Repeat the phrases in the left column several times and notice how your attitude seems to be pulled down. Then repeat the phrases in the right column several times and notice how your attitude picks up.

Negative Self-Talk	*Positive Self-Talk*
I can't do anything right	I make good decisions!
Nobody cares about me.	My life has meaning!
I don't deserve this.	I can handle anything!
Why me? Why me? Why me?	I can, I can, and I can!
I can't stand this job.	My job is very rewarding!

(For more examples and a good activity for students refer to page 209 in the appendix)

2. **Affirmations come in many forms**. Pictures, words, writing, emotions, and actions all can be very effective. We use affirmations everyday, but often don't realize it. A picture of your loved ones, your bathroom scale, a brochure about that new vehicle, your music, meaningful numbers, and your classroom bulletin board are all examples of affirmations. Take control of how you program your mind and surround yourself with positive messages. For example, these numbers can be powerful, positive, affirming reminders.

145#   20/80   4/15/06
24/7   9/11

3. **Keep your affirmations private.** To be effective, your statements must be personal and relate directly to your goal. Sharing them will cause misunderstanding and interfere with your success. Let's say you get frustrated rather easily and have a tendency to snap at students when you are stressed. Have a written goal plan to be more patient and understanding. A key word to post might be "patience." Pictures reflecting the same concept and occasional soft, soothing music will serve as effective reminders. Consider keeping a stress ball on your desk or talking with others who are positive and stay relaxed.

4. **Assimilate your affirmations.** In order to make a difference, you must internalize the message by focusing on the end result. Concentrate on a mental picture of the person you wish to become. In the previous example, actually visualize responding to student actions in a calm, controlled manner.

5. **Believe in your ability to change your thinking.** Look at affirmations as investments, and find the time to bombard your senses with positive images. Too often we allow past experiences to dictate the future. It's like saying, "My mother was very emotional and grandmother was a high-strung person, so I'm just a chip off the block." This becomes a self-fulfilling prophecy. Since your actions are controlled by your dominant thoughts, changing your thinking is the key to changing your actions.

6. **Affirmations do not have to be true.** Remember, you expect to reach your goal. In order to experience success you must see and anticipate success. Use affirmations as tools to help you build your goal plan. Let's say you have a written affirmation, "I stay calm and in control in stressful situations." This is a state you desire to reach. The more your repeat it, the more likely it will be come to pass.

7. **Use spaced repetition** to sub-consciously restructure how you perceive people and events. When something is repeated over and over, we become more likely to believe it and act accordingly. This is the basis behind advertising. Think of a common television commercial or your favorite jingle. After awhile it will influence you to investigate or purchase the product. Teach the alphabet song to a child, and she will refer to it for the rest of her life.

8. **The length of time necessary to realize positive change varies based on the nature of your goal and types of affirmations.** Big goals require more time, patience and persistence. When I first took over the football program at Seymour, the goal to have a winning season seemed highly improbable to most people. Affirmations helped the team to build belief and confidence to stay with the goal and eventually become a winner.

9. **Construct and use affirmations according to these research proven methods.** The steps presented here are time-tested and research proven. While other methods may be workable, shortcuts and impatience may lead to disappointment.

10. **Remember the P's when constructing affirmations.** They must be personal, positive, on paper, and deal with the present.

--Remember --

- *Affirmations must contain the first person pronoun "I."*
- *Affirmations must be written in the present tense.*
- *Affirmations must be stated positively.*
- *Affirmations are fun!*

When practicing visualization and affirmation have a clear image of the desired state you wish to reach. Whether your goal relates to teaching, a personal relationship, athletic contest or

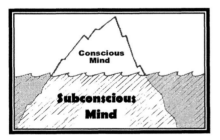

any other activity, focus on seeing yourself completing the task successfully. Research has indicated that events recorded in the sub-conscious are recognized by the brain and central nervous system the same as actual physical experiences.

The power of the sub-conscious mind is colossal. It has been compared to an iceberg where ten percent is visible with ninety per cent hidden. Always remember: A person is caused to act by the way he or she programs his or her personal computer (The brain). When you control input you also control what can be accessed in time of need.

A look back - See it, Believe it, Do it!

I've always believed most students are capable of performing at a level beyond that which they expect of themselves. This is true in the classroom and in extra-curricular activities. During my career I spent a lot of time and effort attempting to determine what made each student tick and what was the best way to reach all the unique individuals in my classroom and in sports.

During the early years at Seymour, we started a strength-building program. The initial purpose was to strengthen our student-athletes to improve their performance in sports. A number of individuals worked very hard and made tremendous gains in their maximum lifts. To keep them motivated and provide new challenges, another coach and I organized a powerlifting team. We traveled around the

> *"Man's reach must exceed his grasp or what's a heaven for?"*
> *Robert Browning*

state successfully competing in a number of meets. Powerlifting consists of three lifts: the squat, bench press and dead lift. Each athlete is given three attempts in each lift with the best in each category being counted. The three best lifts are then added to provide the individual with a competitive total. The dead lift was the last lift and consisted of pulling the bar up and holding it at arms length below the waist.

We were in Fort Atkinson, and because of the number of lifters and the use of only one platform, the meet was concluding around 11:00 PM with the final dead lifts. Jeff Braun, our heavyweight competitor, was leading his division. He opened up with 450 pounds and was attempting 500 for his second lift. I was surprised when he grabbed the bar, gave out a massive yell, but the bar remained anchored to the platform. Subsequently, his main competitor pulled 500 pounds on his last lift and moved into first place. Now in order to win his weight class Jeff needed to hoist 520 pounds. I doubted his ability to do it, but recalled several articles I had read about visualization, affirmation and peak performance.

I instructed Jeff to see himself lifting the bar and took him through the process step by step as described in this chapter. The big thing was to eliminate self-doubt and focus on the end result. "Keep your eyes on the prize." After not being able to budge 500 pounds, and as the crowd cheered him on, he pulled up 520 and locked it out. This experience more than any other convinced me that most students just don't realize what they are capable of doing. It taught me to continually challenge students to transcend previous levels of accomplishment in and out of the classroom.

🔴 *Hot Tip!* *Page 206 contains many good tips for promoting creative thinking in your classroom.*

My Personal Commitment to Personal Growth
(Check the items that apply to you.)

☐ *I recognize the uniqueness of every student and encourage creative thinking.*

☐ *I reflect on my childhood and welcome the joy of play into my daily life.*

☐ *I build a positive relationship with my students, and help them develop their strengths.*

☐ *I find the time to keep my imagination razor-sharp by reading and attending workshops.*

☐ *I understand the procedure for successful visualization.*

☐ *I practice the art of visualization and affirmation to improve the quality of my life.*

☐ *I make it a practice to internalize the process and share appropriate parts with students.*

☐ *I use spaced repetition to build belief and confidence.*

☐ *I have memorized:* ***Thoughts→ Feelings→ Actions→ Habits→ Attitudes→ Behavior.***

☐ *I control my thoughts, visual keys and self-talk to remain positive.*

Goal Setting for Success

Chapter 5

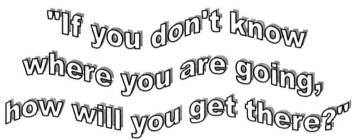

"If you don't know where you are going, how will you get there?"

> "Two roads diverged in a wood, and I –
> I took the one less traveled by,
> And that has made all the difference."
> *Robert Frost*

> "Keep your face to the sunshine and you cannot see the shadows."
> *Helen Keller*

> "It is not enough to be busy, the question is: What are we busy about?"
> *Henry David Thoreau*

Objectives
- To explain why people should set goals
- To give examples of successful goal setting and execution of the plan
- To explore why people don't set goals
- To describe the use of a checklist to follow correct goal setting procedure

Goal Setting for Success

The time is always right to do what is right.
Martin Luther King, Jr.

Ben Franklin said: "Going through life without a goal is like shooting without a target." Goals give direction to our dreams and meaning to our lives. A person should establish short-range, intermediate and long-range goals. Short-range goals include the things you wish to accomplish today, tomorrow or within several weeks. These provide direction to our daily lives and give us targets to aim for in the future. Intermediate goals refer to the challenges several months or possibly even years in the future. It is difficult to accomplish immediate goals without laying a foundation of short-range goals. Short-range goals give us a sense of accomplishment, provide encouragement, and help build confidence. Long-range goals are more like dreams. They may represent a desired state five or even ten years in the future.

Ideally a person should goals in six areas of life. These include:

- **Family and Home** – Find the time for your spouse and children. Schedule them in to your busy life and make it a point to do the little things that send the message to your loved ones that you care about them. Your presence is more important than your presents.

- **Spiritual and Ethical** – Regardless of your religious affiliation live in a state of mind where you are at peace with yourself. One of the best ways to guarantee this is to treat others as you would like them to treat you and to possess a high degree of integrity.

- **Mental and Educational** – Experience intellectual growth in order to keep your mind sharp. Make it a point to set a minimum of 30 minutes aside everyday for professional reading in your field. This doesn't sound like much, but in one year it adds up to 24 eight-hour days.

- **Physical and Health** – If you don't take care of your body, where will you live? Too often we can get wound up in our work and play and forget about keeping in reasonably sound condition. Schedule a yearly physical and establish a maximum bodyweight and follow a plan to stay within the proper range for your height and body type.

- **Financial and Career** – Keep your profession in proper perspective. Peak-performers are not workaholics. Find the time to schedule in free time so your job doesn't dictate your life. It is best to pursue a profession you enjoy, so your work actually becomes part of your play.

- **Social and Cultural** – Enjoy time with your friends, appreciate nature, and take advantage of a variety of entertainment opportunities. Take pleasure in reading, value art, and treasure music.

Keep Your Wheel Round

To visualize the proper development of each area in your life, think of them as spokes on a wheel. In order to guarantee a smooth ride the spokes must be of the same length. If any one area is neglected or receives too much attention, the ride through life becomes quite bumpy. Develop a plan to keep the wheel as round as possible.

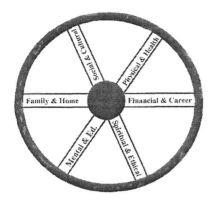

Whenever any spoke is getting too long or too short adjust your life to get back to a smoother ride. Financial and career gain at the expense of the family or physical health is certainly counter-productive.

> *Obstacles are something you see when you take your eyes off your goals.*

Benefits of Goal Setting

By establishing goals in these six categories of our lives, we give more meaning to our daily actions. Our life has more purpose. The goal serves as a magnet pulling us in the direction of our dreams. Goals help kindle our fire of desire, and provide the foundation for motivation. To be effectively motivated, a person must have a reason for doing things. A carefully thought out, well-designed goal crystallizes our thinking and helps keep us on target.

An Introduction to Goal Setting

My introduction to formal goal setting took place with our move to Seymour and the teaching and coaching position at Seymour High School. Dick Tepp, the curriculum coordinator, who was an outstanding teacher and wrestling coach, was a representative of the Success Motivation Institute. He taught classes in goal setting at the technical college, and he invited me to sit in on a class. I had set goals during my teaching/coaching experience at Antigo and UW-La Crosse, but never took the time to write them down and establish a plan for life. The class was a real eye opener, and made me realize what a powerful tool goal setting could be.

I have always been interested in motivation and peak performance. Having been previously exposed to the principles of motivation through Roger Harring, the Head Football Coach at UW-La Crosse, my interest was stimulated even more by listening to Earl Nightingale's "Motivational Moments" on the radio. I purchased his tapes, and read everything I could find on goal setting and personal motivation. Tepp asked me to co-teach the goal setting class at the technical college. A couple years later, through the efforts of Coach Harring, I began teaching a summer graduate class at UW-La Crosse. The planning and research necessary to teach the principles of goal setting for success, built up my confidence to incorporate more goal setting in my history classroom. Excited about motivating students, at a staff meeting I suggested that all teachers teach weekly motivational lessons in their homerooms.

Persistence is the Key

My proposal to the faculty was met with little enthusiasm, primarily because a number of the teachers felt unqualified to teach motivational principles in their homeroom. Others objected because they failed to see the relationship between personal growth, and success in their particular subject. We gave it a feeble attempt for a semester, but the challenge to expose all students to the principles of goal setting and motivation was unsuccessful. Convinced the program was valuable, Tepp encouraged me to join him in moving the program to a site off campus. We made arrangements to use a meeting room at a local bank. With the support of Seymour merchants, we purchased twenty-four sets of tapes and materials from SMI, and began to recruit students to participate in the program.

The Joy of Success

We organized four two-hour classes for each group of 24 students. Two sections were held every year. Other teachers and coaches were encouraged to participate. The program received rave reviews from the students. Within a short time the atmosphere in school improved and virtually every extra-curricular activity took a great leap forward. Our anemic athletic program was transformed, culminating in several state championships. Student leaders emerged and the "Making of a Champion" program received much of the credit. Once the corner had been turned, many of the concepts were incorporated into the athletic programs. There is no question in my mind that much of the success can be attributed to the "Making of a Champion" program. Teachers/coaches who believed in the program, and made the commitment to see it succeed, made the difference.

This chapter is based on proven strategies used when teaching the goal setting class at the college and high school level. Since I followed this procedure in my life, personal examples will be cited to make the process more meaningful. If you are one of the 97% who don't take the time to write down goals and act on them, follow this formula to bring more joy and meaning into your life while keeping your "wheel round."

> **Once begun, you're half done!**

Why Most People Don't Set Goals

Research indicates that peak performers in all walks of life are goal oriented. And yet, according to the Success Motivation Institute only three per cent of people actually have written goals. If goal setting has so many rewards, and if it is an uncomplicated process, why do so few people have written goals?

- **Lack of Belief** – It is difficult for many people to comprehend how an organized system, that includes writing out your dreams and then devising a system to reach them, can make a difference. Most people are capable of achieving much more than they give themselves credit for, but they lack the key ingredient – belief. Suspend judgment, and initiate a goal setting program with the belief that you will be successful. Belief comes from positive practice and preparation. Instead of saying, "I'll believe it when I see it." Revise your thinking to, "I'll see it when I believe it."

- **Lack of Understanding** – Many people just don't know how to set goals and follow a plan to achieve them. Following a dynamic goal setting process is often thought to be a complicated procedure. The system explained here is time-tested and takes it step by step with a number of checkpoints along the way. The 12-point checklist, that I will share with you, provides immediate feedback to determine if your goal is sound.

- **Lack of Experience** – Often children follow in the footsteps of their parents. If the parents didn't set goals it is highly unlikely that their children will be goal setters. Our school systems are so busy teaching facts, figures, formulas, and testing, that teachers usually don't have the time, and are even discouraged from teaching personal improvement and motivation. It is incomprehensible that the school day is structured around goals, objectives and standards, but most students receive little or no instruction on how to set and attain goals.

- **Fear of Criticism** – Goals are personal and don't have to be shared with others. Some people are quick to criticize, and the average person is more likely to point out why something cannot be done than why it can be accomplished. Because of negative feedback, people are often discouraged from setting lofty goals. Keep your goals to yourself and stay focused on the positive results.

- **Fear of Failure** – I've actually had people say to me, "I don't like to set goals because then I'm not disappointed when I don't reach them." This kind of an attitude is what Zig Ziglar called "Stinkin' Thinking." It is beginning with the expectation of failure in mind. That is unacceptable and can be overcome with an understanding of the principles of visualization and affirmation as explained in the previous chapter. Be aware that temporary failure is just a speed bump on the road to success.

Dealing with Failure

Failure is often viewed as the end result when in reality it should be seen as a stepping-stone to success. The greatest people in history are those who have failed most often. It is not how seldom you fail that counts, the most important thing is how often you get up and go again after getting knocked down. There are many examples of this in history including: Susan B. Anthony, Thomas Edison, Abraham Lincoln, Henry Ford, Eleanor Roosevelt, and in the more contemporary world, Mia Hamm, Hillary Clinton, Lance Armstrong and Brett Favre. If you wish to rise to your full potential you must have the persistence to bounce back from adversity. You find the true content of your character by how you respond to adversity. A key to a positive experience with your goal setting plan, is to view obstacles and temporary setbacks as unavoidable components in the process. I once read an article that stated failure should be looked at the same as fertilizer. It may not be the most agreeable thing, but it helps us grow.

> *"Failure is only the opportunity to begin again more intelligently."*
> *Henry Ford*

Prior to the days of computers, a student printed Theodore Roosevelt's popular statement about criticism in poster form and presented it to me. I displayed it on the front wall of the classroom throughout my teaching career. I committed TR's quote to memory and would occasionally refer to it in class. It was fun to notice the students following along with the poster as I related the passage.

The Man in the Arena

"It is not the critic who counts, not the man who points out how the strong man stumbles or where the doer of deeds could have done them better. The credit belongs to the man who is actually in the arena, whose face is marred by dust, and sweat, and blood; who strives valiantly; who errs and comes short again and again because there is no effort without error and short-comings; but who actually strives to do the deed, who knows the great devotion; who spends himself in a worthy cause, who at best knows in the end the high achievement of triumph and who at worst, if he fails while daring greatly, knows his place shall never be with those timid and cold souls who know neither victory nor defeat."

Theodore Roosevelt

Goals Help Us Focus

When people don't have concrete goals to work toward, all their energy, imagination, time, skills, decision-making ability, and concentration just fly around without purpose. Goals help us focus on the mission and accomplish tasks through providing direction and rationale.

No Goals - Lack of Direction

Goals Give Us Direction

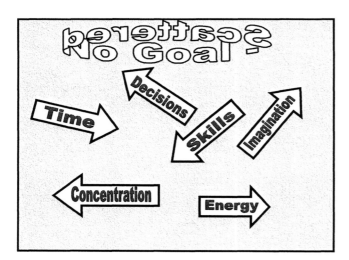

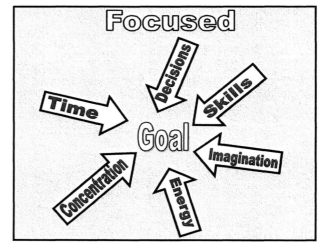

Reflections

When I was in high school my major goals were to have a good time, excel in sports and be popular. The possibility of college seemed remote. I didn't study much, and it looked like my immediate future would be tending bar for my dad and working construction. Mr. Newhouse, my high school history teacher and football coach, took me aside one day and convinced me that I could play football at UW-La Crosse and do college academic work. My motivation and goal became to play football at La Crosse and major in Physical Education since I thought that would be easier than anything else. I became the first "Collar" to attend

> *"To gain strength, courage and confidence, you must do the thing that you think you cannot do."*
> *Eleanor Roosevelt*

college. During the first week of practice I broke my ankle and decided to drop out of school and go home. I was young, homesick and heartbroken. Fortunately, my college football coach, and my dad convinced me to stay in school and focus on my education. Now I had a new mission – survival. I lacked direction, skipped class, partied too much, and managed to eek out a 1.8 grade point. With a 2.2 second semester, I survived and my overall 2.0 GPA made me eligible to return.

When I returned home with my broken leg several patrons of the tavern reminded me how much tougher college football was and maybe it wasn't for me. That was just the motivation needed and I became determined to prove them wrong. Once I got over the self-pity and "poor old me" thinking my life had more meaning.

Viktor Frankl

Years later when I read Viktor Frankl's book, ***Man's Search for Meaning***, I realized how important it is to have positive goals. Frankl, who wrote about his experiences in a Nazi prison camp during WWII, noticed that people who had a mission, a reason to live, who had somebody to return to, were more likely to survive. Those who gave up hope and had a life with no meaning were more likely to die. After his liberation, he went on to become a world famous psychologist. While most inmates were just surviving from day to day, he was acquiring a foundation of knowledge that would serve him well after the war. He was practicing the key motivational principle of identifying with the expected result. It was enough to keep him going. Similar stories are told about American prisoners in Korea and Viet Nam who actually learned to play a musical instrument, or improved their golf game while incarcerated in a small cell. When released and questioned, the common response was that they practiced in their minds. The prisoners visualized being back home in a friendly environment. Goals give meaning to our lives!

Getting Serious

During the summer between my freshman and sophomore year in college I realized it was time to get serious and apply myself in school and in football. With the help of a rigid conditioning program, my body muscled up, and a switch to a social studies major provided me with new vigor in an enjoyable subject area. Even though I didn't have written goals, life now had direction. A college degree seemed within reach, and a career as a teacher/coach like Mr. Newhouse seemed reasonable. The word "Goals" can serve as a reminder to help us get started and stay with a goal setting plan.

G-o-a-l-s

Go for it! Sometimes the most difficult part is to get started. Organize your thinking, decide what you want to do, and establish a plan to get it done! If I had done this earlier, my first year of college would have been more productive. Because of my lack of commitment as a freshman, I was required to attend college an extra semester to earn my degree.

Opportunity! Once you decide on what you want to do, channel your energy to take advantage of the opportunities available. After earning my degree, I planned to get married, but my future wife had another semester to go in school. Instead of seeing this as an obstacle, it became an opportunity for me to go to graduate school while she finished her education.

Action! When the opportunity presents itself take action. Too often we can get paralysis through analysis. Certainly think things over, gather all of the information, evaluate the evidence, consider the consequences, but when you make a decision, don't look back! Take action and stay away from, "Ifa, woulda, coulda, shoulda" thinking. After two years of high school teaching, I took a college administrative position and worked as associate director of housing for four years. Discovering that I missed the classroom, against the advice of others, I returned to high school teaching for the next 29 years.

Love what you are doing! It took me some time to realize this, but true happiness in life means enjoying every day that you are alive. This includes the time you spend working. Make your work and play as similar as possible. For example, I enjoy sports, communicating with people, and history. I spent most of my life coaching sports and teaching history. In other words, I never worked a day in my life! I coached and taught. It was difficult and demanding, but extremely enjoyable and rewarding. If I had it to do all over again, I would do the same thing.

Success! When we accept the definition that "Success is the progressive realization of worthwhile predetermined personal goals," we acknowledge that we must have direction in our lives to help us get where we want to go. Do what you want to do rather than what others think you should do. At various times in my career, people I respected advised me to take a job that was considered to be a promotion, and I declined. After reflecting on these decisions, I know the course of action taken was best for our family. Even though I passed up more money and ostensibly more prestige, the family came first.

Take Action

 These are the words and phrases to keep us focused on our goal-setting plan. Remember, *"G" is Go for it!* Get started. "Once begun you are half done!" Sometimes the most difficult thing is to overcome inertia. *"O" is for Opportunity.* Don't wait for things to happen - cause them to happen. *"A" is for Action.* Thinking without action is just daydreaming. Goals help turn your dreams into results. *"L" is for Love.* Enjoy each day to the fullest and appreciate the people with whom you interact. *"S" is for Success.* When you make a positive difference in the lives of others you are living a successful life. The goals you choose will determine the quality of your life. Years ago when I was teaching at Antigo this refrain was passed on to me.

> *Hot Tip! A key goal setting principle is to identify with the expected result. It is highly motivational when we keep our eyes on the prize.*

Success

"Success is in the way you walk the paths of life each and every day. It is in the little things you do, and in the things you say. It is not in reaching heights of fame. It is not alone in reaching goals that all people seek to claim. Success is being big of heart, clean and broad of mind. Success is being faithful to your friends and to the stranger kind. Success is in your family and your teammates and what they learn from you. Success is having character in everything you do."

Potential

The power of goal setting and the potential of students became clearer to me as a result of working with Jeff Braun. Jeff was a 6'2 200 pound cherubic sophomore who had good size, but little athletic ability. Realizing that football is a game of numbers, much time was spent recruiting students who seemed to have some potential, and Jeff was one of my projects. As a sophomore he came out for football and played with little distinction on the JV team. He then participated in wrestling and was pinned every time except once. As a weight man in track, Jeff put the shot just over 32 feet. Needless to say he didn't seem to have much potential.

Commitment

At the conclusion of our winless football season, the coaches met with all the underclassmen and encouraged them to make a commitment in the weight room to get bigger and stronger for the next season. I opened the room at 6:15 AM and Jeff was the most conscientious lifter. He believed

> *"In order to have a winner, the team must have a feeling of unity; every player must put the team first – ahead of personal glory."*
> *Paul "Bear" Bryant*

in what the coaches said, and made the commitment to lift weights in the morning three times a week. As a junior he played some varsity football, won a few wrestling matches and put the shot 50'2". The football team won a couple games and lost a few close ones. The improvement was rewarding. Since I coached the field events, after Jeff's junior track season, we sat down and had a talk about establishing some goals for his senior year. When I asked him what he was capable of doing for his final year, Jeff was extremely optimistic. He said, "Coach I want to be all conference both ways in football, go to state in wrestling and win the state championship in the shot put." I was startled with his high goals, but replied, "You can do that in football, but remember the team comes first, let's win the conference championship first and if you are all conference – fine. In wrestling going to state is a good goal. However, to win the state shot put title you will have to throw over 60 feet. That will take a lot of work during the off season." He replied, "Coach, I'm willing to do it!"

The Plan

We drew up a workout plan and focused on the shot put, which was his favorite event. We designed a program with an emphasis placed on weekly and monthly goals and never missing a workout. When Jeff reported for football his senior year, he stood 6'3 and was a strong 230 pounds. He earned all-conference both ways on the first winning football team in 24 years. He didn't make it to state in wrestling, but did win most of his matches. In track, Jeff won the state shot put title with a toss of 63'1¼". That earned him a scholarship to the University of Wisconsin where he won seven indoor and outdoor Big Ten Titles.

> **Plan your work – Work your plan!**

Reflecting back on that experience, the plan we followed was consistent with the **"GOALS"** procedure explained earlier. Jeff realized the opportunity was present, he decided to "go for it," and took the action necessary for success. Most of the time he loved what he was doing even though it was hard work.

This reaffirmed my belief that hard work can be fun when it is directed toward an admirable purpose with a measurable result in mind. I finally began to understand what was meant by the phrase, "It's the journey, not the destination." The most important thing in keeping Jeff motivated was the establishment of short term (weekly) and intermediate (monthly) mini-goals that served as stepping-stones to his final goal.

The Process

A similar procedure has been used with students in class, our daughters, in my personal life, and virtually in anything where structure and advance planning is advantageous. Writing down goals for the future provides us with a concrete plan. To simplify the goal setting procedure, I came up with several forms and a step-by-step process to follow. For your convenience all the documents are included in the appendix.

The Wish List

In the previous chapter you were encouraged to set your imagination free and use the powerful tool of visualization to help generate ideas and solve problems. During a goal setting workshop, when I was in my early thirties, I was advised to come up with a "wish list" of all the things that I would like to accomplish in my life. The purpose of this was to encourage creativity, and assist in structuring goals in the six categories previously described as spokes in the wheel of life. Workshop participants were encouraged to be uninhibited, and write out their wildest dreams, even though they may seem unattainable at the time. For example, even though Seymour High School had never won a conference championship in football; that was on my list. I also included such things as taking a trip to Washington, D.C. and speaking at the state social studies convention.

When you begin your goal-setting program, start with a wish list. That will help prepare you for the brainstorming activity that will assist you in getting more specific. To help you follow along with the steps necessary for successful goal setting, I will use a number of examples from my life.

Brainstorming

The next step in your goal-setting plan is to use the "Dream List" to brainstorm goals in the six categories of your life. Listed below are a few examples from my original brainstorming sheet. Without getting too personal I've listed four or five items in each category. My original sheet had 18 items listed under "Financial and Career." My career goals just kept growing as the list was put together. Eventually they included developing classes in contemporary issues and in Native American History. A commitment was made to utilize involvement activities and restructure history class to promote more cooperative learning. By brainstorming and listing the goals on paper it gave the goals more meaning and provided an opportunity to periodically review previous thoughts. When you don't find the time to write goals out, great ideas seem to just drift away like smoke from a campfire, and there is nothing left to grab.

A Partial "Dream List"

Physical Health – Follow a regular exercise program at least 3 times a week. Maintain my weight at 210 or less. Adhere to a sensible eating plan. Limit the consumption of alcohol. Etc.

Mental and Educational – Do at least 30 minutes of reading every day. Attend workshops for personal growth. Have a weekly plan to improve my vocabulary. Establish a Prof. library. Etc.

Family and Home – Find the time for my wife and children. Schedule in family vacations. Build a family room on the house. Maintain contact with our parents. Sunday is family day. Etc.

Spiritual and Ethical – Serve on the church council. Pay our church dues. Attend church on a regular basis. Provide the children with a religious foundation. Be honest in all things. Etc.

Social and Cultural – Go out to eat at least once a month. Start a discussion group. Invite friends to our house on a periodic basis. Attend the theater and movies when interested. Etc.

Financial and Career – Start a TSA. Save a certain percentage of income monthly. Earn additional credits. Integrate history and literature. Teach history in reverse chronological order. Etc.

Prioritize

Once the brainstorming has been done, take a few days to reflect on potential goals and then rank them **"S"** short term (within a year), **"I"** Intermediate (within three years), and **"L"** Long Range (more than three years). This provides you with a sense of order and helps you take action. For example: In the "Financial and Career" category "starting a TSA (tax sheltered annuity) might earn an **"S"** while "saving a certain percentage of income may be ranked **"L",** since it is difficult to do both when you have a young family. Examine the form where you have prioritized your goals and be prepared to take action on at least one goal in each category.

If you have trouble meeting your deadline, revise your timeline, but stay with the project. It is acceptable to modify the goal and deadline. The most import thing is to be persistent and make steady progress.

Establishing the Goal Plan

The goal-planning guide, in the appendix, has been helpful in formulating a plan of success. When planning to achieve a major goal, following this form is highly recommended. Begin by stating your goal. It must be personal, positive and deal with the present. I'm using a career goal from 1980 so you can follow along and better understand the process. This is when I decided to teach history in reverse chronological order. **"I, Bill Collar, have developed a method to teach**

history in reverse chronological order." Always include your name and state the goal as if you have already accomplished it, and then establish a target completion date. A deadline will help raise your level of concern and encourage you to take action. Remember, if necessary, it is acceptable to revise the completion date. Many obstacles will come up as you begin to work on your goal and share it with others. To be prepared for these hurdles, brainstorm as many obstacles as possible, and devise a plan to overcome each one.

Obstacles:		
1. Very non-traditional.	6.	What if I leave Seymour?
2. Confusing for the learner.	7.	Research available?
3. Scheduling conflicts?	8.	Other teacher's views?
4. Students switching classes?	9.	How to organize?
5. Any books available?	10.	How to handle criticism?

Be as specific as possible when listing the solutions to the obstacles. I discovered *"The Backward History Project,"* a study that was done by Indiana State University. They sent me a copy and their research answered many of the questions that had come up. Being prepared with the evidence, I organized a scope and sequence study and became more convinced our students would benefit from the change. It was time to thoroughly examine the expected benefits.

Once the list of expected benefits has been compiled, the degree of belief in the goal will increase. If not, go back and reexamine the goal. It has been my experience writing out the obstacles, brainstorming solutions, and then making a list of expected benefits makes it is easy to determine the wisdom of staying with the goal.

Expected Benefits:
1. Increased motivation for students.
2. Higher test scores.
3. Renewed teaching enthusiasm.
4. Better understanding of contemporary affairs.
5. An opportunity to break away from the book.
6. History will be more relevant.
7. Study about the future.
8. Unlimited potential for improvement.
9. Concentrate on significance of current events.

"Keep your eyes on the prize!"

Verbal Affirmations

It is important we control the content of the messages we send ourselves through self-talk. Since we speak with ourselves more than anyone else, these messages must be positive. The concept of positive affirmations was addressed in the previous chapter. Affirmations assist in improving our degree of belief in the value of the goal. More than anything, positive affirmations will help you determine that your goal is a good one. If you have trouble forming affirmations that support your goal, it might be necessary to revise the goal. For example, when I set up the goal to teach history in reverse chronological order, I needed to convince myself that it was a good idea. I knew there would be criticism and others would give reasons why it wouldn't work. Listed here are some of the actual written affirmations that helped convince me that it was a great plan.

 Hot Tip! *The worksheet on page 190 helped me organize the goal setting process.*

> **Affirmations:**
> 1. I believe in the value of the backward history project
> 2. I know the backward history project will improve student understanding of history.
> 3. I'm certain teaching history backward will increase student motivation.
> 4. I'm enthused about the creativity this project offers students and the teacher.
> 5. I'm excited about getting started and implementing this project.
> 6. Teaching history in reverse order provides me with more flexibility and allows students to focus on contemporary issues.

My experiences on the golf course tell me setting a goal is much easier than its execution. It is easy to stand at the tee and visualize that perfect drive right down the middle. Follow up with a nice two iron to the front of the green, a great chip shot, and one putt for a par four.

The Plan - Par 4!

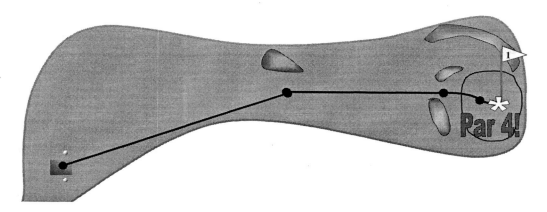

In reality my golf game just doesn't always work out the way I plan. It seems like I get out that hazard seeking ball and pretty soon I'm in the rough, a trap, a pond, across the green, and then a score of thirteen.

Execution!

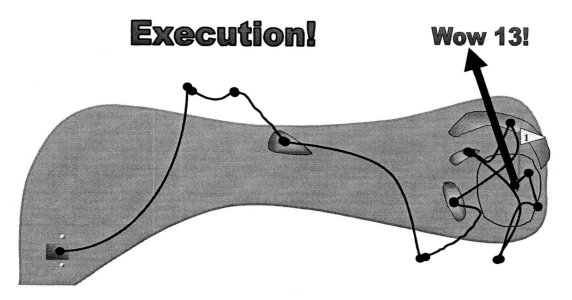

Goal setting in life works much the same way as on the golf course. Advance planning is not enough. It takes time and patience to follow a success path. This includes the ability to bounce back from adversity and treat each new experience as a learning experience.

In golf there are three ways to improve: practice, take lessons, or cheat. Cheating is the most expedient and offers an immediate reward. In the long run it will ruin your character and destroy your

> *"To win you must have talent and desire, but desire must come first."*
> *Sam Snead*

self-image. The same is true with following your goal setting plan. It takes time, effort and determination. Shortcuts are possible, but most often you will benefit the most by taking the time to do it right.

The Goal Checklist

When I was teaching goal setting to students, this checklist was prepared to simplify the analysis and evaluation of the goal plan. The document is included in the appendix on page 191. It is an excellent tool for subjecting your written goal to close scrutiny. When you can answer "yes" to all of the questions, you have a workable plan. Thought must precede action, but taking action on your plan is the real key. This is up to you!

- ☐ **Have I stated my goal clearly? Do I really understand what I plan to accomplish?**
- ☐ **Is this goal challenging for me and yet realistic for a person with my potential?**
- ☐ **Can this goal be measured? Will I be able to tell when I have reached my goal?**
- ☐ **Have I established a deadline to aim for in reaching this goal?**
- ☐ **Do I understand the <u>visualization</u> process well enough to use it to help me reach my goal?**
- ☐ **Have I written <u>affirmations</u> to help develop a positive attitude toward reaching my goal?**
- ☐ **Am I willing to take the time necessary to drill and practice as I work toward my goal?**
- ☐ **Do I honestly <u>believe</u> I am capable of reaching this goal?**
- ☐ **Am I willing to make the personality changes necessary in order to reach this goal?**
- ☐ **Is this goal really mine? Do I have the desire to achieve it?**
- ☐ **Am I prepared to view ridicule, failure, and temporary setbacks as stepping-stones toward reaching my goal?**
- ☐ **Do I possess the patience and determination necessary to maintain a concentrated effort toward reaching this goal?**

After going through the checklist, if you are uncertain about any of the statements, go back and take a close look at your goal. Perhaps your plan needs some revision so you can check an unequivocal "yes" to all the statements. This instrument is a tool to help you understand the process necessary to successfully complete your goal. When you are able to agree with all the statements, indicate on the goal sheet that you are willing to invest the necessary time and effort to realize your goal. To affirm this, sign the document and date it.

Time Management

Another benefit of goal setting is that it helps you make better use of your time. Many educators feel overwhelmed with balancing schoolwork and responsibilities at home. By making a list and prioritizing the tasks, you become better organized and waste less time. Periodically reflect on your wheel and make sure it is as close to round as possible. When we have significant, important, valuable goals to accomplish, we find more energy and become more creative. Instead of reacting to what happens to you, be proactive and cause good things to happen through advanced planning.

My wife doesn't like it when I go grocery shopping. I have a tendency to grab whatever looks good and put it in the grocery cart. If I do go shopping, she will insist that I follow the list she provided. Can you imagine going grocery shopping without a list or any advanced planning? Think of the money you would spend and the calories you would consume if you just walked down the aisle and tossed what looked good to you in the cart. Organized goal setting is the answer.

A Look Back - Concentrate on the Little Things

Roger Harring reminded me to concentrate on doing the little things right and the big things will happen. In other words, when executing your goal plan, pay attention to detail. Or as Coach Harring would say, "Don't worry about the score. Concentrate on blocking and tackling and doing the little things right, and the score will take care of itself." Keeping this in mind, in the classroom my attention was drawn to a student (Butch) who was struggling in a class of high achievers. The student felt he was outclassed

> *"A strong, positive self image is the best possible preparation for success."*
> **Joyce Brothers**

and was reluctant to participate for fear of saying the wrong thing. I decided it was time to give him some positive feedback in front of his peers. We were making progress when I determined it was time to expedite the process.

He was a hard worker who had difficulty grasping historical concepts. I opened the weightlifting room in the morning before school and Butch was a regular lifter. On this particular day in class, we were going to discuss the impeachment trial of Andrew Johnson. I approached

Butch in the weight room and mentioned what the topic would be for the day. Then I said, "I'm going to ask the class the name of the man who saved the entire checks and balances system by casting the deciding no vote against the impeachment of President Johnson. The answer isn't in our book, and no one will know. I'll look around the room and wait a couple seconds. Then raise your hand and I will call on you, and you say, 'Edmund G. Ross'."

I'll get all excited and ask, "How did your know that Butch?" Then you reply, "I've been reading a lot in the library lately." I emphasized how impressed the other students would be and that this will be his chance to really shine. We rehearsed and he was excited about the idea. Butch's class was in the afternoon so I made sure he remembered the name by pointing out how "Ross rhymed with La Crosse." Over the lunch period he came up to me and repeated the name just as we rehearsed. Butch was ready!

Everything went exactly as we planned. The top students didn't know the answer and when Butch's hand went up they kind of scoffed. Then he said, "Edmund G. Ross," I went wild, the students were impressed, and then I asked, "How did you know that?" Remember, we hadn't rehearsed the last part of the ruse since before school. Butch innocently replied, "You told me the answer in the weight room this morning!"

My plan backfired because I didn't take care of the little things, in particular reminding Butch about how he was reading a lot in the library! When following your goal setting plan, always take care of the little things, and the big things will happen.

Hot Tip! *When working on a goal-setting plan with students, take the time to check for understanding to make sure you are in agreement on the steps necessary to reach the desired result. After a discussion with a student, I often asked them to explain to me what we just talked about. Many times the student interpretation was considerably different than mine.*

My Personal Commitment to Goal Setting
(Check the items that apply to you.)

☐ *I realize that written goals give more organization and meaning to my life.*

☐ *I have established goals in all six areas of my life.*

☐ *I possess the drive, persistence and determination necessary to follow up on my goals.*

☐ *I believe in the value of goal setting and understand the process necessary to reach them.*

☐ *My "Dream List" assists me in setting my imagination free to establish challenging goals.*

☐ *I understand that obstacles and setbacks are stepping-stones to achievement.*

☐ *I use the "Goal Checklist" to assist me in attaining my goals.*

☐ *I find the time to make the necessary effort to follow a structured goal-setting plan.*

☐ *I remain confident in spite of temporary setbacks along the way.*

☐ *I identify with the expected result to build my confidence.*

Attitudes Are Contagious

Chapter 6

"It's Your Attitude, Not Your Appitude, That Determines Your Altitude."

Energy is contagious!

➢ "In soloing, as in other activities, it is far easier to start something than to finish it."

Amelia Earhart

➢ "The greatest discovery of my generation is that a human being can alter his life by altering his attitudes of mind."
William James

➢ "Adopting the right attitude can convert a negative stress into a positive one."

Hans Seyle

Objectives

- To provide personal examples of dealing with adversity
- To define the state of mind necessary to develop a positive attitude
- To establish personal qualities necessary to maintain a PMA
- To describe how to use a master affirmation as a motivational device

Attitudes Are Contagious

"Our attitude toward life determines life's attitude towards us."
Earl Nightingale

It is difficult to pinpoint when I first began to live my life in a manner that was based on maintaining a positive mental attitude. My father emphasized the value of competition and stressed a "never say die" attitude in sports. He coached the city baseball team and volunteered his time to coach youth sports in addition to umpiring and refereeing all over northeastern Wisconsin. I often traveled with him, and we would talk at length about winning and losing, attitude development, teamwork and confidence. He instilled in me a sense of pride in performance and high expectations. To this day I can still hear his mantra: "If you can't do a job right, don't do it at all." I was raised under the principles of "Do it right the first time" and "Be proud of your performance."

> *"Do it right the first time."*

Through my participation in athletics and experience tending bar at my parent's tavern, by the time I entered college my outgoing personality was pretty well developed. Like most college freshmen at the time, I lacked direction and confidence, but did have belief in my ability to communicate and possessed some natural leadership skills. During my upper class years, as my thoughts turned to a career in education I became intrigued with motivational principles and how to influence others to perform at a high level. A class on the principles of successful coaching peaked my interest even more. The instructor promoted the book *Building a Championship Football Team* by Paul "Bear" Bryant, the highly successful coach at the University of Alabama. It reinforced my belief that football was much more than X's and O's, and it influenced me to dig deeper in the area of peak performance.

Positive Mental Attitude

The more I read, the more I began to subscribe to Napoleon Hill's positive mental attitude philosophy. He summed up his approach to life with the statement, "Whatever the mind of man can conceive and believe, the mind of man can achieve." To me this meant having confidence in yourself and never giving up. It is an approach to life where instead of seeing barriers, see hurdles, instead of obstacles, see opportunities, and instead of problems, see solutions. It is a method of controlling one's thinking and actions by always looking for the best in every situation, no matter how dismal things may appear. This is difficult to do and it takes time to

> *"Whatever the mind of man can conceive and believe, the mind of man can achieve."*
> *Napoleon Hill*

develop, but is a great way to go through life. All of us have had classes where the students seemed to be disinterested and unmotivated. A teacher with a positive mental attitude will see this as a challenge and devise methods to bring out the best in each individual. The greatest reward occurs when students have actually altered their attitudes to meet the teacher's expectations. This takes planning, patience and persistence. While it is challenging and time consuming, it is gratifying. View each student as being gifted in some way, and help each discover his or her gifts.

Now let's take that same challenging class and view it from the perspective of a teacher who lacks the proper mental outlook and has negative expectations. That teacher often will complain in the lounge to colleagues how incorrigible the class is and actually develop a negative expectation of the students. Negative self-talk often ensues and eventually the teacher becomes so frustrated he or she tells the class, "This is the worst class I have ever had in all my years of teaching." Students tend to live up to or down to the expectations of the teacher.

> *Students tend to live up to or down to the expectations of the teacher.*

Change is a Challenge

After four years as Assistant Director of Housing at UW-La Crosse, I realized I belonged back in the high school classroom. Several people with whom I worked tried to convince me that it would be a "step down" to go from a university position to teaching in high school. I was determined to do what I wanted to do, and was eager to get back to teaching history and coaching high school football. During the early 1970's, there was a high demand for teachers. Considering a number of opportunities, we chose Seymour High School. At Seymour, I had the opportunity to have my own classroom and teach U.S. History, which I thoroughly enjoyed.

> **Hot Tip!** *It took me about five years to figure this out, but once I became comfortable doing what I wanted to do, instead of what others thought I should do, I was much more content. There is a myth in our society that one must continually be moving "upward" in order be successful. I've known teachers who became principals and regretted the move out of the classroom. When you really like what you are doing, you don't have to "work" a day in your life.*

The Early Years in Seymour

Seymour had a beautiful new facility, but the athletic program was struggling. In fact, the football team had gone 22 years without a winning season. At one time they lost 37 games in a row, and actually went one season without scoring a point. In spite of the advice from respected coaches who said, "Seymour is a graveyard for coaches. You will never win there." I took the job. My young wife and I, and two small children moved to Seymour to begin a new adventure. Little did we realize at the time, the biggest challenge was not coaching football or teaching history, it was changing people's attitudes. In a short time I realized it wasn't the students who were the problem; it was the attitude of many of the faculty and parents.

After signing my contract with the superintendent of schools, I was walking down the hallway and I noticed a teacher coming toward me. Enthusiastically I extended my hand and said,

> *"You're going to be sorry you came to this damn school, kids around here don't want to win."*

"Collar's the name. Football's the game. I'm the new football coach." He limply took my hand and replied, "You're going to be sorry you came to this damn school, kids around here don't want to win." I thought, "Kids who don't want to win? I never heard of anything like that." At that moment I pledged to work to show the negative thinkers that Seymour athletes could compete successfully.

A Disastrous Season

The first year our football team compiled a five and four record. We lost five games on the road and four at home. That's right! We were zero and nine, and the saddest thing was that our team was actually worse than the record indicated. If we had played 90 games, we were capable of losing all of them. Discipline was lacking, the players didn't make a commitment, and "teamwork" was a foreign word to most of the players. When I walked down the hallway a number of teachers would look at me with the attitude, "I told you. What did you expect?" It was extremely difficult to stay positive, especially when players were quitting the team and we had numerous discipline problems.

Homecoming

The problems peaked during the seventh week of the season when the school was celebrating Homecoming. I had informed the team that the customary Homecoming activities would not be followed. I took time to explain what was expected; and throwing vegetables, throwing eggs, toilet papering, and wrecking floats were not acceptable.

 We reviewed the athletic code and reminded the players of the 10:00 curfew during Homecoming week. The following Monday I was informed that a big party was held the previous night to kick off the Homecoming activities. After investigating the incident, seventeen players, including all the seniors but one, were suspended for the game. In the past, incidents had taken place, but they were usually covered up. Many parents felt there was nothing wrong with the players "having a few drinks." On Wednesday the student unrest at school peaked when over half of the student body of 800 walked out of school, sat down on the lawn, and refused to come back to class until the football players were reinstated. Of course, the Green Bay TV stations had been contacted and the media was having a big local news day.

Changing Attitudes

Meanwhile an administrative meeting took place, and I was the featured guest. Pressure was exerted to reinstate the players so conditions could get back to normal. My mind was made up that a statement must be made with regard to expectations of the athletes, and past traditions must be changed. I was so convinced that earlier I had called my wife and told her, "If the administration backs down, I'm resigning and we are leaving town." She was shaken up, but I was determined that to make the football program competitive, we must first have a commitment from parents and players to follow the rules. Definitely my positive attitude was being challenged. Just when the Superintendent of Schools began to waver, it started to rain. I had learned from my experiences at UW-La Crosse during the anti-war protests, that the strength of a movement could be determined by the degree of conviction displayed during a thunderstorm. Gradually the students drifted into school, and the impasse was over. The suspensions were maintained, our marriage was saved, and we took a step in the right direction by not backing down to the students and pleas of many parents.

Disaster

The Homecoming game was a disaster. We trailed 39-0 at halftime. Consideration from the opposing coach limited the score to an embarrassing, but forgettable 45-0 margin. The entire season was a bust. Players didn't show up for games, suspensions were common, players quit, and we even had an alcohol-drinking incident in the back of the player bus after our final game. Perhaps the most creative incident was when identical twins (who I could never tell apart) switched jerseys and played different positions. Meanwhile, the JV team lost all of their games, finished with 15 players, and in one game a substitute refused to play. The outlook was bleak, but with the support of the principal, a handful of parents, a small core of dedicated sophomores, and a determined group of coaches, we believed Seymour football could be competitive. The big challenge was to convince the rest of the faculty, parents, and players.

Keep the Faith

We coaches made it a habit to be positive in everything and to preach the success formula:

Desire + Belief + Positive Practice = Peak Performance!

I offered to speak to the Lion's Club, the Kiwanis, the Women's Club, Chamber of Commerce, and anyone who regularly had meetings. Since the team hadn't won a game yet, people often were critical and asked difficult questions. Some people even believed Seymour athletes weren't capable of competing successfully against players from the city schools. People used every excuse imaginable such as, "Everyone in town is related and our kids are physically inferior to those in other communities." Another one I heard more than once, "So much gas has leaked into the water supply that our athletes are not as strong or fast as others." I know they sound unbelievable, but I heard them.

Criticism

Often when a person is unsuccessful at a task, he or she has the tendency to go into a shell and hide out. It is best to do the opposite. Make it a point to get out in the district and be visible. Be positive and preach the success formula. It doesn't make any difference if we are talking about drama, music, classroom activities, a building project, or athletics, make it your mission to spread the message! Communicate your positive attitude.

Being a new teacher, I had a heavy teaching load and a study hall to supervise. Most of the students were great, but when I would stop in the faculty lounge or eat lunch with the rest of the staff, it seemed like the main topic was how bad everything was. Eventually I couldn't take it anymore, and feeling that my attitude was being pulled down by all the negative talk, I started eating lunch with the students in the commons area. Some colleagues interpreted the move as my thinking that I was better than they were. Eventually the principal suggested that I spend more time with the rest of the staff in the lounge. Perhaps that was the only time an administrator had to convince a teacher to spend more time in the lounge!

Attitudes are Contagious

Whether it is called "the lounge" or "the faculty workroom," most teachers perceive it as an area where they can relax for a bit, get some work done, and engage in conversation with other staff members. That is critical in the workplace. Everyone needs a place to ventilate and commiserate. However, some teachers thought it was their right to spend all their "free" time in the lounge. It was difficult to understand how people could justify in their minds, starting out every day with a 30-minute break. These individuals actually got offended when the principal found the need to remind them that the time before class in the morning was set aside for preparation and meeting with students. Some of the same people finished their day the same way, with a 30-minute "break" in the lounge. Fortunately the number of teachers who possessed constructive views outnumbered the purveyors of pessimism and in time the more upbeat attitude prevailed. New staff members were more upbeat and positive. Attitudes picked up and the lounge became a friendlier place.

The Law of Attraction

Maintaining a positive mental attitude is the key to enjoying life. Program your subconscious mind to expect success and the "Law of Attraction" will do the rest. The "Law of Attraction" simply states, "You become that which you think about the most." If you want to be an outstanding teacher, see yourself as an outstanding teacher.

All teachers are in the sales business. By viewing your students as customers you see yourself a being responsible for selling your product – education. Some students are more enthusiastic about buying your product

> *The Law of Attraction: You become that which you think about the most.*

than others. The challenge is to utilize a number of methodologies to attract the attention of all students. There is no doubt that the profession of teaching requires a complex set of talents and skills. The talents must be diverse to reach a wide range of students. At times you must be a coach, a counselor, a consultant, a friend, a problem solver, an expert, an artist, an explorer, a judge, a warrior, a speaker, a facilitator, and a persuader. Remember: Attitudes are contagious; make sure yours is worth catching!

Selling Your Product

One Harvard Business School study determined that there are four factors critical to success in sales: information, intelligence, skill and attitude. When these factors were ranked as to importance, this particular study found that information, intelligence and skill combined amounted to 7% of the sales effectiveness. Attitude amounted to

> *"Sales are contingent upon the attitude of the salesman – not the attitude of the prospect."*
> **W. Clement Stone**

93%. If 93% of success in sales can be attributed to attitude, it seems the same can be said about teaching.

Make it a point to wear a smile and offer a friendly greeting as you pass students in the hallway. Students appreciate it when you recognize them even though they may not show it. This is especially true of high school students who often are just too "cool" to acknowledge a greeting. I liked to stand next to the door of my room as students came to class. As students entered, I said, "Good morning" or "How are you today?" Other common greetings included, "Let's have a good one" or "Are you fired up for class?" Invariably students smiled and make some reply. Around the first of November, I stood in the same spot, but didn't say anything to the students. Out of 25 individuals maybe four or five greeted me first. As I started class, I asked, "What was different today?" The students replied, "You didn't talk to us as we came in the class." My next question was, "How many of you greeted me?" Perhaps four or five hands went up.

As I inquired about their reluctance to acknowledge my presence at the door, I made the

> *You get from people that which you give people.*

point that you get from people that which you give to people. The response was usually a quizzical look as if I was from another planet. I encouraged the students to improve their communication skills by building a friendly personality and reminded them, "If you want to be treated with dignity and respect, treat others with dignity and respect." It was a teachable moment that made a lasting impression on the students. Of course the next day most of the students were over zealous in their greeting.

Teach the Student

The many lessons we all teach in social skills and relating with others will not be on the vast battery of tests students are required to take. We must continue to make the commitment to teach the student in addition to the subject. It is easy to look the other way when a teachable moment is at hand. Suppose you are out in the hallway and a student yells out an obscene comment to another student. Stay calm and simply say to the student, "That kind of language is very offensive to many people, please think about what your are saying before you speak." Another appropriate comment might be, "Please use language that is acceptable here in school." The vast majority of the time students will realize the language was inappropriate and they will learn from it. In fact, often they don't even realize what they said, and when you bring it to their attention they will apologize and move on. A key point is to always make a statement rather than ask a question. If you ask, "Why are you using that kind of language?", It gives the individual the opportunity to come back with a wise remark.

Too often, I've observed teachers who apparently are afraid of a confrontation, just ignore foul language as if they didn't hear it. That is unacceptable. The language used influences the overall attitude in the school and the way people interact. Use your positive attitude to influence others and you improve the school climate.

Do Your Best

As a young teacher/coach, a difficult thing to accept was the lack of positive feedback from others. I sensed I was doing a fine job and felt good about my teaching, but administrative evaluations were usually centered on what could be done better, rather than building on what was being done right. For some reason most of the administrators with whom I interacted seemed to subscribe to the philosophy that it was not an effective evaluation (assessment) of the teacher unless suggestions were made for improvement. I tired of the typical "sandwich" where something positive would be said, then suggestions for improvement and then positive comments again. What was wrong with just reinforcing all the positive things that took place? The most effective principals know which teachers need help to improve their effectiveness, and which teachers simply need encouragement to keep doing what they are doing.

I felt like I was just drifting and trying to please the evaluator rather than concentrating on doing what I felt was most effective with the students. The worst thing was that I began to compare myself to others to see how I was shaping up. That is a no win situation. Why waste time and energy worrying about something out of my control? It took me some years to figure out that it is best to focus on the things over which I had the most control – **my** preparation and performance. Once I started concentrating on what I was able to control, my days became more productive.

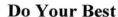

> *"One of the things my parents have taught me is never listen to other people's expectations. Live your own life and live up to your own expectations."*
> *Tiger Woods*

Lead by Example

Realizing that I experienced less stress and became more productive by concentrating on that which I could control, I felt obligated to share the message with students. Many students evaluate themselves by how they compare to others. Have you noticed what students do when papers are corrected and returned? They usually ask their friends what their grade is. Sometimes an "A" student will be disappointed with a "B," but when he or she discovers the other top students earned "C's," suddenly the "B" doesn't look so bad. Why allow someone else to determine the level of performance you accept? I have often used the following diagram to help students comprehend the value of concentrating on their performance rather that on that of others.

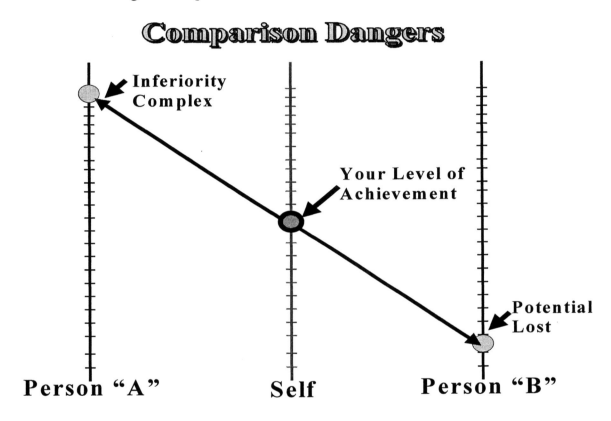

The vertical lines represent the level of achievement. This could be in sports, music, drama, etc. or in the classroom. Person "A" has a very high level of achievement, perhaps the best in school or in the state. Person "B" is struggling and has a low level of achievement. Your performance is somewhere in the middle. When you compare yourself to people who are struggling, it is easy to get complacent and lose potential for growth. Conversely, when you compare yourself to the very best, it is easy to acquire an inferiority complex. You might think that no matter how hard you work, you are not capable of reaching that level. Comparing yourself to others is a lose – lose experience. Only one person can be the best, but all of us are capable of doing our best.

> *Only one person can be the best, but all of us are capable of doing our best.*

Keeping a Positive Attitude

During staff development workshops, teachers have asked, "How do you manage to keep a positive attitude when you have negative students?" I've always believed that deep down all students want to learn, and when the teacher is enthused about the class, the students will be enthused. Unfortunately a few students are always difficult to reach. Most often, eventually they will come around. Provide an assortment of activities, communicate with them individually, and always maintain your composure.

Positive Feedback

In 1977 I was nominated by students and named Wisconsin Social Studies Teacher of the year. It was a significant experience since the DAR, who sponsored the contest, sent me a copy of the letters of recommendation written by my students. After reading what the students wrote, I was shocked to realize my influence on them. One of the most difficult things about teaching at the high school level is that it isn't fashionable for students to tell you how much they enjoy your class or to what degree they value your efforts. Keep in mind your students appreciate your hard work, but seldom do they take the time to express their feelings. *I share some of the comments with you to verify how important it is to maintain a great attitude and set a positive example in the classroom.*

Student Comments

…"Mr. Collar's success in education is in part due to his energy and enthusiasm. He employs a variety of teaching methods to avoid boredom and to give each student the maximum opportunity to excel. He does not lecture. Instead he presents material in a knowledgeable and interesting manner. He often employs projects such as historical recreations, verbal presentations, debates and competitions to enhance more general group instruction and discussion.

Mr. Collar's attitude has also insured his success in the classroom in both teaching and maintaining control. He continually stresses the positive and impresses upon his students that learning is the primary goal of school despite the distractions found in modern education. He is an avid supporter of school activities, but does not allow them to interfere with academics

…For me, Mr. Collar has made history come alive. History is not a collection of past incidents which are locked up in old books. We are living it. Knowing this my interest in and awareness of history grew, and I did better in history than I had previously done…"

This excerpt, written by a junior history student early in my teaching career, points out what makes a difference to students. Notice the reference to "energy and enthusiasm" and "attitude" and "being positive." Theses are character traits an individual has the ability to control. Everyday we have the opportunity to make a decision on what kind of a day we are going to have. Your attitude in class is the number one factor that will influence the classroom atmosphere.

Let's jump ahead eleven more years to 1988 and look at an excerpt from a letter written by a student supporting my nomination for Wisconsin Teacher of the Year.

Be Yourself

"…When you step into his room you can see how involved he is with history. Pictures of the presidents line the walls. Posters showing famous people, the horrors of war, the industrial revolution etc. are on the walls. The front of the room is lined with old newspapers proclaiming famous events. From the ceiling are hung flags of America, models of planes, ships and other artifacts …

...Once Mr. Collar starts teaching all eyes are on him. He never has any trouble with problem students as he has everyone's respect. Each class day is different from the last, and is usually full of surprises. People in history come alive as Mr. Collar comes to class dressed as that person. ...It's not unusual to walk in class and hear him singing a song of historical significance....

Mr. Collar taught us much more than just what is in our history textbooks. He believes that if we understand our heritage and opportunities we have, we will be less likely to be negative in our thinking and develop a positive attitude...."

This selection, written eleven years after the first one, refers to the leadership, enthusiasm and dynamic attitude of the teacher. Notice the reference to "each day being different from the last" and once again citing the importance in developing a "positive attitude." Teaching is hard work. In fact it is exhausting. You must think on your feet as well as on your seat. Planning lessons that are motivational and vary from previous classes is a challenge and a responsibility of every professional educator.

> *"The way of progress is neither swift or easy."*
> *Marie Curie*

Here is a letter received in 1993 from a student who graduated several years earlier. In order to meet a requirement for a college education class, he was required to write a paper describing an "effective and inspirational teacher."

An Effective and Inspirational Teacher

"...Your methods of teaching helped me learn and definitely epitomizes the way that I want to teach. The thing that I remember most about your class was the role-playing and group projects. These learning methods gave me a unique perspective on historical events from different key historical figures and also promoted teamwork within groups. Your periodic dressing as famous men from history helped the past come to life as well as providing comic relief. ...The textbook became just another source of information and not the sole source.

...You could always see the opposing side to everything. Taking a knee in front of a student's desk to maintain eye contact, leading a class clap when a student did an admirable job in something, and using exaggerated hand and facial gestures with great enthusiasm created a positive and healthy learning environment. ...Your classroom was definitely alive and full of energy.

I am sending you this letter because I want you to know that I appreciate your dedication to the teaching profession. As I learn more about the right ways to teach, I frequently remember your teaching style. I want to thank you for instilling in me a positive attitude and sound morals. Finally I want to thank you for being you."

How thoughtful it was of the former student to mail me a copy of what he wrote for a college assignment. What made an impression on me was the reference to "comic relief." Too often we get wound up with facts, figures, formulas, standards, and benchmarks that we forget the most obvious – that we are teaching students. Young people have impressionable minds and need a break from the routine in order to digest all the daily details. Once

> *"Even if you are on the right track, you'll get run over if you just sit there."*
> *Will Rogers*

again a reference was made to an abundance of enthusiasm and a classroom "alive and full of energy." What better memories can a teacher have other than a former student remembering your teaching style and modeling themselves after you?

During my final year of teaching high school (2001) a student from the previous year walked in my classroom handed me a paper and said, "Here Mr. Collar, I think you should read this." She was applying for a scholarship and was required to write an essay about someone who was an inspiration in her life.

Enthusiasm

"On any given day the enthusiasm is contagious in Mr. Collar's history class. He never fails to encourage all students in their learning. To me Mr. Collar has been an inspiration. …His success with students is due to his dedication to excellence. He will not accept excuses or discouragement; instead he works with the students to develop their self-esteem. This helps them complete their own work and be proud of their accomplishments. Everyday his attitude in class is inspirational…

…In his class he taught me that I must learn from my mistakes and all of my life experiences while keeping a positive mental attitude…"

Again notice the reference to "enthusiasm" and "keeping a positive mental attitude." It was always my plan to "flame out" and not "burn out." I never understood the teachers who would complain about virtually everything and then make comments like, "I only have six more years left and I'm out of here." It sounded like they were in prison, and it was just a matter of completing their sentence. When we start counting the years or days left before retirement, we lose sight of our greatest challenge – bringing spirit and enthusiasm to the classroom everyday.

> "Teachers teach because they care. Teaching young people is what they do best. It requires long hours, patience and care."
> Horace Mann

The question is, how do we maintain a positive attitude in spite of adversity? That is the prevailing theme of this entire book. Use the checklist below to help determine where you are now and which areas need the most improvement.

How to Develop and Maintain a Positive Mental Attitude

Directions: *Review the keys to a positive attitude listed below and rank yourself from 5 (High) to 1 (Low) to determine your strengths and weaknesses. If you rank 2 or below in any of these categories, develop a plan to improve that area.*

1. **Be enthusiastic!** Move vigorously; use expressive gestures when talking. Maintain eye contact. Walk with a confident stride.
   Rank_____ My plan: _____

2. **Speak in a loud, clear voice.** Always use affirmative statements. Work in the phrases "I can" and "I will" into conversations.
   Rank_____ My plan: _____

3. **Professional pride.** Top teachers view themselves as professionals. When you feel pride in your profession, you strive to live up to your positive expectation.
   Rank_____ My plan: _____

4. **Invest in yourself.** Find the time to take classes, attend workshops, conferences and seminars. Continue to grow as a professional and you feel better about yourself. *"Any living thing that quits growing is dead".*
Rank_____ My plan: _____

5. **Be an active listener.** Make it a point to focus on the person who is speaking and use eye contact, body language and brief comments to affirm you are listening. Demonstrate interest in the ideas and actions of others.
Rank_____ My plan: _____

6. **Wear a smile.** People often form their first opinion of others by their facial expression. A warm friendly smile and personal greeting can be contagious. We cannot control our age, but we can control our expression.
Rank_____ My plan: _____

7. **Set goals.** Goals give us direction and by helping organize our lives, reduce stress. Having a daily, weekly, and monthly plan helps put meaning in our lessons and lives. *"Plan your work, work your plan."*
Rank_____ My plan: _____

8. **Be polite.** Say "please," "thank you" and "you're welcome." Compliment your students on their good points. When you treat them with respect, they will treat you with respect.
Rank_____ My plan: _____

9. **Have a plan to deal with criticism.** Students, parents and other educators may criticize your actions. Be prepared for this, and develop a plan to follow when criticized.
Rank_____ My plan: _____

10. **Positive persistence.** Some students may not be as excited about learning as you are about teaching. Maintain a belief that all students have a desire to learn, and your goal is to help them develop to their full potential.
Rank_____ My plan: _____

11. **Always maintain your composure and self-control.** Remember, you are the professional! You have been trained to solve problems. Students may act out and make cruel statements; the best way to diffuse a volatile situation is to remain calm.
Rank_____ My plan: _____

12. **Exercise your mind and body on a daily basis.** Be a life-long learner. Set a time aside for personal growth. Even thirty minutes daily of professional reading will help you remain innovative. Physical exercise will invigorate the body and refresh the mind.
Rank_____ My plan: _____

13. **Remember the "Golden Rule."** This means more than doing onto others as you would have them do unto you; it means refraining from doing unto others that which you would *not* like them to do to you.
Rank_____ My plan: _____

14. **Learn from failure.** Perhaps this is the most important. Teaching is one profession where failure is a daily reality. You must develop the courage and persistence to learn form your disappointments and view failure as a stepping-stone to future success.
Rank_____ My plan: _____

(The form on page 187 provides many hints about maintaining a PMA.)

Remember life's greatest secret: *"You become that which you think about the most."* In order to keep a positive attitude, you must continually engage in positive self-talk. Daily affirmation of your self-worth and acceptance of your uniqueness is necessary in order to expect the best from others. A positive attitude is one of the most important characteristics to guarantee your effectiveness as an educator. With a PMA you will enjoy life more and help others get the most out of theirs. Attitudes are contagious. Make yours worth catching!

My Master Affirmation

During the summer of my third year at Seymour, Dick Tepp, the curriculum coordinator, offered a workshop on personal and professional development with an emphasis on goal setting.

> *"To love what you do and feel that it matters – how could anything be more fun?"*
> *Katharine Graham*

The process was based on the principles introduced in Chapter 5. He encouraged the participants to write a "Master Affirmation." He further elaborated that we should form a mental picture of the teacher we wish to become. Dick directed us to write in the first person and not be concerned if the statements are true. He emphasized describing the person we wished to become. Here is what this struggling teacher wrote in 1976, years before I received any awards or recognition.

> *"I am an exciting and energetic teacher. I use my imagination and creativity to continually come up with new ideas to challenge my students. I constantly search for new methods to teach certain concepts. I emphasize student involvement in the learning process.*
> *I enjoy the feeling I get when I witness students demonstrating their achievements to others. I begin each day with a positive expectancy. I realize I am an extremely important person in the lives of the young people I work with...*
> *I thank the Lord for guiding me into the field of education. It is challenging and constantly changing. I am willing to take creative risks to contribute to the development of new teaching strategies...*
> *I am sincerely interested in the welfare if each student and do everything I can to allow for individual differences. I see obstacles as opportunities, barriers as hurdles, and instead of problems I see solutions. I enjoy every day I am alive."*

He then told us to sign the statement and keep it handy for future reference. Dick then directed us through the process to make our dreams come true. This experience was one of the most meaningful and memorable of my teaching career. It provided direction and has helped me become the person I envisioned. Have you ever taken the time to write out your philosophy of education? How about writing your own "Master Affirmation" and describe the person you plan to become.

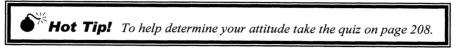

Hot Tip! *To help determine your attitude take the quiz on page 208.*

A Look Back - Reinforce the Positive

Educational experts remind us to reinforce the behavior we would like repeated. Being a perfectionist, as a young coach I tended to focus too much on negative actions. After a loss I was inclined to have a film session and point out how bad the team was playing and even criticize individuals as I ran the film back and forth. While it may be necessary to get personal at times and appeal to a team's pride, a coach must be careful to remain positive.

A number of times in my coaching career, after a bad loss the coaches told the team, "We are better than the way we played. The game is over so we are concentrating on the next opponent." If fact, we explained the team is not even going to look at the game film. Adjacent to our game field the boosters erected a "spirit rock." It was a huge boulder engraved with "We **ARE** Seymour." It was our "rally rock" around which we would gather prior to games. The players

> *"When the going gets tough, the tough get going."*
> **Frank Leahy**

were reminded of what it meant to represent their family, school and community. They would touch the rock and then take the field. At this particular practice we brought out the game film from the bad loss and a shovel and proceeded to bury the film under the rock.

We used the rock on many other occasions. The coaches emphasized that our backs always hang on to the ball. If we had a game where we fumbled, we stressed that was out of character for Seymour teams and out came the shovel and a symbolic "fumble ball" that we buried under the

rock. On a couple occasions we had a trumpet player on the team who played taps as we disposed of the "fumble ball." One of the assistant coaches had a pair of green coaching shoes. Prior to a game with a major rival, whose colors were green and gold, we took his shoes and buried them. Throughout the years we periodically used the rock to anchor in a key point. After "burying the negative," the rest of practice was positive with an emphasis placed on the skill we wanted to reinforce.

The players enjoyed the break from routine and it served the purpose. We usually responded with an excellent performance. An important point is to do this type of thing sparingly otherwise players come to expect it and it loses effectiveness.

Hot Tip! *For an example of coaching with a positive attitude, a handout from our coaches' meeting at the beginning of football season is on page 211.*

My Personal Commitment to Maintaining a Positive Attitude
(Check the items that apply to you.)

☐ *Instead of seeing barriers, I see hurdles, instead of obstacles, I see opportunities and instead of problems I see solutions.*

☐ *I have the determination and persistence necessary to overcome any problem.*

☐ *The "law of attraction" helps me move in the direction of my dreams.*

☐ *I wear a smile and present a positive image every day.*

☐ *I have deep down desire to be the best educator that I can be.*

☐ *I focus on my performance and find the time for self-evaluation.*

☐ *I realize that "attitudes are contagious" and make it a point to be a positive role model.*

☐ *I completed the "Positive Mental Attitude" checklist and have identified my strengths.*

☐ *I have developed a personal improvement plan to follow in the pursuit of excellence.*

☐ *I have written my "Master Affirmation" and am taking action to make it come true.*

Personal Motivation and Maintaining a Positive Attitude in the Classroom

Chapter 7

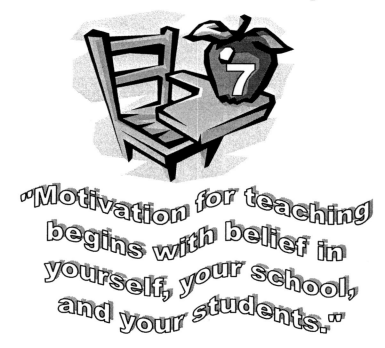

Hippie from the 1960's

> ➤ "It's not whether you get knocked down. It's whether you get up again."
> *Vince Lombardi*

> ➤ "If there was just one word I could use to describe a successful person, that one word would be attitude."
> *Bart Starr*

> ➤ "When you banish fear, nothing terribly bad can happen to you."
> *Margaret Bourke White*

Objectives

- To define personal and classroom motivation
- To identify the principles of effective motivation
- To illustrate the connection between PMA and motivation
- To examine the common barriers to motivation

Personal and Classroom Motivation

"Throw your heart over the fence and the rest of your body will follow"
Norman Vincent Peale

The previous chapter defined a positive attitude as, "An approach to life where instead of seeing barriers, see hurdles, instead of obstacles, see opportunities, and instead of problems see solutions. It is a method of controlling one's thinking and actions by always looking for the best in every situation no matter how dismal things may appear." The chapter then states, "This is difficult to do and it takes time to develop, but is a great way to go through life." This chapter will point out the difference between having a positive attitude and being personally motivated to maintain and spread that attitude.

Motivation is actually two words, motive and action. It is our motive for action, our reason for doing things. We have a positive attitude because we are motivated to see the glass half full instead of half empty. The main theme of this chapter is the origin of motivation and its application in our lives. That application includes maintaining a positive attitude. Positive attitude and positive motivation always go together. It is impossible to be effectively motivated without belief in a positive result. When the teacher is motivated, the student becomes motivated. This chapter addresses teacher and student motivation from a personal point of view, and in the classroom.

The Challenge

The greatest challenge in education is to bring enthusiasm and a positive expectancy to the classroom every day. Since attitudes are contagious, students usually pick up the outlook of the teacher. At times personal problems or family concerns can be on the teacher's mind. In spite of this, the teacher must focus on the task at hand and promote the proper classroom climate. This is difficult to do, but is essential in order to provide students with the best possible educational experience. The attitude we bring to school is the most important factor in determining the overall climate in our classroom. Most often when we are enthused about teaching and excited about the lesson, the students become enthused about learning. While some "experts" say it is impossible to motivate another person, experience indicates the teacher plays a vital role in providing the conditions for effective motivation to take place.

Motivation

Most definitions of motivation include some variation of one I first learned at a workshop many years ago. According to the Success Motivation Institute motivation is, "A desire held in expectation with the belief that it will be realized." Picking the definition apart we see "desire" is a vital ingredient. No one can give us desire; it must spring from within. We must have an innate desire to teach; it is a gift. "Belief" is much different; it can be developed. Belief in yourself as an educator is directly related to the principles of effective classroom leadership.

The key to being effectively motivated is to focus on the objectives for the day. Realize you are an influential person in the life of every student. When you made the decision to become an educator, your motivation probably was to make a positive difference in the lives of others. Always keep that in mind. You are a difference maker everyday! That in itself should be your "motive for action."

Three Types of Motivation

- **F**ear – Fear motivation is sometimes needed. It gets some of us out of bed in the morning. It makes some people obey the law. It can influence students to be in class on time, or pressure them to do their homework.
  > *Strengths: It is quick, decisive and causes action.*
  > *Weaknesses: It is temporary and comes from an external source.*

- **R**eward – We all need a pat on the back at times. Certainly a kind word and recognition for achievement will keep us going. Many students work for high grades and a potential scholarship or college acceptance.
  > *Strengths: It is immediate and recognizable.*
  > *Weaknesses: It is temporary and must come from an external source. Too often it becomes expected and after time it can limit production when the person does just enough to get the reward.*

- **A**ttitude – Attitude motivation is superior to any other type. You control it! It is internal, an "inside job." Positive attitude motivation must be worked on every day. When you control your attitude, you control your thoughts, feelings, actions, habits and behavior. **Go for it!**

Since attitude or internal motivation is personal and long lasting, it forms the foundation for positive action. Unfortunately, fear and reward motivation are easy to administer, while attitude motivation is complex. Because of this, it is often expedient to offer numerous incentives or to engage in intimidation. These may offer a quick fix, but lasting change requires attitude motivation.

Change

Research indicates that "burnout" or the tendency to "get in a rut" often rears its ugly head somewhere between the sixth and twelfth year of teaching. If this does occur, the best antidote is to do a self-analysis and take a close look at how you are doing things. Perhaps it is a time for change. Change can be very refreshing. Examine how and what you are teaching. Simple modifications in procedure can lead to renewed spirit and enthusiasm. During various stages of my career, I was refreshed by teaching history in reverse chronological order, integrating history with literature, utilizing new technology, developing a new class or by making other minor changes such as revising a unit or employing new methodology.

About twenty years ago, I started presenting staff development programs for school districts. The most common concern of teachers was how to maintain a positive attitude and stay motivated in the classroom. Teaching is a very rewarding profession, but at times we can get into a rut, and develop the feeling that our extra efforts are not appreciated. To summarize the major points of the presentation I created the following handout. These vital points are just as important today as they were then. Consider applying each of them to your life. They are condensed on pages 204-205.

Twenty-Five Time-Tested Tips for Maintaining a Positive Attitude and Personal Motivation in the Classroom

1. **Self-Esteem - You must believe in the value of your teaching and your impact on youth. You are an important person. Feel good about your accomplishments and wear a smile. It's contagious!**

Concerned educators expect all their lessons to be successful. In reality the best teachers are those who experience some failure on the road to success. When a teacher is well prepared and puts the necessary planning time into the lesson, the class is set up for success. The most effective teachers are innovative and look at each day as a

> *If you are not failing on occasion you are not being very innovative.*

challenge. At times people will expect you to solve all of society's ills and undue blame will be assessed for things that you really can't control. Take charge of your feelings, maintain high expectations, but realize there will be challenging times.

Always remember, you control the thoughts that determine how you will act. Positive thoughts lead to positive actions. See yourself as being a member of the world's most important profession. Be proud to be a teacher. Many people see self-esteem (the way you feel about yourself) as being strengthened by success. Actually meaningful self-esteem is built through struggle and self-actualization.

2. **Goals - Establish a number of concise, written goals and develop a plan to reach them. You should include short range, intermediate, and long term goals. Consider all areas of your life when planning for the future. It is important to keep your "wheel" round.**

Just as you have goals and objectives for your lessons, it is essential to have direction in your personal life. Time management is vital for getting the most out of each day. By establishing goals in the six areas of your life and following a logical goal completion plan, you will experience a sense of organization and efficiency.

My life became much more organized after taking a class in goal setting and time management. Keep your eyes on the prize, and live each day to the fullest. It is extremely rewarding to move in the direction of your dreams and to constantly challenge yourself. As Robert Browning said, "Man's reach must exceed his grasp."

3. **Imagination - Set your imagination free. Continually search for new ideas that will help make your lessons more appealing. Develop a "constructive discontent" with the status quo. Utilize various approaches to reach all learning styles.**

Much research has been done in recent years to determine how students learn. It is necessary to stretch your teaching style to reach all learners. Research indicates the typical attention span in minutes, is age, plus or minus two minutes. This means it is essential to include a wide variety of methodologies to enhance motivation and concentration. In order to do this, constantly search for ways to invigorate your classroom and

> *"It is the supreme art of the teacher to awaken joy in creative expression and knowledge."*
> *Albert Einstein*

put more zest into activities. Remember: The greatest barrier to creativity is the perception of not being creative.

4. **PMA - Develop a positive approach to life. Begin each day with a positive expectancy. Program your subconscious mind to expect success, and the "law of attraction" will do the rest. An essential ingredient to a great attitude is to maintain a sense of humor. Laughter in the classroom helps promote an atmosphere conducive to learning.**

> *"The most extraordinary thing about a really good teacher is that he or she transcends accepted educational methods."*
> *Margaret Mead*

You get from students what you give to students. When you are fired up and enthused about the day's activities, your students will be enthused. Greet your students by name, show interest in them outside the classroom and expect success. Control your self-talk and inspire your classroom through displaying positive sayings, inspirational posters and examples of quality work. The law of attraction says, "You become that which you think about the most."

5. **Motivation - Be a self-starter. Your goal-setting plan will help you develop enthusiasm toward each day. Believe in your value to the system. Internal motivation will serve as the spark to get you started for another day of achievement.**

Your desire to provide the best possible learning environment in your classroom is the key to stimulating learners. Since most educators enter the profession driven by a sincere concern for young people and an altruistic sense of serving humankind, disappointment is not uncommon. Appreciate the small victories, realize there will be frustrations, but remain focused on success. Believe that deep down every student wants to learn, and view your leadership as a vital cog in the educational machine. Take pride in seeing that "aha" look on a student's face when the lesson is finally grasped.

6. **Adversity - Grow with each hardship in your life. Rededicate yourself to overcome fear, worry, doubt and anger. These will sap your strength and smother personal growth.**

Take control of your personal life.

> *"What is necessary to change a person is to change his awareness of himself."*
> *Abraham Maslow*

When you are happy in your relationship with others outside the school day, it is much easier to bring a sense of achievement and positive expectation to school. It is said that 40% of the things people worry about won't happen, and another 40% we have no control over. That only leaves 20%, so why worry? Confidence is simply overcoming fear, worry and doubt. Use the powerful tool of visualization to glance at adversity and then concentrate on success.

Anger causes one to act on emotion rather than reason. Always control your actions through considering the consequences and taking personal responsibility for your actions. We discover the true content of our character by how we respond to adversity.

7. **Decompression Routine - It is important to get away from school and get your mind off teaching. Take a vacation, follow an exercise program, take up a hobby. All of these are important to your mental health. These will help you avoid "burnout." Physical exercise is a must to help combat lethargy. Peak performers are not workaholics.**

Whether you jog, lift weights, paint, knit, work with wood or read, find the time to clear your mind and get away from the stresses involved with education. Take a stress-reduction break at work when you are able to clear your desk and arrange to spend at least 10 undisturbed minutes in a relaxed state. This is different from dropping in the lounge and having a cup of coffee with friends. It is time you have reserved for progressive relaxation involving deep breathing and guided imagery.

In a busy work setting, finding time for yourself can be tough to do. One must be creative and schedule in the time. When I needed some down time, I often would retreat to the coaches' office during my prep period.

8. **Relaxation - Set aside a time each day when you can put your mind at ease by "thinking black." A 15-minute relaxation session can be refreshing and beneficial.**

This relates back to the "decompression routine." By "thinking black," just clear your mind of all worldly thoughts. This may be done at home in your favorite chair at a time when you can get away from the rest of the family. Try it, and you will find it invigorating,

> *Find the time to relax!*

especially when you focus on clearing your mind and reaching a state of total relaxation.

9. **Gratitude - Teachers must cultivate a sense of satisfaction for a job well done. This internal reward is essential when working with teenagers who are usually too self-centered to express thanks for all the effort and assistance granted.**

This is a difficult concept for inexperienced teachers to understand. The phenomenon is most common at the high school level. You may have put a great deal of time and effort into planning an outstanding unit. You sense the students enjoy the experience, learning takes place, there is excellent classroom interaction, but no one takes the time to tell you how much they appreciated your efforts. If you are so inclined and need the feedback, it may be advisable to have the students complete a reaction form. Unfortunately, the problem with an evaluation form is even if only a few students reply negatively, the sensitive teacher will focus on those comments.

One of my most vivid memories as a young teacher was when my wife, who was teaching seventh grade, was overwhelmed with Christmas presents, while my cupboard was bare. Most high school students are reluctant to express gratitude.

10. **Positive Feedback - Keep any letters or notes from students praising your teaching or expressing thanks for the efforts you have made. File them in a special place and refer to them when you have a "down day." This will help you realize a sense of purpose and keep your self-esteem high.**

An experienced teacher passed this tip on to me at a workshop early in my career. Most educators receive little positive feedback, and when it does happen we are so busy we often toss the note or letter aside and forget about it. I kept all communication in a desk drawer in my home office. Periodically over the years when my sense of purpose needed a boost, I would review these tidbits. It was always inspirational and a real ego boost to realize my efforts were appreciated and that I made a significant difference in the lives of numerous students.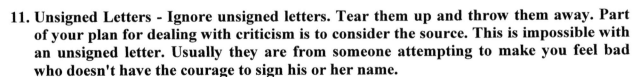

One may expand on this concept by including letters from parents and comments from colleagues. As Mark Twain said, "If no one gives you a pat on the back, give yourself one." Too often positive feedback isn't there when you need it the most.

11. **Unsigned Letters - Ignore unsigned letters. Tear them up and throw them away. Part of your plan for dealing with criticism is to consider the source. This is impossible with an unsigned letter. Usually they are from someone attempting to make you feel bad who doesn't have the courage to sign his or her name.**

I often make this point when presenting at workshops for teachers, and it is fairly common for someone to question the wisdom of this action. The reasoning is based on the principle of having a plan to deal with criticism. My plan for handling criticism is to consider the source. If it comes from someone

> *"The art of being wise is knowing what to overlook."*
> *William James*

who is respected, I'll speak with the person to get things ironed out. If I don't respect the person, I'll ignore it. This may have to be done tactfully, but why would I allow someone who I don't respect affect my feelings?

Keeping this procedure in mind, how can one consider the source when the person doesn't have the courage to sign a name? This procedure was particularly helpful when I was coaching. If a letter was signed "A Concerned Fan," I ripped it up and threw it away without reading it. It felt good!

The value of this course of action was reaffirmed a number of years ago when a woman with whom I was team teaching tearfully stopped by my room after class. She shared a note left by her "6th hour class." It was critical of her and said some very nasty things. Being a sensitive person, she took it to heart and felt the entire class was criticizing her. When I explained it was probably just one or two disgruntled students, she regained her composure. She wouldn't have had the problem if she had first looked for a signature. In reality, she was an outstanding teacher who expected quality work from her students.

12. **Communicate With Parents – Telephone, e-mail, or send letters to parents of your better students. They deserve recognition, and you will feel good about the positive comments you have made.**

All educators know how important it is to stay in touch with parents. Too often in the classroom most of the attention is given to those who are struggling or causing problems. Make sure you find the time to recognize the children who are achieving.

I found it rewarding to telephone the parents of marginal students who had demonstrated considerable improvement. Usually the parents were surprised and elated to receive positive news from school.

> *Communicate with parents about positive things.*

13. **Teamwork - Support other teachers. Congratulate your colleagues for their achievements and the successful programs they generate.**

All teachers need some type of a support system. We like to be recognized for our achievements and be given encouragement when struggling. Make it a point to attend school functions and recognize the extra efforts of your colleagues. Upon occasion, slip a note into the mailbox of a teacher who is the advisor to an activity or supervises a unique project. Yes, even coaches can use a pat on the back at times.

You are part of the educational team, and everyone at school benefits through the support of extracurricular activities. You will feel good about helping raise the self-esteem of your colleagues.

14. **Administration – Work with the administration to build the best possible learning experience for students. When you have concerns or suggestions, speak with the people responsible. Be persistent with concepts you believe will be beneficial to all.**

There is no place for top-down management in a progressive educational setting. Clear lines of communication must be open between the faculty and administration. Classroom teachers must realize everyone has the same end in mind, and when mutual respect exists everyone benefits.

When controversial issues develop, resolve differences through discussion and compromise. Keep the atmosphere in the teacher's workroom positive and know school concerns must remain at school. It is counter-productive to sit at the local bowling alley or restaurant and speak negatively about school issues. Instead of criticizing, talk about all the positive things that are happening at school.

15. **Respect Students – Mutual respect between student and teacher is ideal. Exercise caution when students seek counseling from you and refer them to professionals for assistance. Beware of "student friendships" and maintain a proper relationship.**

Student privacy must be respected at all grade levels, but it is vital at the middle school and high school to understand a certain degree of distance must be maintained between the student and teacher. Teenagers are experiencing many changes, and it is not uncommon for a favorite teacher to be considered a "friend." It is up to the professional to guarantee the proper relationship is maintained. When a student would begin to confide in me and share personal matters, my goal was to refer them to a professional counselor as soon as possible.

While a teacher may be pleased that the student thinks enough of him or her to share personal concerns, the teacher must realize his or her limitations, and the possible undesirable consequences of creating a too familiar relationship. When I was faced with that type of situation, I escorted the student to the counseling office and introduced them to the person who was capable of giving assistance.

> *Maintain a professional relationship with students.*

16. **Extra-curricular Activities – Students appreciate teachers who are sincerely interested in them. Your support of activities tells them you care about their accomplishments. Find the time to work as a coach or advisor. It keeps you young.**

You send a positive message to young people when you take the time to attend and comment on their performances. Whether it is a dramatic production, musical presentation, National Honor Society induction or sports event, your presence, is appreciated. With children at home, and parents multi-tasking, it is difficult to attend many evening events at school, but the rewards are many.

With the complex nature of today's society, because of time commitments, it is virtually impossible for everyone to coach or advise a club or organization. Sometimes duties can be shared between two individuals, and more teachers will have the opportunity to interact with the students outside the classroom.

17. **T.L.S. – Avoid the "Teachers Lounge Syndrome." Keep your comments upbeat in the lounge. It is easy to become critical of just about everything when you have a challenging day. Associate with optimistic people, and avoid the "if'a, would'a. could'a, should'a, and yeah-buts!"**

Take care to view each obstacle as an opportunity. By refraining from negative talk and criticism of students, a climate is maintained that is conducive to problem solving. It is acceptable occasionally to ventilate and share your concerns with colleagues. Everyone needs to do this at times, but nobody likes to be around a chronic complainer.

During one stage of my career, I found the lounge (workroom) such a negative place I seldom visited, and I even chose to eat lunch with the students. An insightful principal encouraged me to spend more time in the lounge. He correctly pointed out that I would benefit more by interacting with other faculty, than by segregating myself.

18. **Professionalism – Teachers often speak about their desire to be treated as professionals. Make it a point to uphold high standards. Always keep confidential information privileged, and school news at school. Use good judgment when socializing.**

It is not enough to say you are a professional. Your dress, talk and actions must convey this message. Think of the professionals you hold in high regard in other occupations. What is it about them you admire? It is up to you to convey that same impression. You only have one chance to make a good first impression. Be careful about keeping school business confidential when interacting with the public.

19. **Community – Be active in your community. Parents and students will appreciate your interest in local activities. Share your knowledge and enthusiasm with civic organizations.**

Because of the mobile nature of today's society, more teachers are commuting to neighboring schools, and it is increasingly difficult to participate in community activities. Efforts can be made to overcome this obstacle through making a commitment to share your uniqueness with school parent organizations and arrange to be a guest at local meetings.

Inviting people of interest in the community into your classroom is another way to help promote good will and understanding. Field trips, participation in local events, parent teacher organizations, youth and church activities, all of these provide us with opportunities to interact with parents and community leaders.

20. Time – Make effective use of your time. It is easy to waste valuable time that could be spent in a constructive manner. Keep a daily "will do" list and prioritize your tasks. To make most efficient use of the hours available to you, consider taking a class in time management.

Each day consists of 24 hours. How you organize yourself and utilize that time will have a huge impact on your level of stress. Just making a priority list and crossing things off as you accomplish them can be very rewarding and provide a sense of accomplishment.

> *"When you put your hand to the plow, you can't put it down until you get to the end of the row."*
> *Alice Paul*

Make a list of the time wasters in your life and develop a plan to overcome them. Most common include, watching television, talking on the phone, surfing the Internet, and chitchat sessions. Write down how you spend your time for a week and then analyze how you can eliminate the timewasters.

21. Personal Growth – An occasional summer class, clinic, conference or workshop can be stimulating. Make it a point to have experiences that will enhance your teaching effectiveness. This will keep you fresh and aware of the latest educational research.

Early in my teaching career a mentor told me, "Any living thing that quits growing is dead." That phrase has been with me throughout the years. It is important to stay out of a rut. Occasionally take the time to clear out your files and revise your unit plans.

These are exciting times in education. With all the research ranging from Multiple Intelligences and Brain-Based learning to Differentiated Instruction and Standards Based Education, numerous exceptional strategies are available to teachers.

22. Change – Look at change as a challenge. Modify your classes through using different approaches and various teaching techniques. Make twenty years' experience pay off rather than repeating one year's experience twenty times. Welcome technology into your classroom. It is stimulating and provides you with the opportunity to reach more students.

The best way to accept change is to help make it happen. A good example is when the computer revolution hit schools. Some of the more experienced teachers refused to learn how to use the new technology. They refered to the fact they only had a few years left to teach and didn't want to take the time to learn. This is a self-destructive attitude and will lead to burnout.

> *"In teaching it is the method and not the content that is the message. It is the drawing out, not the pumping in."*
> *Ashley Montague*

When students began making innovative PowerPoint presentations in my classroom I didn't want to get left behind. Several students took the time to teach me the basics so my toolbox could continue to grow.

My teaching improved with the realization that students are great resources. They enjoy sharing their knowledge and asking for assistance helps develop rapport.

23. **Student Behavior – The teacher has the responsibility to maintain a classroom atmosphere favorable to learning. No one has the right to destroy the learning environment for others. Make sure you find the time to establish proper behavior guidelines for the classroom.**

While this topic has been addressed in other chapters of the book, it cannot be stressed enough. Over the years I spent very little time on classroom discipline. It is critical during the first week of class to establish an environment of mutual respect and to uphold that during the course of the year. The key is to place the responsibility in the hands of the students. Explain how vital it is to make every day a learning experience and no one has the right to sabotage learning for anyone else.

At the high school level I found it meaningful to emphasize to the students that they will be competing against students from other schools in the conference not just in activities, but also for jobs, college and in life. Their level of concern was raised when they realized what they invested now would pay dividends later. Use examples from daily life to illustrate the value of making the most of the time spent in the classroom.

24. **Enthusiasm – Take time to plan lessons you are enthusiastic about. Enthusiasm is contagious. Make an effort to obtain maximum student involvement in learning. Be the "guide on the side" and not the "sage on the stage." Decrease the gap between what you teach and what the students learn.**

When you are excited about your subject and your classes, your students are more likely to get excited. Be an active teacher. Move around the room, use effective gestures, vary your voice, ask the right questions, and plan great activities. At least once a year, video your class and do a self-evaluation.

I found it helpful to have the students complete a class evaluation at the conclusion of the year. Having had juniors, most took this seriously. I explained they could be a big help in my improvement as a teacher and please be sincere. Over the years this was extremely valuable. This is explained in more detail in chapter one.

25. **Patience – Always keep your composure when dealing with students. It is best to reason things out without resorting to emotion. Allow individuals a way to avoid public embarrassment when they put themselves in a difficult position.**

Keep in mind that you are the professional and you have been trained to defuse potentially explosive situations. Speaking with students one on one is the most effective form of communication. Most people will demonstrate respect when treated with respect. Some students bring much baggage to school. Keep your cool in potentially volatile situations.

By wearing a smile you convey a warm, caring attitude. Do your best to keep non-school problems out of school and maintain a positive attitude. There are days when family problems or health concerns will be wearing heavily on your mind. It takes a special person to put their personal concerns behind them when arriving at school.

Sense of Humor

The most common question that comes up is, "Bill, how come you haven't included maintaining a sense of humor on your list?" Actually, when I originally came up with the list I

> *A laughing classroom is a learning classroom.*

never thought of including humor as a separate category. To me it is a given. Humor must be included in everything we do. When interacting with students, see the humor in daily developments. Develop the ability to laugh at yourself and with students. Take the time to explain to students what is appropriate humor and model that behavior in your teaching. Be sure students understand what constitutes hurtful humor, and why it is unacceptable. A lesson that includes humor is a memorable learning experience. Always remember: "A laughing classroom is a learning classroom." Chapter Nine will examine the use of humor in education in more detail.

Thoughts on Motivation

Keep in mind that coaching is teaching and teaching is coaching. The only thing that changes is the location. Developing teamwork is essential in the academic classroom, on the stage, the athletic field, gym or wherever education takes place. Over the years the application of these motivational principles has led to success in the classroom and in coaching. What is success? The following definition works best for me. "The progressive realization of worthwhile, predetermined, personal goals."

Stay away from the thinking that it is impossible to motivate another person and that all individuals are responsible for their own motivation. To me this is an excuse; it is a way of saying the teacher is not responsible

> *"Always do more than is required of you."*
> *George Patton*

for motivating the class. The effective teacher can and does utilize motivational principles to establish a non-threatening classroom climate that is conducive to learning and the free exchange of ideas. Consider these fundamental motivational thoughts that I followed for personal, student, and classroom motivation. A summary sheet on self-motivation is in the appendix on page 193.

Motivational Principles

- **Motivation can be learned or developed. A person doesn't have to be born with it.**

     When provided with a goal or mission in life, one is more apt to take action. This is why it is important to speak with students about their future and to explain the reason why they are being required to learn the lesson being taught.

     Educational application: Educators have an obligation to assist students in establishing classroom and personal goals.

- **To be effectively motivated, a person must possess a desire to act, have high self-esteem, and a positive mental attitude.**

     Effective motivation is extremely difficult without belief or self-confidence. Once again, this concept points out the value of teaching the student first and then the subject.

Educational application: Educators must provide a variety of learning experiences that will give students many opportunities to realize success. As students struggle to overcome setbacks, they experience more success and their self-esteem improves. With improved self-esteem comes a renewed vigor to transcend previous levels of achievement.

- **Belief in one's job and in one's purpose is the essence of motivation.**

  When a person believes his or her daily work is valued, he or she is more likely to do more than is required. This is true of students and teachers.

  Educational application: Educators must help students see the relationship between learning and life.

- **What a person really needs in life is not a stress-free state, but the striving and struggling to accomplish a goal that provides a feeling of accomplishment.**

  The only people who are absolutely tension free are in the grave. A certain amount of stress means a person is concerned about doing the best job possible.

  Educational Application: Educators are compelled to help students develop a procedure to deal with setbacks and disappointments. Teachers need to have many safety nets in place to provide students with many avenues to success.

- **A person should not attempt to motivate another with the reverse of an idea. Example: "Don't do drugs. They mess up your mind."**

  People tend to act on their dominant thoughts. By telling someone what not to do, you actually introduce that thought into his or her mind. This topic is addressed in more detail in chapter three.

  Educational Application: Always speak with the expected end result in mind. Explain to students what you expect them to do and how they may act to reach the desired result.

- **We become what we think about the most.**

  The human brain is like a heat-seeking missile. When a person concentrates on success and possesses mental images of achievement, he or she is more likely to be successful. More discussion of this principle is found in chapter four.

  Educational application: Help students understand how to use the powerful tool of visualization. Convince them to believe "The body can only achieve what the mind can perceive."

- **To the degree you provide others with what they need, they will give back to you what you need.**

  The more you do for others, the more others will do for you. Some people have difficulty with this concept; however, when you really believe in doing things for others because you feel good about doing them, many rewards will come back to you. Of course most people don't keep track of what they are doing for others, or even expect something in return. It is just a beneficial attitude to carry through life.

  Educational application: See yourself as a "servant leader," one who is in the business of helping others experience peak performance. Your motivation comes from the intrinsic rewards you reap as your students achieve.

- **When you fear a possible outcome, you actually set it up as your sub-conscious goal.**

  Since we are moved by our dominant thoughts, fearing an outcome or event and concentrating on that thought actually moves one toward that end.

  Educational application: Assist students in using positive, affirmative thoughts and language. Instead of saying, "I really get nervous when I have to speak in front of the class," convince them to think, "This is a great opportunity for me to experience personal growth."

- **People do things for their reasons, not your reasons. Those reasons are usually emotional and determined by the way a person feels.**

  Keeping this in mind, it is best to remember when attempting to influence a person, a teacher/coach should approach the individual by indicating how he or she will benefit from the experience.

  Educational Application: When attempting to recruit a student for a team or activity, too often educators will explain to the individual how much the student will be able to contribute to the activity. Most often the potential recruit will respond better when it is clearly explained how he or she will benefit from team participation.

- **It can be difficult to motivate others. However, you can arouse and stimulate those inclinations within others that steer their thoughts and actions.**

  This gets back to the issue of motivating others. Once again, you may not be able to motivate another person, but you can help establish the conditions that enable people to motivate themselves. Relate this principle to multiple intelligences and brain-based learning.

  Educational Application: Always remember, "Attitudes are contagious." Teach who you are first and then what you know.

> *"America's future will be determined by the home and the school. The child becomes largely what he is taught; hence we must watch what we teach, and how we live."*
> *Jane Addams*

Frustration

Many skilled educators have experienced the frustration of doing everything possible to motivate a student with little to show for it. At a regional social studies conference in Chicago, I asked a nationally recognized educational expert what could be done to motivate students who just don't show any interest in learning. Expecting a solution, I anxiously waited with my pen in hand for his well-researched response. I was shocked when he replied. "Oh, you mean the brain dead?" He explained that no matter how hard we work, sometimes it is impossible to reach all students. His response reminded me how easy it is to give up on a student. At that time I made the commitment to do everything possible for student success, but to realize some of the responsibility for learning rests with the student. We are fortunate that schools have many special programs and safeguards in place. It behooves every educator to identify students with special needs as soon as possible.

Barriers to Motivation

All educators have to deal with students who lack the motivation to experience success. We spend countless hours attempting to determine how to reach each student. By being aware of the most common barriers to motivation, an educator is equipped to devise a plan for remediation. I found Mel Levine's book, *A Mind At A Time*, thought provoking and practical. Levine, a psychologist, cites a number of reasons why students lack motivation.

Most Common Barriers to Motivation
(Condensed from Mel Levine's book: A Mind At A Time)

1. **High levels of performance anxiety.** Students must be taught how to study, take tests and overcome fear, worry and doubt. Too often we assume students have capable study and test taking skills.
   - It is not the purpose of this book to elaborate on study skills and test taking, but most chapters address overcoming fear, worry and doubt.

2. **A total lack of concern.** When a student is frustrated or has experienced too much failure an, "I don't care" attitude may develop and failure becomes an expectation.
   - This student will benefit from a practical goal setting plan demonstrating how it is possible to attain goals.

3. **A lack of self-esteem.** Self- esteem is earned through a series of accomplishments. The student who has had few successes in school can be easily discouraged.
   - Teachers can assist this student through providing choices that take into consideration multiple intelligences and individualized instruction.

4. **A negative self-fulfilling prophecy.** Continual failure leads to more failure, just as success promotes more success.
   - The obvious answer is to coordinate the level of difficulty of the task with the ability level of the student. A number of examples follow this section.

5. **Misunderstood learning disabilities.** Teachers must be aware of "red flags" that are indicative of special needs.
   - Find the time to become knowledgeable about how to identify these students.

6. **The presence of serious family problems.** It is difficult for students to maintain a positive attitude in school when a negative attitude exists in the home.
   - Get to know you students and their family structure.

7. **Physical health problems.** Teachers must be aware of the warning signs and report any unusual circumstances to the proper resource person.

Boiling a Frog

I've often been asked, "Bill, what is the best method to motivate kids?" I like to sum up my philosophy by using the example of boiling a frog. If you have a pot of boiling water on the stove and you drop the frog in, it will jump out because the water is too hot. If you put a pot of cool water on the stove and drop in the frog, the frog will "frog around" and feel comfortable. As the frog is enjoying the water, gradually turn the heat up and pretty soon the frog will be boiling without even realizing it.

While frog advocates may not like the story, it does make the point about how teaching is most effective when the student is feeling comfortable and task is not too difficult. Catch students being successful and then gradually increase the level of difficulty.

> *"Flatter me, and I may not believe you. Criticize me, and I may not like you. Ignore me, and I may not forgive you. Encourage me and I will not forget you."*
> William A. Ward

For those readers who are more comfortable with a graph or chart perhaps the following example will be more acceptable.

Student Success

The Challenge Zone

The goal is to keep as many students as possible in the "Challenge Zone" by aligning the level of difficulty with the ability level of the student. If the level of difficulty is high and the ability level is low, the student ends up in the "Panic Zone." If the level of difficulty is low and the ability level is high, the student ends up in the "Drone Zone." I believe the most challenging aspect of teaching is to individualize instruction to the point where the maximum numbers of students are in the "Challenge Zone." It takes a master teacher to meet this goal. You can do it!

It is much easier to motivate a student to learn when he or she feels capable of accomplishing the task. Remember the definition of motivation that we stated early in the chapter, "A desire held in expectation with the **belief** that it will be realized."

A Look Back - Motivation for Fire Drills

It was one of my best classes ever. You know how it feels; you're in the zone, it's a great lesson, the students are exhibiting all the signs of active listening and you're on the verge of driving home the main concept. Everything in the lesson has led up to this point, and now you're anticipating the "aha" moment when the students finally get it. That's what keeps us excited about teaching. The student light is about to go on and your hand is on the switch. Then it happened, "aa-nt, aa-nt, aa-nt." It was a fire drill at the least propitious moment. Deeply chagrined, I felt like I just struck out with the bases loaded. I followed the students out the door and sauntered lethargically down the hall past the principal to the exit.

Of course the penultimate moment was lost. All the set up was wasted, the period ended as the students returned to the room and I felt like I was left alone at the

> **"Life is what we make it, always has been, always will be.**
> *Grandma Moses*

altar. Later, when I picked up my mail, I noticed a note from the principal. "Bill, see me about the fire drill." He greeted me with the statement, "I would like to see you show more enthusiasm for fire drills." He then explained that I was not setting a very good example for the students. Of course he was right. I explained myself and assured him it wouldn't happen again. I proceeded to the lounge for lunch and ventilated to my colleagues. For the next several days I was kidded about showing more enthusiasm for fire drills.

While shopping for a birthday present for my daughter I spotted a fireman's hat complete with a flashing red light on the top and a siren. Yes, I did it. At the next faculty meeting I had the

 hat in a bag next to my chair, and when the principal asked if anyone else had anything to add, I said, "I have an idea how we can all show more enthusiasm for fire drills." I took out the hat, put it on with the light flashing and siren wailing and said, "What do you think?" He said, "Collar, it's not in the budget! Sorry!" Everyone had a good laugh and we moved on. A principal with a big ego could have made an issue out of the incident, but he took it as a joke and ended the meeting with some humor. I never heard about it again, and from that time on I showed great enthusiasm for fire drills. We had worked together for about 15 years and had a great relationship.

My Personal Commitment to Positive Motivation
(Check the items that apply to you.)

☐ *I believe every student has the ability to learn.*

☐ *I believe I am a member of one of the most important occupations in the world.*

☐ *I know people support what they create and I strive to provide students with ownership.*

☐ *I constantly relate learning to real life experiences.*

☐ *I identify with the expected result when faced with a challenging task.*

☐ *I put fear, worry, doubt and anger behind me and focus on success.*

☐ *I've read the 25 Time-Tested Tips and plan to apply them in my classroom.*

☐ *I never allow anyone else to determine how I feel about myself.*

☐ *I know attitudes are contagious and always keep a positive outlook.*

☐ *I make a consistent effort to keep every student in the "challenge zone".*

Using Emotional Intelligence to Teach Students with Multiple Intelligences

Chapter 8

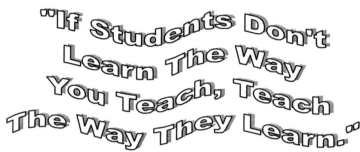

"If Students Don't Learn The Way You Teach, Teach The Way They Learn."

"One if by land, two if by sea ..."

➤ "Many intelligent people are poor thinkers. Many people of average intelligence are skilled thinkers."
> *Edward De Bono*

➤ "What I want when kids get through a K to 12 education is for them to have a sense of what their society thinks is true, beautiful and good; false, ugly and evil; how to think about it and how to act on the basis of your thoughts."
> *Howard Gardner*

➤ "Emotional Intelligence is the primary indicator of success."
> *Daniel Goleman*

Objectives

- To define Emotional Intelligence and Multiple Intelligences
- To offer an Emotional Intelligence self-analysis activity
- To trace the origin and growth of the Multiple Intelligences movement
- To portray the teacher as a successful salesperson

Emotional Intelligence

"All learning has an emotional base."
Plato

During my freshman year in high school my parents built a tavern. Actually it was an early "sports bar" before the phrase became popular. When the tavern was completed, my dad named it "Elmer Collar's Dugout." Dad insisted that his name would be featured since "everyone knew him" and the moniker "Dugout" conveyed the message that it was a gathering place for everyone interested in baseball. The interior was decorated with paintings and pictures of sports scenes with an emphasis on the Milwaukee Braves. Upon entering, one was impressed by the cleanliness of the place and predominant baseball décor.

Poised behind the U-shaped bar was the proud owner in front of his most cherished possession, a four by eight foot painting of the Braves slugger, Eddie Mathews. The realistic painting, portraying the muscular Mathews finishing his home run swing, was a popular conversation piece. Three by five foot pictures of high-kicking pitcher, Warren Spahn and the right-handed ace, Lew Burdette flanked the main entrance. The horseshoe structure of the bar encouraged patron interaction and aided the bar tender in more efficiently serving the customers.

Emotional Intelligence in Action

Emotional Intelligence is defined as, "the capacity to create positive outcomes in the relationships with others and with yourself." Little did I know it at the time, but my father was the perfect example of emotional intelligence in action. I have to smile when I recall the training sessions he had with my older brother and me.

> *Every patron was greeted with a warm smile and a friendly, "How are you?"*

"Always greet everyone. Ask, 'What can I do for you today?' And be sure to thank people when they leave." And remember, "This one is on the house." The purpose of buying a round of drinks was to show appreciation and encourage customers to return. While this is a simplified explanation, it is an example of the application of emotional intelligence. In this case, a satisfied clientele and return customers reflected the positive atmosphere that was created.

First Impressions

In the business world, emotional intelligence is considered to be a key characteristic in customer relations. Sam Walton raised the bar when he introduced the concept of greeting and thanking people at a corporate level. Successful sales people appreciate the value of making a good first impression and gaining the confidence of the client. The ability to problem solve, empathize with the customer, monitor and adjust, and establish trust; these are all examples of emotional intelligence. A recent visit to the atrium area and Hall of Fame in renovated Lambeau field reminded me of the value of creating positive outcomes for others. The atrium has something for everyone, games for the

> *You only get one chance to make a good first impression.*

children, a huge shopping area, Packer history, stadium tours, a food court, adult beverages and many opportunities for vicarious experiences. People who are outgoing and friendly present all of this with a warm smile and kind comment.

Daniel Goleman

The work of psychologist Daniel Goleman, author of ***Emotional Intelligence***, establishes the premise that intelligence is much more complex than what IQ tests can measure. Goleman traces the history of the study of personal intelligence and identifies self-awareness, self-management, social awareness and relationship management as essential skills.

> *"You can't shake hands with a clenched fist."*
> *Golda Meir*

In his book ***Primal Leadership***, Goleman teams with renowned researchers Richard Boyatzis and Annie McKee to explore the role of emotional intelligence in leadership. The authors argue that a leader's emotions are contagious. If a leader exhibits energy and enthusiasm, the organization thrives; if a leader spreads negativity and discord, it flounders. Of course, teachers realize this, and it is an essential part of classroom leadership. This is something that is not tested, but the more EI we can pass on to our students, the greater the likelihood that they will experience academic success. Self-control, initiative, coping skills, teamwork and collaboration, these are all skills we strive to develop in students and are integral components of EI.

School Climate

Evidence indicates after emotional intelligence training of the staff, school discipline and academic performance improve and overall school climate is enhanced. Numerous studies by Caine and Caine, Eric Jensen and others, indicate that emotions are critical to learning and the retention of knowledge. Goleman identifies eighteen emotional leadership competencies in four categories. I've taken Goleman's principles and adjusted them a bit to make them more specific to the teacher. For a meaningful exercise in self-analysis, read through each statement and determine your degree of mastery. Rank yourself from 5 (high) to 1 (low).

Self-Awareness

_____ ***Emotional self-awareness*** - Teachers high in emotional self-awareness are tuned in to their inner signals, recognizing how their feelings affect them and their job performance.

_____ ***Accurate self-assessment*** - Teachers with high self-awareness typically know their limitations and strengths, and exhibit a sense of humor about themselves. They exhibit a gracefulness in learning where they need to improve and welcome constructive criticism and feedback.

_____ ***Self-confidence*** - Knowing their abilities with accuracy allows teachers to play to their strengths. Self-confident leaders can welcome a difficult assignment. Such leaders often have a sense of presence, a self-assurance that lets them stand out in a group.

Self-Management

_____ ***Self-control*** - Teachers with emotional self-control find ways to manage their disturbing emotions and impulses, and even to channel them in useful ways. A hallmark of self-control is the leader who stays calm and clear-headed under high stress or during a crisis

_____ ***Transparency*** - Teachers who are transparent live their values. Such leaders openly admit mistakes or faults, and confront unethical behavior in others rather than turn a blind eye.

_____**Adaptability** - Teachers who are adaptable can juggle multiple demands without losing their focus or energy, and are comfortable with adjusting to unforeseen circumstances.

_____**Achievement** - Teachers with strength in achievement have high personal standards that drive them to constantly seek performance improvements—both for themselves and in their students.

_____**Initiative** - Teachers who have the quality of initiative believe they have what it takes to control their own destiny. They seize opportunities—or create them—rather than simply waiting. Such a leader does not hesitate to cut through red tape, or even bend the rules slightly when necessary to create better possibilities for the future.

_____**Optimism**. A leader who is optimistic can roll with the punches, seeing an opportunity rather than a threat in a setback. Such leaders see others positively, expecting the best of them. Their "glass half-full" outlook influences them to expect that changes in the future will be for the better.

Social Awareness

_____**Empathy** - Teachers with empathy are able to attune to a wide range of emotional signals. Such people listen attentively and are able to identify with the perspective of others. Empathy enables a leader to get along well with people of diverse backgrounds.

_____**Organizational awareness** - A teacher with a keen social awareness is able to understand the various forces at work in a school and realize the value of developing positive relationships.

_____**Service** - Teachers high in service competence maintain a classroom climate that fosters an overall feeling that guarantees the free exchange of ideas. They also make themselves available as needed.

Relationship Management

_____**Inspiration** - Teachers who are inspirational interact in a manner that brings out the best in each student. They offer a sense of common purpose beyond the day-to-day tasks and make learning exciting.

_____**Influence** - Indicators of a teacher's powers of influence range from finding just the right appeal for a given student, to knowing how to build buy-in from administrators and other educators. Influential leaders are persuasive and engaging when they address a group.

_____**Developing others** - Teachers who are adept at cultivating people's abilities show a genuine interest in those they are helping along with understanding their strengths and weaknesses. Such leaders can give timely and constructive feedback and are natural mentors or coaches.

_____**Change catalyst** - Teachers who can catalyze change are able to recognize the need for a different approach, challenge the status quo and champion the new order. They also find practical ways to overcome barriers to change.

_____**Conflict management** - Teachers who manage conflicts best are able to draw out all parties, understand the differing perspectives, and then find a common idea that everyone can follow

_____**Teamwork and collaboration** - Teachers who are team players maintain a classroom atmosphere of mutual respect and are models of respect, helpfulness, and cooperation. They draw other teachers and students into active, enthusiastic commitment to the collective effort, and build school spirit and identity.

I realize funds are limited, and most schools don't have the time or resources to in-service their entire staff in emotional intelligence. The other option is for every educator to accept the responsibility of addressing the EQ (emotional quotient) along with the IQ, in his or her classroom. I'm sure most educators do this since it is pays many dividends to address classroom management and positive expectations during the first week of class. In order to maximize the educational experience for each student, teachers at all grade levels must inform students what is expected of them.

As discussed in Chapter Three, at the eleventh grade level I found it helpful to give each student a four by five card titled "Twelve Keys to Success in U.S. History." The students were

> *"When the only tool you have is a hammer, you tend to see every problem as a nail."*
> *Abraham Maslow*

instructed to keep the card in their textbook as a bookmark. Periodically we would review the main components of the card. I referred to this as "setting the students up for success." Of course, the information on the card will not be on the standardized test, but application of the material will aid the student in learning essential content that will be tested. Notice the twelve keys for success are similar to the components of emotional intelligence. For example **"Respect Others"** and the explanation that goes with it is similar to a number of the EI statements under **"Relationship Management."** **"PMA"** and the application of that concept relates to what can be found under **"Self-Awareness."**

The point is, as an effective teacher you realize the value of emotional intelligence even though you may call it something else. In spite of the recent emphasis on standardized tests, teachers must remember we don't have "standardized students." Continue to do the procedures in your classroom that set the students up for success.

Multiple Intelligences

The greatest revolution that took place in education during my 35 years as a teacher was the research that was done in the area of multiple intelligences (MI). MI acknowledges that people do learn, represent, and utilize knowledge in many different ways. It was particularly meaningful to me because while the concept was introduced, our three daughters were in school. As I worked with our children, I noticed a considerable difference in learning styles. Then I had the opportunity to attend a workshop put on by Bernice McCarthy, the creator of The 4MAT System, a framework for organizing learning. 4MAT is a natural cycle for identifying the diversity of learners, for enhancing communication, teaming and problem solving, and for designing learning at all levels.

> *"Never be afraid to sit awhile and think"*
> *Lorraine Hansberry*

The next leap forward was when I attended a three-day creative thinking workshop where I was exposed to the application of right and left brain thinking in learning. The 1980's were very productive for me, since I was working with a principal who encouraged professional growth. I had the opportunity to attend Dr. Roger Taylor's Advanced Curriculum Design Conference, and the annual Wisconsin Council of Social Studies Conventions where I interacted with the top social studies teachers in Wisconsin. Eventually the work of Dr. Howard Gardner, a Harvard Psychologist and researcher was brought to my attention. Prior to this I believed in providing students with learning options and did my best to employ a wide variety of methodologies. Gardner's early works such as *Frames of Mind (*1983) were complex, and when I attended one of his speeches I realized he was a brilliant man who was excited about his research and how it would improve learning. Unfortunately because of my learning style and unfamiliarity of some of the topics he addressed, I didn't get as much from the speech as I hoped.

Howard Gardner

Seeing the man up close and witnessing his passion, I decided to investigate his work more thoroughly. In 1993 he published a book that fit my style and appealed to my interests. *Creating Minds*, *An Anatomy of Creativity Seen Through the Lives of Freud, Einstein, Picasso, Stravinsky, Eliot, Graham, and Gandhi*; is a remarkable book. It answered many of the questions I had about MI. In the book he explains how people can be brilliant in different ways. For example, in comparing Picasso with Freud, he contrasted people who exemplified different intelligences: linguistic and logical in Freud's case, spatial and bodily in Picasso's. Obviously Einstein, with a logical and spatial dominance, would be much different than Gandhi, who was strong in the personal and linguistic areas. He also emphasized how each of the seven "gifted" personalities also had their weaknesses, Freud linguistic and spatial, Gandhi, artistic, etc.

> *"It is of the utmost importance that we recognize and nurture all of the varied human intelligences, and all of the combinations of intelligence."*
> *Howard Gardner*

Keeping this in mind I realized it would be beneficial to me to know more about the dominant intelligences of the students in my classes. I then discovered the book *7 Kinds of Smart* by Thomas Armstrong. This was just what I needed to construct a multiple intelligence survey for my students. Prior to administering the survey, I distributed a sheet explaining the intelligences and why it is important to be tolerant of others who may think differently. I also hoped that it would help students discover their gifts. Since I originally did this, Gardner has announced his eighth intelligence – nature.

After a discussion about the characteristics of the different intelligences, I handed out the MI survey to all students. I emphasized that the purpose of the exercise was simply to provide them with an idea of their interests. With a possible ten checks in each category, students were directed to check the ones that referred to them, and then total each sub category. Of course, it is important to inform the class that there are no right or wrong answers. The main objective of the activity is to have

> *"I dream for a living."*
> *Steven Spielberg*

the students realize the heterogeneity of the class and to have tolerance for the views of others.

I then surveyed the class and asked the students to notice the varied interests in the room. It was not uncommon for some students to have nine or ten items checked in music or spatial, and only two or three checks in linguistic or logical. With multiple intelligences in mind, I planned lessons knowing, "If students don't learn the way you teach, teach the way they learn." For the purpose of a better understanding of how this was used, I have reproduced the categories of logical-mathematical intelligence and interpersonal intelligence. For a more complete analysis of this topic refer to Armstrong's book *7 Kinds of Smart.* Check the statements that apply to you.

Logical-Mathematical Intelligence
(Condensed from 7 Kinds of Smart by Thomas Armstrong)

Core components: Sensitivity to, and capacity to discern, logical or numerical patterns; ability to handle long chains of reasoning.

End states: Scientist, Mathematician or Engineer

_____ I can easily compute numbers in my head.

_____ Math and or science were among my favorite subjects in school.

_____ I enjoy playing games or solving brainteasers that require logical thinking.

_____ I like to set up "what if" experiments to see what happens when I vary components.

_____ My mind searches for patterns, regularities or logical sequences in things.

_____ I'm interested in new developments in science.

_____ I believe that almost everything has a rational explanation.

_____ I sometimes think in clear, abstract, wordless, imageless concepts.

_____ I like finding logical flaws in things that people say and do at home and work.

_____ I feel more comfortable when something has been measured, categorized, analyzed, or qualified in some way.

_____ **Total number checked. This is my Logical-Mathematical Intelligence Score.**

Interpersonal Intelligence

Core components: Capacity to discern and respond appropriately to the moods, temperaments, motivations, and desires of other people.

End States: Salesperson, Therapist, Teacher or Politician

_____ I'm the type of person that people come to for advice and counsel.

_____ When I have a problem, I'm more likely to seek out another person for help than attempt to work it out on my own.

_____ I prefer group sports like badminton, softball, volleyball or softball to solo sports such as swimming and jogging.

_____ I have at least three close friends.

_____ I favor social games like Monopoly or Clue over video games that I play alone.

_____ I enjoy the challenge of teaching another person, or groups of people, what I know how to do.

_____ I consider myself to be a leader (or others have called me that).

_____ I feel comfortable in the midst of a crowd.

_____ I like to get involved in social activities connected with my school, church or community.

_____ I would rather spend my evenings at a lively social gathering than stay at home alone.

_____ **Total number checked. This is my Interpersonal Intelligence Score.**

After the students completed all seven categories, I asked them to share which categories received the most checks and which had the least. It is interesting to note how the students look around to see who has a similar or much different score in the various categories.

I always collected the signed survey sheets from the students and entered their scores in my record book next to their name. You may wish to do this on your computer. This will give you a little more insight into each student and the information will come in handy during the course of the year. I remember Dr. Roger Taylor saying, "The ideal school would have a Director of Multiple Intelligences who would inform the teacher of the dominant learning style of each student."

> **Hot Tip!** *An investment in EI and MI will pay huge dividends in your classroom. Add books in these subjects to your professional library for reference.*

When working on projects, I usually had groups of five and started building the clusters with students strong in musical, spatial, and linguistic intelligence. To expedite the process, I stated, "I need five students who have some musical ability," and then "artistic" ability and finally "someone who likes poetry." This would guarantee that we have three of the most difficult categories represented in each group. When I didn't get five volunteers for each of the categories, students were directed to put their hand in the air

> *"The ideal school would have a Director of Multiple Intelligences who would inform the teacher of the dominant learning style of each student."*

and on a count of three point to someone who has artistic talent, etc. This always worked. Since the projects were set up with Multiple Intelligences in mind, the mixed composition of each group was important.

Multiple Intelligence in the Classroom

While the purpose of this book isn't to go into great detail on Multiple Intelligences, I hope the reader is curious enough to do additional research. Listed below are examples of how the concept was utilized in my high school history classroom.

Logical-Mathematical – Calculate stock market prices and profits. Assist the group in organizing and presenting the activity. Lead a problem solving experience. Help in meeting time requirements. Use scientific reasoning and problem solving.

Verbal-Linguist – Write and deliver a speech or poem for the group. Play the role of a comedian in a skit. Engage in debate over a controversial issue. Communicate the results of the group's work. Write creative letters from great inventors.

Visual-Spatial – Design a poster to represent a historical event. Help design a set for a reenactment. Create a PowerPoint presentation. Draw an image of a new invention. Lay out a magazine or historical newspaper. Build a collage from a historical decade.

Musical-Rhythmic – Design and coach a dance from a historical decade. Perform a musical selection portraying an event or historical period. Play background music for a skit. Choreograph a performance with a historical theme.

Bodily-Kinesthetic – Perform as an actor in a production. Demonstrate games and activities of an era. Demonstrate a dance from a historical period. Participate in a period style show. Present a charade type activity. Be active in anything that involves physical movement and performance.

Intrapersonal – Engage in self-evaluation. Assist the group in coming up with unique ways to perform. Help design a review activity to determine how the production connects with what has been previously learned. Keep a journal.

Interpersonal – Serve as leader to help the group stay on task. Communicate with the teacher on the group's progress. Work with the group to implement assessment. Interpersonal intelligence is required for teamwork and cooperative learning.

Naturalist – Look for connections with the environment and how those connections influence historical events. Establish the relationship between geography and history. Explain the how and why of the ecological movement.

> *"Do not train youth to learn by force and harshness: but direct them to it by what amuses their minds. So that you may be better able to discover with accuracy, the peculiar bent of genius of each."*
> *Plato 427-347 BC*

Once we determine the dominant intelligences of each of our students it is much easier to catch the individual being successful. We can structure and organize lessons to take advantage of the gifts of each student. The converse is also true. Students should be challenged to participate in activities that are not considered strengths. When this is done, student's minds are stretched and as a result, the individual experiences personal growth.

Be a Salesperson

When speaking with sales groups, I often begin by asking: "I imagine you are wondering, what does a teacher/coach knows about sales?" My answer? "For 35 years, I was selling a product that most of  my customers didn't even want – U.S. History. I had to convince the students that it was important to learn about history." So actually I was in sales, marketing, quality control, prospecting and consumer relations. It is fascinating to watch the expressions as people realize teaching is selling a product and dealing with people. Consider the similarities between selling a product and teaching school. Many of the principles necessary for success in sales also apply in the classroom. Consider these effective sales techniques to add more zest and personal relationship to the classroom experience.

Selling Yourself and Your Product

Whether you are selling real estate, automobiles, stocks, insurance, or teaching a class, first you must convince the customer/student you are trustworthy and committed to doing what is best for them. They don't care how much you know until they know how much you care. A successful salesperson/teacher knows people do things for

> *"Many of life's failures are people who did not realize how close they were to success when they gave up."*
> *Thomas Edison*

their own reasons. In other words, the recipient of your product must see the benefits involved and how losses may be avoided. Notice how the principles of effective selling apply in the classroom, by applying each of the following to education.

Principles of Effective Sales

1. **Maintain a professional appearance.** Look sharp, be prepared, and get a good night's sleep. When you are interacting with and serving people, you must have unbounded energy and the will to go the extra mile. You have only one opportunity to make a good first impression.

2. **It's your attitude that makes the difference.** Attitude is everything. When you are enjoying yourself, the customers can sense it. Great attitudes are contagious; make sure yours is worth catching.

3. **Personal motivation is a must.** You must have an intense burning desire to constantly improve your drive and determination. Learning as much as possible about your product and how you may help the customer benefit will increase your level of belief. Belief in your product helps maximize the faith you have in yourself.

4. **Self-Confidence is a given.** When you control your feelings and utilize attitude motivation, the end result is self-confidence. Confidence gives you the energy necessary take on challenging tasks. When you successfully complete a demanding mission, you experience personal growth. To build trust you must exemplify competence and good character.

5. **Have a deep down desire to succeed.** Internal motivation to be the best you can be, will assist you to develop the courage necessary to overcome obstacles and take advantage of opportunities. Use the powerful tool of visualization to see yourself being successful.

6. **Persistence is a valuable characteristic.** Have a plan to deal with criticism and rejection. Understand that rejection may mean correction, and that follow-up is critical to reaching some prospects.

7. **Do Your Follow-up.** Develop a master list of prospects and determine the best approach to use for each. Keep thorough records and review your latest entries so you know what you need to do next.

8. **Know your product.** Make an effort to continually work on building your knowledge base. Classes, workshops, and reading about your product will enhance your degree of belief.

9. **Be a goal setter.** Goals give direction to our dreams. Ben Franklin said, ***"Going through life without a goal is like shooting without a target."*** Short range, intermediate, and long-range goals are essential for success.

10. **Master the art of sales.** Study various approaches to reach diverse people. Know that individuals may comprehend facts and statistics differently. Utilize a wide variety of methods to communicate and close. Have as many tools in your toolbox as possible.

11. **Empathize with the customer.** Put yourself in the other person's shoes. How do you like to be treated? The ability to identify with the feelings of others is essential.

12. **Have fun!** Enjoy interacting with people and providing them with the education and service vital to improving the quality of their lives. Always remember Henry Ford's statement, *"Failure is only the opportunity to begin again more intelligently."*

Once again we can readily see how the effective teacher must be a person who possesses well-developed people skills consistent with the concept of emotional intelligence. Whether the student/ customer is a child or an adult, he or she deserves our respect and attention. While some teachers may find the concept of sales difficult to accept, perhaps it is time for all educators to acknowledge that it is their responsibility to adjust their methodology to best meet the needs of all students. Everyone can relate to that well-skilled salesperson who earns our respect and confidence through employing techniques that grasp our attention. You are a salesperson who is selling a valuable product, and your commission is the growth you witness in each student. Improve your emotional and multiple intelligences to increase your monthly commission.

Hot Tip! *When we take the time and make the effort to understand the learning strengths and weaknesses of our students we individualize instruction more effectively. Effective teachers acknowledge the value of students teaching each other with the instructor serving as the facilitator. It is an effective way to change the routine and allow students to develop their interpersonal skills. Educational research indicates retention is improved when students actively participate in learning.*

A Look Back – Emotional Intelligence

Previously I mentioned that my classroom was filled with props, artifacts, posters, pictures and various other teaching materials. My nature was to trust students and I liked to operate that way. I seldom locked my classroom door. Students appreciated having access to the maps and

resources in my room. They respected my personal materials and over the years I seldom had any problems. However, there was one time when I was deeply disturbed by an incident that took place.

I left the room open over the lunch period, and when I returned my life size cutout of President Kennedy was decapitated. That's right. His head was off and missing! I left him in front of the room and announced to each class that a crime had been committed. At first the students thought it was funny, but after awhile they realized it was flagrant destruction of property. I sensed the students

> *"Teaching was the hardest work I had ever done, and it remains the hardest work I have done to date."*
> *Ann Richards*

were upset, and they wanted the vandal apprehended. One day I received a hot tip and sure enough the police liaison officer spotted JFK's head taped to the dash of a student vehicle in the parking lot.

A former student who thought it was cool to exhibit his trophy on the dash of his car had taken it. The student was told he could be charged with breaking and entering, disorderly conduct and destruction of property. Eventually we sat down and had a good discussion about the prank.

He came up with the idea of replacing the damaged president and said he would take care of everything if I wouldn't press charges. I gave him the catalogue from which I ordered the cut out, and agreed to forget about the incident if a new, intact JFK appeared. I believe it cost him $42.00 plus shipping and handling and his pride!

Some may wonder why we didn't punish him more severely. We felt that he learned his lesson, was genuinely remorseful, and took corrective action. There was no need to take any stronger action. Students will make bad decisions sometimes, and there should be logical consequences, but one must be cautious to keep the indiscretion in perspective and not be excessively punitive.

Hot Tip! *I've never been a fan of "no tolerance policies" when dealing with students. Unfortunately, young people are going to make some bad choices. The consequences of those choices must be logical and a learning experiences for the perpetrators. Coaches must think all the possible circumstances through carefully before establishing a policy of one offense and the player is finished for the season. I've known a number of outstanding young people who made a bad choice, but had the opportunity to learn from the mistake.*

My Personal Commitment to Teaching with EQ and MI
(Check the items that apply to you.)

- ☐ *I strive to create positive outcomes in my relationships with others.*
- ☐ *I realize IQ is just one measure of intelligence.*
- ☐ *I promote self-control, initiative, coping skills, teamwork, and collaboration.*
- ☐ *I recognize that my emotional state and feelings affect students and their performance.*
- ☐ *I interact in a manner that brings out the best in each student.*
- ☐ *I stay calm when under stress or during a crisis.*
- ☐ *I have the ability to empathize with my students and colleagues.*
- ☐ *I believe in finding the time to provide positive feedback to coworkers.*
- ☐ *I understand the concept of multiple intelligences and use it in my daily teaching.*
- ☐ *I utilize successful sales techniques in teaching my subject.*

Humor: The Universal Language

Chapter 9

"Yeah Baby!"

"A laughing classroom is a learning classroom."

➢ "A sense of humor is part of the art of leadership, of getting along with people, of getting things done"
 Dwight D. Eisenhower

➢ "The shortest distance between two people is a laugh."
 Victor Borge

➢ "Laugh at yourself first, before anyone else can."
 Elsa Maxwell

Objectives

- To explain the relationship between the use of humor and your health
- To give examples of the use of humor in the classroom
- To list and explain how to add more humor to your teaching
- To examine why some people are humor impaired

Humor: The Universal Language

"Laughter is a form of internal jogging"
Dr. Lee Berk

Do you know people who are fun to be around because they make you laugh? Have you ever been in a tense situation when something humorous happens, causing people to loosen up and communicate more effectively? How about those memorable classes where the knowledge seemed to flow as students laughed and learned together? Research indicates positive humor and laughter can contribute to improved health and overall quality of life. When you are cheerful, upbeat, playful, and light-hearted, you tend to relax and unwind, which reduces stress.

A lighthearted spirit always has the power to see us through. When we are troubled, feeling low, depressed, or down, the experience of laughter, if even just for the moment, banishes feelings of loneliness, anger and fear. Humor and laughter can transcend any predicament with feelings that are lighthearted, carefree, and hopeful. Humor has the power to turn any situation around by drawing our

> *"Laughter is an instant mood changer that can erase fear, anger, anxiety and depression."*
> **William Fry, M.D. Stanford University Medical School**

attention away from things that upset us. When we experience more laughter and smiles, and feel carefree, our happiness increases with the spirit's energy, and powers the will to live a more positive life.

During my years at Seymour, Keith Swett, an English teacher who was also the wrestling coach, possessed an infectious laugh. I just loved it when we shared the same lunch period. Keith, who was a bear of a man, always had a story or would relate a humorous incident from his teaching and coaching experiences. Within a short time he would have the entire lounge erupting in laughter. His attitude carried over to the classroom where students enjoyed his quick wit and ability to inject laughter into learning. Think back on your educational experience and I'm sure there is a special place in your heart for those unique teachers who appreciated the value of humor. When you

> *"Laughter conditions the heart muscle, exercises the lungs, works the abdominal muscles, boosts the immune system and increases adrenaline and blood flow to the brain. Laughter can increase alertness, creativity and memory, increase pain tolerance, lower blood pressure and improve breathing."*
> **Lee Berk, M.D. University of California Medical School**

think of your colleagues, often the most effective and stimulating teachers value the use of appropriate, timely humor. In his book **The Learning Brain**, Eric Jensen emphasizes the importance of using emotions to lock in learning. My experience indicates students recall key facts more effectively when they are associated with laughter.

When speaking with educators about the use of humor, one of their major concerns is the fear of losing control of the class. This is a good point, and a valid concern. Chapter One addresses the value of establishing the desired classroom climate during the first week of school. This is when it is critical to review proper classroom behavior and the expectations you have for the students. Take the time to explain about humor, how you enjoy it, and what constitutes appropriate and inappropriate humor. Develop some type of visual signal (I used raising my right hand) as a gesture that says, "Serious up, your attention is needed." This is an effective way to get students back on track and continue on with class. Moving to a certain position in the classroom can also serve to increase the level of attention of the students. When I was behind the podium, students knew it was time to listen closely. Facial expression, gestures, walking about the room, visual and verbal keys, and body language are all valuable in sending messages.

> *"Negative emotions have a negative effect on health. Positive emotions a positive effect."*
> *Norman Cousins*

I'm sure you can recall numerous examples from your classroom experiences where the use of humor helped sell the lesson. All teachers, unless totally burned out, employ methods to utilize humor to enhance lessons. These methods take time to perfect, but you know you have mastered the use of humor, when you can take wise cracks or negative comments from students, and turn them into a meaningful part of the lesson. Here is an example of a humorous educational strategy used every year, and it always worked.

When I taught about the Cold War many students had trouble understanding the concept of "**containment**". I came up with the idea of hanging a stuffed arm out of a large storage cabinet with a piece of wood between the handles securing the doors, but allowing the arm to hang out as if it was attached to someone in the cabinet. I started the class as usual and invariably a student would draw attention to the cabinet and ask what was going on. I responded with something like, "Don't worry about it." A little later I would walk over toward the cabinet, pound on it and say, "Quiet down in there."

At the appropriate moment, I paused and said to the students, "Well, I guess I should tell you what happened. Last night while up at school doing some work, I caught this Communist going through some files in my room. Being a peace loving person, I didn't want to kill him, but I certainly wanted to keep him from spreading to other rooms. That's when I had the idea to **contain** him in the cabinet. You see, I don't mind if he exists in there, but I certainly don't want him to get loose all over school." I then asked the question, "What is that called if I allow him to exist, I want to keep him from spreading, but I'm not going to wipe him out?" Of course a couple students yelled out, "**Containment**". I responded, "Hey that's it!" Then we investigated the concept in more detail.

This may seem like a time-consuming and unusual way to present the concept of containment, but every student was engaged and it was a simple way to demonstrate a difficult concept. In fact, to add a little more drama, some years I would add a tape recording featuring a voice from inside the cabinet that was set to begin about ten minutes into the period. The drama was enhanced, and attention was even more acute. In this "politically correct" and "no tolerance" era, one must be careful to make sure all classroom techniques conform to accepted standards.

The Rest of the Story

Here is the rest of the story. After the dramatic lesson, I was totally convinced, every student in class now understood "containment," and the critical role it played during the Cold War era. At the end of the unit on the Cold War, I included a short essay question, "Describe the role the policy of containment played in the relationship between the United States and the Soviet Union." At least two or three students, who were in class for the lesson, responded, "I don't know." Or something like, "Containment was the foreign policy of the United States during the Cold War." Some students just didn't get it! I did my best job teaching, and put my heart and soul into in, but for some reason two or three out of 100 students were left behind. This is why it is critical to maintain a sense of humor and don't self-destruct. After further probing, students may say, "Oh I was having a bad day," or "I just don't like history." Think about a similar situation in your classroom. If the student is not engaged or might be "having a bad day," it is extremely difficult to teach that person. The teacher can check for understanding and do everything by the book, but sometimes the

> *If the student is not engaged or might be "having a bad day," it is extremely difficult to teach that person.*

student is just not receptive to learning. It is frustrating, but it is impossible to reach all of the children all of the time. Often times there is a big difference between what is taught and what is learned.

The Healing Power of Humor

Yet, in the same classroom sits the student who has an intense desire to learn and processes knowledge rapidly. How do you adjust your teaching to reach all students and keep all of them engaged and challenged? This is what most people, who are critical of education, just don't understand. That is why it is so important to glance at criticism, but focus on success. The best response might be to just lighten up and laugh. Your sense of humor has the power to manage, endure, and lighten any load. By not allowing yourself to take things too seriously, you gain a

> *"Humor is another of the soul's weapons in the fight for self-preservation. It is well known that humor, more than anything else in the human makeup, can afford an aloofness and an ability to rise above any situation, even if only for a few seconds."*
> *Victor Frankl*

greater ability to see criticism as challenging, not threatening. It gives you the capacity to cope with stress and difficulties in ways that are positive, uplifting and successful. Humor and laughing help detach us from our daily problems and encourage us to enter into the proper state of mind to be most effective in the classroom. Here are just a few of my most memorable failures to effectively communicate with all the students.

Did I Teach This?

Q. Who developed the polio vaccine? A. **Marco Polio**

Q. Why did Lincoln give the Gettysburg Address? A. **He didn't want anyone to know his real address.**

Q. Name the two Houses of Congress. A. **The Capital and the White House**

Q. Why did G. Ederle swim the English Channel? A. **Her father promised her a red rooster. (Roadster)**

Q. What changes took place during the Ind. Rev? A. **People quit reproducing by hand and started reproducing by machine.**

Q. What National Monument features four heads? A. **A VCR**

Q. Who was Lenin? A. **One of the Beatles**

Q. Who said, "Speak softly, but carry a big stick?" A. **Babe Ruth**

Then there was always World War Eleven (WWII) and Malcolm 10 (X)!

These represent just a few of my favorites. I know they sound strange, but are all true. Imagine the challenge I was faced with to keep a serious attitude and redirect the question. All teachers experience these types of answers. Remember, don't judge your overall effectiveness by a limited number of unrelated responses. Rather than getting upset with the inability of the student to comprehend and digest the information, lighten up and look for the humor.

The Toolbox

With experience, all teachers acquire tools to utilize when the class gets a little sluggish and needs to be tuned up. We all have certain gimmicks to help advance classroom motivation. While some educational purists may preach that a well-planned lesson will carry itself, it has been my experience that a number of educational tools are of great assistance. Examine your subject matter, consider the grade level of the students, and build into each lesson motivational devices to be drawn upon when needed. I kept a cabinet stocked with hats,

props, fun rewards, and a wide assortment of magic tricks. The room was decorated to be a trip back in time with an assortment of pictures, maps, flags and posters on the wall. My personal gimmick was to wear a different tie every day of the year, each conveying some historical or contemporary message. The students were told they could ask about the historical significance of any tie and I would relate an appropriate story. When I retired, the students suggested having a silent tie auction, and we earned over $500.00 for the local food pantry. Fun activities help build the proper non-threatening atmosphere that encourages the free exchange of ideas. Build up your personal toolbox and utilize it as needed!

Dr. Humor

A friend of mind, Stuart Robertshaw, a former college professor, became so convinced that some people lack a proper sense of humor that he started the National Society for the Humor Impaired. Dr. Humor speaks to a wide range of audiences throughout the United States. He has a client list that ranges from the FBI to major corporations. He told me teachers are great audiences because they are around humor all the time. His website, www.drhumor.com, states that a review of research led him to conclude that, "fifteen percent of people in America are humor impaired, and another fifteen percent are 'at risk', and it's no laughing matter." Stay out of the dirty thirty per cent, by encouraging positive humor in your classroom for motivation and peak performance. In his book, ***Dear Dr. Humor: A Collection of Stories for all occasions***, Dr. Humor stresses the value of seeing humor in our daily lives. He says, "A healthy sense of humor is a wonderful gift from God that needs to be exercised daily and shared with others – never leave home without it."

> *"A smile is the curve that sets everything straight."*
> *Phyllis Diller*

Hot Tip! *How is your sense of humor? Do you need to give Dr. Humor a call? Check your personal H.Q. (Humor Quotient) by taking the H.Q. test on page 192.*

Your Classroom Humor Quotient

I'm sure you will find the humor quiz in the appendix to be of interest, but let's take a quick look at how your classroom shapes up from a humor point of view. Listed below are ten essentials for promoting positive interaction and fun in the classroom. Check those that apply to you.

_____1. I welcome humor in the classroom.

_____2. I tell jokes to help students lighten up.

_____3. I use my sense of humor to add interest to my lessons.

_____4. I laugh easily.

_____5. I search out articles about the proper use of humor.

_____6. I'm building my "toolbox".

_____7. I'm comfortable making fun of myself.

_____8. I'm able to defuse volatile situations through humor.

_____9. Any humor I use has a positive purpose.

_____10. Sometimes I regret using negative humor.

Let's hope that you have checked at least seven or eight blanks and you are doing your best to stay away from number ten.

The Proper Use of Humor

Students can be cruel to each other. Every teacher has the responsibility to monitor classroom humor to insure it doesn't get out of hand. This is a topic that must be addressed during the first week of school and constantly modeled by the teacher. We must be conscious of cruel humor disguised as fun. If one student is hurt or offended the humor is inappropriate. At times I was guilty of making an off the cuff remark like, "I see the dog ate your homework again." The class may laugh, but the student certainly didn't feel very good about being the subject of the joke. We must make a sincere effort to eliminate name-calling, sarcasm, and stereotyping. Take some time to reflect on your relationship with your students and how they interpret your sense of humor.

> *If one student is hurt or offended the humor is inappropriate*

● *Hot Tip! Some educators are hesitant to utilize humor in teaching because they fear losing control of the class. Address humor early in the school year and explain to the students what your signal is to get serious once again.*

Keeping in mind that appropriate classroom humor can improve learning and enhance retention, make a concerted effort to improve your humor quotient. Consider some of these techniques to bring more appropriate humor into your classroom.

25 Tips for Improving Your Humor Quotient

1. Keep working on building up your "toolbox" full of props.

Set your imagination free and work on developing your own style. Discover what works for you and have the courage to experiment with new ideas. Make sure when you reflect back on your teaching career you see 30 different years of experience and not one year repeated 30 times.

2. **Speak with other teachers who seem to have a great gift for utilizing humor.**

   Notice which people on staff seem to have a great relationship with their peers and students then do you best to find out why? It is important to be yourself, but you can learn a lot from others.

3. **Begin each day with a quip or quote that is relevant to the lesson for the day.**

   Let's say you are going to teach a lesson in geometry that relates to techniques the Egyptians used to build the pyramids. A significant quote about the enormity of the task or facts and figures comparing the pyramids to modern day structures certainly will grasp their attention. Prior to reading a book by F. Scott Fitzgerald, introduce a quote by him or one of his contemporaries. This procedure can be used periodically with success.

4. **Loosen up and participate in dress up days, homecoming and other activities.**

   While it may be quite a bother or seem silly, students at all grade levels enjoy seeing the teachers participating in school events. Challenge your colleagues to tap into their creativity and allow their child side to come out.

5. **Empower students through being tolerant toward appropriate classroom humor.**

   Students have a tendency to come up with absolutely hilarious comments, which may at times disturb the class, or break up the continuity of the lesson. Take advantage of these and turn them around to become part of the lesson, or at least make sure they provide a break from the routine. Your reaction to what is said is often more important than what is actually stated. Keep your cool and lighten up and laugh!

6. **Edit yourself into a classroom video or visual presentation.**

   I used this gimmick only once or twice a year, but it was effective. Through the course of the year a number of videos were used that were rich in content, but not very motivational. To spice them up, about halfway through I edited in a brief segment of Mr. Collar encouraging everyone to pay attention. I reviewed a few critical attributes up to that point and encouraged the class to pay attention. Including a few rhetorical questions and providing insight for the remainder of the program, seemed to get everyone's attention. For some reason, I found this technique to be much more effective than stopping the program and inserting a few "live" comments. Another twist off of this, is to do a "voice over" on part of the video.

7. **Keep puppets, manikins, cardboard cutouts and other props in the room.**

   During the course of my teaching career various life-sized cardboard cutouts graced the front of the room. These ranged from James Dean to John Kennedy. I found it helpful to have them present when the class wasn't responding very well to questions or when students weren't eager to participate in discussion. I would simply turn to President Kennedy and ask him several questions, or pause and redirect a question toward our celebrity guest. This served as an successful diversion and the students usually perked up.

8. **Decorate your room in a bright, inviting and unique style.**

   I wanted the students to be overwhelmed with history when they walked in the room. A huge 7 x 12 foot colored map of the world dominated the back wall. Seldom would a day go by without some reference to the map. The walls were filled with pictures of the presidents, inspirational posters, and pictures of historical events. The front wall included large reproductions of the front pages of newspapers, a collection of campaign buttons, and my personal favorite, an oversized poster of Woodstock. The walls were a history lesson, so I designed an "Off the Wall" test. Students were divided

into groups and spent ten minutes on each wall before they rotated. The object was to complete the 50-point exam by finding the answers on the walls. It was amazing how they would get into it and how much historical data came from off the wall.

Over 50 historical models hung from the ceiling. Students assembled all of them from kits that I provided. Each year I would pick up seven or eight plastic models of varying degrees of difficulty. Some students who were not strong in verbal or research skills, were gifted in constructing and painting the models. Almost every significant military aircraft was displayed in Room 120. Students who didn't have me for a teacher stopped in to view the models. During basketball games or other events graduates would ask if they could visit my room to see the plane they assembled years ago. Of course, some completed models were deemed not authentic enough to be displayed, like the time a B-29 was decorated with bright flames and racing stripes!

9. **Sing, recite poetry, play a musical instrument, or use other methods to capture interest.**

When I was in the grade school church choir, the teacher asked me to just move my lips. She said I was tone deaf. As an adult I discovered I was a great singer because whenever I would sing in church, many people would turn around and look at me. Since the lyrics of many songs have historical significance, occasionally I broke out in song, or recited the lyrics in poem form. For example, The Coal strike of 1902 would be introduced with a few verses from Tennessee Ernie Ford's *Sixteen Tons* and World War I was launched with *Over There*. I discovered when I risked ridicule and laughed at myself, students were more likely to do some creative risk taking.

I even took guitar lessons for a year. My goal was to be able to strum well enough to accompany the class on songs, to introduce units, and emphasize key facts. *Home on the Range* introduced a unit on westward expansion, and *Wabash Cannonball* emphasized the impact of railroads. Unfortunately, it was difficult for me to learn the guitar, but I did develop appreciation for musicians. It also made me realize, just as I struggled with the guitar, some students found the study of history difficult to comprehend. I believe the experience assisted me in becoming more patient and understanding.

10. **Use creative examples, illustrations, and visual aids to introduce or summarize lessons.**

Many students are spatial or kinesthetic learners. Because of this, it behooves the teacher to continually be in search of appropriate examples, illustrations, and visuals. During the course of studying the origins of the Civil War, students were introduced to the impact of the cotton "gin" on southern agriculture. The concept was anchored in by passing bolls of raw cotton around the class. Students were challenged to see how long it took them to extract ten seeds from the cotton. After this experience, the fact that the cotton "gin" could do the work of 50 slaves was more relevant. It was intriguing to see the reaction when I asked if Whitney's  invention increased or decreased the need for slaves. Invariably most students would say "decreased," then a hand shot up and I saw the reaction that causes many of us to be life-long teachers. A student who had an "aha" moment said, "It increased the need for slaves, because now cotton could be processed so much faster, and more slaves were needed for planting and harvesting."

This is just one example. As you reflect on your teaching style, consider how often you utilize a similar procedure. Make sure you take the time to analyze each lesson thoroughly to determine what methods may be used to capture the interest of as many students as possible.

11. Make a commitment to read books on creativity, humor and using your imagination.

When I make presentations at staff development programs, teachers sometimes comment, "This may work for some people, but I'm not very creative, what do I do?" Creativity is addressed in Chapter Four, but the question I ask in return is, "What have you done to improve your imagination and creativity?" Like anything else, **we must do the drills to experience the thrills.** Find the time to read books that stimulate your creative mind and you will enjoy the benefits.

12. Give students the "face" through a wide variety of expressions.

I was at a workshop in Wisconsin Dells with a number of other educators. We were informally discussing classroom strategies when someone I had just met said, "It is so important to give them the face." I had never heard that phrase before and asked what he meant. He proceeded to elaborate on the value of facial expressions and non-verbal communication. The gentleman was a math teacher, who was recognized several times for excellence. He then spoke in some detail about what he did to bring life to his classes. We talked several times over the next couple days and I witnessed his dynamic interaction with students. His toolbox was full, and his specialty was performing "magic tricks" with a piece of cord during which he continually gave the students the "face"!

13. Vary your voice and act out scenes from your lessons.

Many accomplished teachers are performers and the classroom is their stage. Use your voice to emphasize essential facts, and gestures and actions to bring attention to things you wish to highlight. Be animated, move about the room, and most of all use your voice to complement your "face". Whether you are teaching kindergarten and reading to the class, or teaching high school algebra, be aware that your voice can help bring the lesson to life. Emphasize critical attributes by raising your voice or by punctuating by changing the modulation or rate of speech.

14. Be willing to take risks to discover fresh methods to teach what could be dull topics.

How do you know what works unless you are willing to experiment? One of the greatest fallacies in education is that every lesson must be a resounding success. When we were investigating the possibility of integrating U.S. History and American Literature many reasons were given why it couldn't be done. Fortunately we were possibility thinkers, and determined to make it happen. The result was the synergy that was experienced as two dynamic teachers combined their skills to offer more options and a better educational experience for students. We witnessed a number of setbacks along the way, but each failure was a seed for a future success.

15. Rise above negative thinking by refusing to spend time with pessimistic people.

When I started at Seymour High School as the new history teacher and football coach, it seemed some of the established faculty members wanted me to fail. As a result of previous experiences I had an optimistic outlook and believed teaching U.S. history and coaching football could be fun. Whenever I would stop in the lounge to eat lunch with the other teachers it seemed the conversation was laced with negative comments about the students and the school.

I just made up my mind that I wouldn't be taken in by the naysayers and the talk in the lounge. Eventually I felt more accepted, but the fact that the football team didn't win a game seemed to validate the prevailing perception of the faculty that our players just couldn't compete successfully in the Bay Conference. I was determined and believed that hard, smart work, and determination, would eventually bring about positive results. Fortunately, several experienced staff members provided support and prevented a fall into the bottomless pit of despair and self-pity.

16. Use recorded music and theme songs to pep up the class.

Students love music. Every classroom should be equipped with a boom box. I built up a comprehensive music library stocked with songs of social significance. Periodically, as students entered the classroom between periods, these songs were played. Themes from television shows were popular with the students. How does one come into class with a bad attitude when the theme from *Gilligan's Island* or the *Beverly Hillbillies* is blasting away? *Snoopy and the Red Baron, Sink the Bismarck, The Battle of New Orleans* and numerous other hits were coordinated with the unit being studied. During the study of the 1950's and 60's a recreation of *Name That Tune* with numerous historical facts woven in was a real hit.

Another musical twist that livened up the class was the use of key words or phrases from popular songs. I made a tape with excerpts from songs such as these in a particular order, "Help," by the Beatles, "Don't Be Cruel" by Elvis, "Stayin' Alive" by the Bee Gees. I asked a question and if the student was having trouble answering, I would ask, "Do you need some help?" Then I would hit the remote and "Help I need someone" would play. The next question might be, "Should I deduct some points?" and "Don't Be Cruel" would play. It was done only a couple times a year in each class, but it always was a slam-dunk!"

17. Do something unexpected to break the routine.

A basic motivational principle is to periodically change the learning environment. If the teacher gets in a rut, the students tend to get in a rut. With this in mind, I made an effort to provide the students with an assortment of learning experiences. Details presented in a humorous matter, subtly coupled with a motivational experience, will be remembered long after facts memorized for a test.

A popular project was to have one student play the role of a famous person from history and write a letter to a contemporary about some incident or development in their life. Another student answered the letter using facts from the era with the option to embellish. The two letters then were analyzed looking for facts and fabrication. Providing the students with an opportunity in inject humor and stray from the truth, motivated them to do more research to differentiate fact and fiction.

18. Use "magic" to brighten up the day.

Numerous props may be purchased for the purpose of stimulating student interest in a lesson. Children of all ages are fascinated with "magic" and sleight of hand. Over the years I became an amateur magician and added a number of tricks to my toolbox. A couple of favorites included, *"The Magic Coloring Book"* and *"Squaring the Circle."* Both of these are simple to perform, but effective in demonstrating a major concept.

 The coloring book trick appears to defy logic, as pages are colored and then made blank again. This was used to illustrate the concept of multiple intelligences. The square that turned into a circle was all about putting pressure on oneself to break out of the comfort zone and welcome new challenges. These and many others were of assistance in bringing out a key point in a simple, but memorable way. The catalog from *The Abbott Magic Company*, in Colon, Michigan offers many simple illusions at reasonable prices.

19. Take the opportunity to "phone a friend."

When Regis and the *Millionaire* Program was a big hit on television I decided to bring the concept into the classroom. Through the years variations of *Family Feud, Wheel of Fortune,* and of course, *Jeopardy*, were all used with varying degrees of success. *Do You Want to be a Millionaire* using PowerPoint, was popular for a while and then the interest waned. I did manage to hang on to the "phone a friend" part, and when the class would have difficulty coming up with an answer, they would perk up when I offered them the opportunity to phone a friend. I gave them the opportunity to call another faculty member to see it they knew the answer. Sometimes this would be arranged in advance, and even though it was used sparingly, we had a lot of fun with it.

20. Keep a variety of small rewards in your desk or cabinet.

Whether or not to give students rewards can be debated endlessly, but I found periodic surprises added a lot of fun and excitement to the day. Pencils, pens, buttons, stickers, etc. are inexpensive in bulk, and are great to have on hand for many different occasions. In fact, occasionally I would put stickers on tests and the juniors loved it. Many of them hadn't had a sticker since elementary school.

21. "Show and tell" can be a hit at all grade levels.

Reaching into the bag of elementary tricks, once a year we had a "Historical Show and Tell Day." Students were encouraged to bring in some item of historical significance and make a brief presentation. They were required to answer the questions, what, when, where, why, and how? The items students presented amazed me. Objects ranged from a father's Purple Heart, to antique kitchen utensils.

This project requires a written explanation of what is acceptable and what is not. Many of the boys wanted to bring in an old gun or a sword. Of course, we would thoroughly explain the school's policy on these items. This can be done in any class. In math class have the students bring in an item that is calibrated, in science an item from nature, English, improper headlines or misused words in the newspaper, etc. Use your imagination.

22. "Stump the teacher" adds variety and enjoyment to the class.

A big red cowboy hat gave me mystical powers and whenever I wore it I knew everything about history. Guidelines were established and the students could ask any questions from within those parameters. They were very creative in their attempt to stump the teacher. A small prize was usually given to the first student to succeed. This idea was picked up from a friend who taught seventh grade.

23. Rearrange the room.

It was important for me to get to know each student's name as soon as possible. Some years I had as many as 150 students and this would take two weeks. During my learning period the students were assigned seating. After I got to know their names they could sit anywhere, but most of the time they stayed in the same place. It was fun to reconfigure the room in a circle or triangle to see how the students reacted. It was a great lesson on how we become creatures of habit.

24. Take advantage of the talent in your classroom.

I became a better teacher when I realized some students in my classroom were smarter than I was. Certainly I knew more about history, but many could out perform me in science, math, music, art, etc. Once a teacher accepts this fact, and turns students loose in a non-threatening way, it is amazing what students accomplish. I've seen remarkable musical presentations, outstanding artwork, incredible dramatic productions, and other student work that amazed me. Students never ceased to astonish me with their talents. Sometimes the talent is hidden and it takes a little probing to bring it out.

25. Keep a treasure chest full of items that may be used by students for activities.

Here is another item I borrowed from elementary teachers. When students are participating in a mini drama or role-play they become less inhibited when they are in character. A hat, vest, shawl, stole, scarf, helmet, and accessories can assist them to get into the role. Often students would bring items from home and donate them to the cause. A couple large containers in the back of the room were available for storage.

All of these activities have been used at one time or the other. I'm sure you have your own favorites, but perhaps you will find some of these interesting. Feel free to experiment with a few of these, and add those that work out the best to your toolbox.

Have Fun Teaching

If you feel things are too serious in your classroom, the old saying, "If you're having fun, you can't be working" might have been drilled into you. Logic tells us this is just not the case. People who truly enjoy their time at school, can't wait to get there and have trouble distinguishing between work and play. This is sometimes confused with being a "workaholic." People who have a fun loving attitude

> *"People rarely succeed unless they have fun in what they are doing."*
> *Dale Carnegie*

toward their work, are less stressed, do a better job, and are filled with pride. They are often among the most popular, are witty, energetic, creative, positive, great teachers, and just fun to be around. Using your sense of humor at work and school is the perfect tool to get more pleasure out of your day. If you feel blocked from doing so, here are six major reasons why this may be the case.

- *You have been raised with the attitude that work and play are separate entities.*
- *You believe you won't be taken seriously.*
- *You fear you might offend others.*
- *You haven't mastered the ability to make the transition from a humorous state to a serious one in a matter of seconds.*
- *You fear the principal will view you as lacking effective classroom management skills.*
- *Perhaps you are nervous about losing control of the class.*

When you use your humor appropriately, in moderation, with respect for the boundaries of your classroom, and give your students time to get used to the idea of initiating humor and having fun; you will be surprised how quickly it is accepted and anticipated. Introduce it gradually with small steps and learn from others who have mastered the art of utilizing humor to make the classroom a fun and exciting place. In our fast-paced world, educators and others are always looking for solutions to combat stress and burnout. Humor is one of the most important tools for you to have in your toolbox to benefit both you and your students. Lighten up and see the humor in the situation.

"Abraham Lincoln became America's greatest Precedent. Lincoln's mother died in infancy, and he was born in a log cabin that he built with his own hands. Abraham Lincoln freed the slaves by signing the Emasculation Proclamation. On the night of April 14, 1865, Lincoln went to the theater and got shot in his seat by one of the actors in a moving picture show. The believed assinator was John Wilkes Booth, a supposingly insane actor. This ruined Booth's career!"

Those who laugh – last!

"A keen sense of humor helps us to overlook the unbecoming, understand the unconventional, tolerate the unpleasant, overcome the unexpected, and outlast the unbearable."
Billy Graham

"In prehistoric times, mankind often had only two choices in crisis situations: fight or flee. In modern times, humor offers us a third alternative; fight, flee - or laugh."
Robert Orben

"Kids aren't happy with nothing to ignore, And that's what parent's are created for."
Ogden Nash

"Forgive, O Lord my little jokes on Thee, and I'll forgive Thy great big one on me."
Robert Frost

"Nobody goes there anymore, it's too crowded."
Yogi Berra

"Wrinkles should merely indicate where the smiles have been."
Mark Twain

A Look Back - Presents and Appreciation

I remembered my cooperating teacher saying, "Never expect gratitude from teenagers. They are so self-centered they won't think to say thank you." Yet as a beginning ninth grade teacher at Antigo, with Christmas coming up, I expected some show of appreciation from my students. After all, we had a lot of fun in class, and I worked hard to make history interesting. Realizing I was strict and sometimes too authoritarian, maybe the students were giving me the cold shoulder. My wife, who taught seventh graders just down the hall, accumulated dozens of cards and presents for the holidays. Why did the students show so much admiration toward her and so little toward me?

We had an upstairs apartment just a block from school. As we finished eating and sat down to read the evening paper, the doorbell rang. I noticed five of my students carrying a huge refrigerator box and grinning from ear to ear. In unison they yelled, "Merry Christmas, Mr. Collar" as they carried the box up the steps and sat it down in the middle of the living room. As I began to open the present, I found it was a box within a box within a box. Eventually our modest living room was crowded with cartons and

> *"I'm not concerned with your liking or disliking me...All I ask is that you respect me."*
> *Jackie Robinson*

wrappings. Finally I arrived at the present tightly wrapped with tape. It was heavy and difficult to open.

After struggling to find an opening I finally got inside and was shocked with the contents. I discovered two six packs of Hamm's beer and a quart of Jim Beam whiskey. Incredulously I asked, "Where did you get this?" One of the class characters replied, "My mother bought it for us. She thought it was something you could use." Remember, this was northern Wisconsin in 1966. Even though I thought it was inappropriate, I graciously accepted their holiday cheer and walked them to the door. What did we do with their gift? We put it to good use!

My Personal Commitment to Classroom Humor
(Check the items that apply to you.)

☐ *I value the power of laughter and recognize its physical and emotional benefits.*

☐ *I work on building up my personal "toolbox" to better serve the students and myself.*

☐ *I lighten up and enjoy moving toward improving my humor quotient.*

☐ *I only use humor in a constructive manner and serve as an excellent role model for students.*

☐ *I periodically review the "25 Tips" and progress toward implementing several of them.*

☐ *I make a concerted effort to bring my work and play as closely together as possible.*

☐ *I embrace change and spontaneity and am willing to break from my routine.*

☐ *I wear a smile – It's the curve that sets everything straight.*

☐ *I make it a point to have at least one good belly laugh every day.*

☐ *I discuss humor with my students, and they understand when it is time to get serious again.*

Positive Parenting for Success in School

Chapter 10

"Presence and support are more important than presents and $upport."

Coach Collar & Daughter - 1983

➢ **"Bias has to be taught. If you hear your parents downgrading women or people of different backgrounds, why, you are going to do that."**
Barbara Bush

➢ **"Education is the transmission of civilization."**
Ariel and Will Durant

➢ **"Children are more likely to be achievers if their parents join together to give the same clear and positive message about school effort and expectations."**
Sylvia Rimm

Objectives

- **To describe parent actions that support student success in the classroom**
- **To share memorable personal parenting experiences**
- **To list the benefits of participation in extracurricular activities**
- **To explain strategies for positive parenting for school activities**

Parenting for Success in School

"Don't worry that children never listen to you; worry that they are always watching you."
Robert Fulghum

Reflecting back on my earliest years as a student, I can vividly recall attending Catholic grade school and being eager to learn. The school, staffed by nuns, had two floors with grades one through four downstairs and five through eight upstairs. I viewed the long stairway to the upper floor with anticipation, as the older students, who I admired most on the playground, spent most of their time up there. Of course the "upstairs" was off limits for younger students. By the time I reached grade four I had developed much respect for the nun who managed to teach all four grades and maintained firm discipline. Even though neither of my parents attended college, both encouraged me to do my best, and when I got home from school, it was standard procedure for me to sit down at the table and complete my homework before I was allowed to go outside to play.

High Expectations

My mother always found time to review my lessons with me, even though I had a brother a year older and another several years younger. Eventually two more brothers joined the family. I was always interested in social studies; and sensing that, the nun occasionally sent age appropriate geography and history books home with me. Since the teacher taught all four classes in one room, I usually listened when she was instructing the other classes in geography or history. I experienced integrated learning and differentiated instruction at an early age!

My parents were in constant contact with the teachers because in a small town with a Catholic school, the teachers knew all the parents, and there was weekly contact at Sunday Mass. I smiled from ear to ear when Sister Francis Agnes patted my head and said, "William is my best geography student." My parents had lofty expectations. Education was held in high regard. The quarterly report card was closely scrutinized and the most important grade was "Effort."

Regardless of the endeavor, I was always expected to "do my best," and that became a prevailing theme during my formative years. My dad often complained about being a factory

> *The quarterly report card was closely scrutinized and the most important grade was Effort.*

worker, and he stressed a sound education as being the ticket to finding a job that was more than just a paycheck. He found the time to teach us the fundamentals of sports and started a grade school baseball, basketball and eventually a football program. They were community wide programs irrespective of denomination. He volunteered his time for the youth of the community. Parental involvement was never a problem for me, since my dad was active in the sports program. We spent many hours together on the baseball diamond and in the old community hall.

 Upon moving "upstairs" at school I became one of the "big guys," and was invited to play on the real ball diamond and participate in the basketball pick up games. Playing tackle football in the knee-deep snow was a real treat. We would come in from recess with our jeans soaking wet and Sister would have us stand next to the radiators to dry out. I wondered why she allowed us to get

soaked and disrupt the classroom by crowding around the radiators with steam rolling off our pants. I now realize she felt the exercise and lessons learned in team play were valuable and worth the effort. Throughout grade school I was a strong student because my parents closely monitored me.

Growing Pains

Because of a sound academic foundation, good study habits established in grade school, and parental commitment, my first couple years of high school were very successful. I earned A's in all of my subjects. Following my sophomore year several things happened that had a negative influence on my academic performance. My father realized a lifelong dream and opened a tavern. Managing the family business was time consuming for both parents, since my mother helped by tending bar and making sandwiches. With only so much time in the

> *"When I was a kid my parents moved a lot, but I always found them."*
> *Rodney Dangerfield*

day, my parents became so committed to making the business a success that they didn't take the time to follow up on their son's progress in school. Due to a number of factors including getting my drivers license, tending bar, and most of all, a lack of parental supervision, my grades began to decline and I was making some bad decisions.

Fortunately, a number of teachers noticed the decline and managed to take preventive measures before I slipped too far. With their assistance, I managed to get back on track and build a decent academic record my final two years. While I haven't gone into a great deal of detail, one can readily see the value of parental support and communication between parents and teachers. Times have changed, and the Internet has replaced weekly personal contact, but it is just as essential to maintain open lines of communication.

In raising our three daughters, my wife and I kept in mind the lessons we learned as teachers. The following suggestions for positive parenting worked for us and are worth considering. Even more important, after 35 years in the classroom additional insight has been acquired. With the benefit of hindsight the key points are listed here.

Positive Parenting for Success in School

1. **Be positive with your child.** Positive expectations lead to positive results. Focus on the accomplishments and exercise caution when dealing with lack of achievement. Always concentrate on improving the performance and not ridiculing the individual. Parenting can be difficult, and tough decisions must be made. Remember, you must do what is best for your child and not what your child wants you to do. You are the adult with mature problem solving ability and a solid foundation of self-esteem.

2. **Establish a time schedule.**  Illustrate to your child how to make a list and establish priorities. Schedule in key activities and explain the need to minimize time wasters such as television, computer games and telephone time. Establish a certain amount of time when television is acceptable. Don't turn off the TV or throw it out, but exercise your parental responsibility to establish proper guidelines.

3. **Keep extra-curricular activities in perspective.** Research indicates students who participate in school activities achieve more academically than those who do not. Encourage music, drama, sports, etc.,

130

but stress that doing their best in the classroom comes first. Help your child to make good decisions in this area, and never threaten to take away participation in activities as a punishment for poor grades. Seldom will a student study during the time normally spent practicing for an activity.

4. **Homework is essential.**  Much has been written about students being burdened with excessive homework. Most often the problem is one of procrastination and poor time management. Check with your son or daughter to guarantee they have a workable time schedule and help them eliminate time wasters. Teachers provide students work time in class and often study hall time is available. Getting a jump-start on homework during the day can be a big help in reducing frustration with a lack of time at home. Talking with friends and straying off task at school can be tremendous time wasters.

5. **Make the commitment to find time to take interest in schoolwork.**  When you ask, "What did you do in school?" or "How is school going?" the customary reply is "nothing" or "good." Ask follow up questions and express interest in seeing your child's daily work and special projects. It is easy to get wound up in your work and have a busy social schedule at the expense of spending quality time with your children. Find the time to schedule your children into your day.

6. **Tell your children you are proud of them.**  Unconditional love is essential and must be expressed, but communicating a sense of worth to your son or daughter is most meaningful. Stress you are proud of who they are and not what they accomplish. Too often children compare themselves with others and invariably come up short. Emphasize that doing their best is more important than being the best.

7. **Help your child find his/her gifts.** Students will display a variety of talents in and out of class. Work with the teachers to help provide your child with opportunities to develop their skills. Music, drama, art, athletics, etc. provide them with valuable learning experiences.

8. **Part time jobs.** Many students work too many hours while attending high school. About two thirds of U.S. high school students hold part-time jobs and work an average of 15 to 20  hours a week. This concept is unique to the United States. Explain to your teenagers their number one job is to do their best in school. Too often, the money earned is used to purchase materialistic goods that are not needed. "Putting money aside for college" is often the stated reason for working, but mostly it is spent in less essential ways. Be sure to investigate the availability of scholarships and financial assistance to attend college.

9. **Spending time with friends.** Students may spend 20 to 30 hours a week just 'hanging out' or wasting time with friends. Your  influence as a parent must be greater than the influence of friends. Socializing may take the time that could be devoted to homework. Obviously teenagers shouldn't be locked in their room, but parents must accept the challenge of positive leadership. Numerous studies indicate teens feel they need restrictions. They value parents who are willing to establish specific guidelines for them to follow.

10. Introduce yourself to teachers. Make it a point to get to know your child's teachers. Too often parents feel they have this responsibility during the primary grades, but become less

visible as the student matures. Continue to monitor your child's progress throughout high school. Always attend parent conferences and if you are unavailable, make an appointment to visit with the teacher at another time. Be there for your child, but keep in mind that he or she needs to learn to make decisions and eventually develop the confidence to live independently.

11. Support the school professionals. If an incident takes place where there is a serious difference of viewpoint between the teacher or principal and the student, have confidence the school professionals are doing what is best for your child. Listen to your son or daughter, but follow up by communicating with the teacher before you jump to conclusions. Set up a conference with the people involved, and establish a plan to work out individual differences. If the teacher has made a mistake in judgment, realize the complex nature of the profession and maintain your decorum while tactfully working out a solution.

12. Allow your child to make decisions. Students develop self-confidence and a sense of

ownership when they help make the choices that influence their lives. Be sure you have taught the proper steps to making good decisions prior to giving your child that responsibility. By providing students with incremental decision-making experiences, you are building a foundation for future growth. Simply saying, "It's your decision to make" doesn't take into consideration the vital steps of gathering information and evaluating the evidence. Emphasize the value of considering the consequences and accepting personal responsibility.

13. Stay calm and keep failures and successes in perspective. Overreaction by parents can lead to a feeling of intense pressure for a child to succeed or the inability to deal with failure. Children must learn at an early age that failure is never fatal and success is never final. When you stay calm in stressful situations, your child will learn to

maintain emotional stability. Each setback should be viewed as a learning experience. Have a logical plan to follow when dealing with disappointments and achievements.

14. Always have logical consequences. Maintain control of the outcomes when discussing consequences with your children. Too often decisions are made in haste and emotion is involved. Simply grounding someone, banning television, dropping extracurricular activities, or invoking some other unrelated penalty, is punitive in nature and doesn't teach life-long lessons. The consequence must be a learning experience and relate to the indiscretion.

"When I was a boy of fourteen, my father was so ignorant I could hardly stand to have the old man around. But when I got to be twenty-one, I was astonished at how much he had learned in seven years."

Mark Twain

If I Had My Child to Raise Over Again

"If I had my child to raise all over again,

I'd build self-esteem first, and the house later.

I'd finger-paint more, and point the finger less.

I would do less correcting and more connecting.

I'd take my eyes off my watch, and watch with my eyes.

I'd take more hikes and fly more kites.

I'd stop playing serious, and seriously play.

I would run through more fields and gaze at more stars.

I'd do more hugging and less tugging."

Diane Loomans

"Oh, what a tangled web do parents weave; when they think their children are naïve."   *Ogden Nash*

A Few Memorable Stories

While the purpose of this book isn't to reveal Collar family secrets or imply that my wife and I were perfect parents, several particularly poignant stories merit sharing. These experiences have become life-long lessons that can be applied to a number of situations.

Dad as the Teacher

Raising three daughters was a challenge. We did our best to stay positive, keep events in perspective and have logical consequences. In past discussions with teachers, I've been asked whether or not a teacher should have his or her children in class. There are various ways to view the issue, but all three of our daughters decided to take their dad's class for U. S. History and my senior elective class, Great Issues. It worked out great. I enjoyed getting to know them as students. In fact, it was a real learning experience, as I discovered more about their learning styles and thought processes. We established several guidelines. The two most important points were to never talk about class at home, and to keep a teacher - student relationship in the classroom. The girls thought I went a little overboard when I insisted that they refer to me as "Mr. Collar" in class.

The Shield

When our middle daughter was in the seventh grade she was going through an awkward stage; wearing braces, thick glasses and wrestling with kinky curls. She wasn't as successful in activities as she would have liked, and was struggling in a few classes. One night she was complaining how some students were making fun of her. She was developing a negative attitude toward school, and wasn't feeling very good about herself.

It was time to take action and work to build up her self-esteem. I cut out a shield from a piece of plywood and lettered it with the statement, "Stop! No one can take my feel good without my permission!" I painted it white with red and black lettering and fastened a little handle on the back. I explained to her how everyone has a good feeling about him or herself inside, and no one can take that away unless you allow them. I encouraged her to take the shield to school, and when she walked down the hallway, if someone made an unkind remark, just lift up the shield and the remark will bounce off. She replied, "Dad that is really dumb! Kids will just laugh at me." I then said,

The "Shield"

"OK let's leave the shield home, but carry one with you in your imagination. When someone says something negative, just think of the shield and don't let them get your feel good." She could relate to that, and along with developing a plan to deal with criticism, her self-worth improved. At numerous times in my career as a teacher/coach I recalled the shield idea to protect my own "feel good!"

> *A number of times in my career as a teacher/coach I recalled the shield idea to protect my own "feel good"!*

Gymnastic Competition

When our oldest daughter was a little girl, she was on the gymnastic team at the Green Bay YMCA. My wife drove her to practice and kept me informed of her progress. Finally her first big meet came up and the proud father was there to encourage her. Since she was a beginner, all the participants were required to perform an identical floor exercise routine to the same musical selection. Our daughter was about the 25th of 30 contestants. Prior to her routine the highest score was a 6.6. As she began to perform, it was obvious to me she was more graceful, agile and coordinated than the other girls. In fact, she was also the prettiest! As she completed her performance I just knew it had to be at least a 7.0. When the judge held up a 5.8, I was shocked and deeply chagrined. Before I made a fool out of myself by taking issue with the judge, my wife reminded me that I knew nothing about gymnastics. Then she pointed out that I

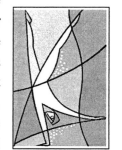

wasn't being very open-minded and was seeing our daughter in a different light than all the other girls.

Then it finally hit me! I was biased because she was our daughter. Furthermore, the experience helped me realize how parents have difficulty keeping an open mind about their sons who were playing football. The gymnastic lesson helped make me a more understanding football coach and made me realize how important it was to communicate with parents.

Guitar Lessons

All three of our daughters participated in extracurricular activities. The oldest and youngest were dedicated to sports. Our middle daughter enjoyed sports, but from a little girl on, lacked hand-eye coordination, and during the middle school years struggled to get much playing time. She had an interest in music. Looking for the opportunity to spend some quality time with her, the two of us took guitar lessons together. She caught on quickly, but I was a real klutz. Even now, every once in a while, she reminds me how thrilled she was when she graduated to the intermediate book and I was still struggling with the beginner program. It was a learning experience. It made me realize that for some students, catching on to history or football was a challenge, just like playing the guitar was for me.

French Contests

As our middle daughter matured, she discovered her gifts in the area of foreign languages. A French teacher took her under his wing and entered her in some state and national competitions. She did outstanding; her confidence zoomed, and she ended up with a degree in French. She now shares her talent by teaching French at the high school level. One teacher made a significant difference in her life. He found the time to make the extra effort to help her find her gifts, and her future career.

Art Education

During her early years our youngest daughter was a real social gal, always surrounded by a bevy of friends. As a high school student, she took an interest in art. Fortunately, the art teacher was a personable individual who allowed much flexibility in class. Struggling a bit to find a career path, she wasn't gifted at art, but continued to take classes. Even as a senior planning to pursue a career in education, she signed up for another art class. My wife and I thought she might benefit more by taking additional college prep classes, but she insisted on the art class and persisted.

Eventually, her educational interest focused on the primary grades, where her artistic ability and experiences in art class were invaluable. Presently she teaches kindergarten and stimulates her students with numerous artistic endeavors. The art teacher deserves a big pat on the back for finding the time to do the extra things that kept bringing her back.

Extracurricular Activities

Looking back on 35 years as a teacher/coach, I believe strongly in the benefits of students participating in activities. Regardless if it is music, drama, foreign language, debate, mock trial, academic decathlon, athletics or any other club or organization, anytime students have the opportunity to interact outside the classroom it is a valuable learning experience. For 25 years I was the advisor to the letter club. It was rewarding to witness students cooperating to plan activities and perform good deeds such as purchasing and wrapping Christmas presents for the less fortunate. Students who participate in these events benefit in ways that can't be tested.

> *"If you want your children to improve, let them overhear the nice things you say about them to others."*
> *Haim Ginott*

Since activities are time consuming, and some people claim they detract from study time, a number of years back I prepared a handout for parents of students who played football. When I met with parents to convince them their son would benefit from playing football, I shared the contents of my handout. When parents could see the benefits of participation laid out on paper, it was easier to communicate with them. Eventually the athletic director distributed that form, and the sheet on positive parenting in extracurricular activities, to parents at the freshman orientation meeting. Reflecting back to Chapter Seven and motivation, keep in mind that people are most easily influenced when they can see how they or their family members will benefit. A summary sheet pointing out the value of participation in a sport, club, or activity, will help parents and students make good decisions based on facts.

The form I used is reproduced in the appendix on page 199. The following list summarizes the key points made in the handout that was distributed to parents.

Benefits of Participation in Extracurricular Activities

- Teamwork
- Commitment
- Work Ethic
- Pride in Performance
- Friendships
- Achievement
- Enthusiasm
- Persistence

- Confidence
- Have Fun
- Identity
- Courage
- Challenges
- Better grades
- Responsibility
- Success in Life

Preseason Meeting

After coaching for several years and witnessing questionable behavior by parents, I felt the need to have a required preseason meeting with all parents. The purpose was to improve communication and eliminate as much parent/coach misunderstanding as possible. During my first three years as a head football coach the following problems surfaced:

❖ Sixteen players were suspended for violating the athletic code.

❖ Two parents came to my house to question why their son wasn't playing more.

❖ A number of players were drinking alcohol on the team bus after a game.

❖ Many students would miss practice for family vacations, hunting, etc.

❖ Players were embarrassed by how loud and confrontational their parents were during games.

❖ Players were working too many hours during the season.

❖ Homecoming activities involved drinking and vandalism.

❖ A parent created a scene during an injury situation in a game.

❖ Players were often eating junk food and not getting enough sleep.

❖ Many students were performing below average in school and causing discipline problems.

❖ Some parents didn't attend the games and even missed "parent's night."

❖ Parents encouraged their son to quit because the coach "hollered at him."

❖ More players were needed to successfully compete with other schools.

❖ A general negative attitude and loser mentality existed.

We required all parents to attend the orientation meeting. I made transparencies and organized the meeting to keep things moving. We demonstrated protective equipment to parents, and the coaches explained proper fundamentals that were taught to promote safe and clean play.

The meeting was a big success. We decided to make it an annual event. Listed and explained here are sixteen points that were presented and discussed. With slight adjustments, the tips for parenting relate to all school activities. The condensed form that was distributed is included in the appendix on page 200.

Sixteen Tips for
Positive Parenting in Extracurricular Activities

- ## Be positive with your athlete

One of the most difficult things to overcome when I first took the position at Seymour was the attitude of the parents. They actually believed the Seymour football team was incapable of competing successfully with other teams in the league. Many parents didn't go to the games and when the players would get home after a game some parents would simply ask, "How bad did you get beat?" It is difficult for players to believe in themselves when the parents don't believe in them. Win or lose, tell your son or daughter you are proud they are part of the team. If the team is struggling in the win and loss column, concentrate on the benefits of teamwork and personal discipline.

- ## Encourage your athlete to follow all training rules

Making the commitment to follow all training rules is a difficult thing for high school students. Parents can be a tremendous help in this area through setting a positive example and discussing the commitment with the athlete. This doesn't mean the parent has to abstain from alcohol, but it does mean the parents should discuss the responsibilities of social drinking with their son or daughter and model acceptable behavior.

Too often a parent may have the attitude, "I don't care if he drinks beer as long as he stays away from drugs." I have even seen situations where the parents will sponsor a party for members of the team and serve alcohol.

> *A positive and proactive approach is to get together with other parents and help organize drug and alcohol free activities.*

Their attitude is, as long as the players stay over and no one drives home there is no harm done. This is hypocritical and has no place in high school athletics. A positive and proactive approach is to get together with other parents and help organize drug and alcohol free activities.

- ## Allow your athlete to perform and progress at a level consistent with his or her ability

Athletes mature and develop skills at different ages. It has been my experience that the best players in middle school are not necessarily the best in high school. Many factors enter into the equation. Some students have growth spurts, others develop better coordination, and unfortunately some acquire bad attitudes that hinder progress.

> *"There are two lasting bequests we can give our children. One is roots. The other is wings."*
> *Hodding Carter, Jr.*

We have had some players who played junior varsity ball as juniors and received all-conference recognition as seniors. It was important for them to get game experience; since they weren't ready for varsity ball. Others, when it was explained playing with the JV's would be a good experience, considered it a blow to their ego and quit. Proper parenting can help the player have confidence that the coaches are acting in the best interest of the player.

- ## Support the coaching staff when controversial decisions are made

Parents must have confidence the coaches are doing what is best for the team. If the parent criticizes the coach, the player may lose confidence in, and respect for the coach. Numerous times in my coaching career a critical decision had to be made in a matter of seconds. When reviewing the game video, or analyzing the game, it is easy for the coach to second-guess himself. The proper approach is to have the attitude, "Considering the information available, I did what I thought was best at the time."

Years ago in a big game, we scored with time running out and our team needed one point to tie and go into overtime. Realizing our kicking game was suspect, and we weren't playing very good defense, we decided to go for two and the win. We had a good play called, and I was confident of the score and the win. The defender made a great play and we lost by one. I felt we did the right thing, but it is a perfect scenario for second-guessing the coach.

- ## Insist on positive behavior in school and a high level of performance in the classroom

Keeping in mind that extracurricular activities are an extension of the classroom and teach life long lessons, parents must monitor their teenager's progress in school. Research indicates students who participate in activities are the most successful in the classroom. Perhaps part of the reason is because of the discipline, organization, and values learned from sports. At times athletes can get preoccupied with their on the field performance and slack off in their studies.

> *"Sports constantly make demands on the participant for top performance, and they develop integrity, self-reliance and initiative. They teach you a lot about working in groups, without being unduly submerged in the group."*
> *Byron R. White*

Concerned parents and coaches can be helpful by keeping activities in proper perspective. Many of the characteristics needed for peak performance in sports are also applicable in academic performance.

- ## Stay calm in injury situations

The Seymour eleven was struggling through a mediocre season. The opponent was a top team and the game was close. I spotted a gap in the defense, and on first down called for a quarterback sneak to the designated hole. The quarterback tucked the ball away and attacked the opening. A lineman slipped behind the blocker and hit the quarterback from the side. The QB grabbed his knee and cried out in pain. As I rushed out onto the field attempting to comfort the player, his father was right behind me. With his son on the ground in pain, the father turned to me and said, "That was the stupidest call I ever saw in my life." His son yelled, "Just shut up Dad."

While this is not typical, it does demonstrate how parents can lose sight of what the game is all about. In injury circumstances it is best to keep emotions under control and allow the situation to be dealt with by the trained professional personnel present. Most often the injury is minor, if it is serious, the parent will be summoned.

- ## Cheer for our team and respect the opponent and referees

Have you ever been to a high school game where fans are verbally abusing their players, opposing players, or the referees? Or perhaps you have noticed spectators who attempt to coach from the stands. These actions detract from the game and focus the attention on the wrong things. Remember, these are high school students playing a game for fun! The referees are performing a difficult task in a pressure filled situation. They will do their best.

- **Promote having fun and being a team player - very few high school athletes receive scholarships**

Allow your son or daughter to concentrate on having fun and being the best team player possible. Parents who are preoccupied with statistics have confronted me. It seems their major goal is to have their son get a college athletic scholarship. Parents must keep in mind, a Division I scholarship offer is rare, and often isn't all it seems to be.

For a fee, recruitment agencies will guarantee a scholarship. These must be thoroughly investigated before any decision is made. Too often they do not meet expectations. Remember, many non-scholarship colleges exist where an athlete can continue to compete after high school without the pressure of meeting scholarship requirements.

- **An athlete's self-confidence will be improved by support at home**

Even though this point is obvious, it deserves mention that parental backing through encouragement and attendance is critical. Some of my worst memories associated with coaching are of Parent's Night when an athlete was not represented by a parent or guardian. One of my most common comments was to remind the players, in particular the offensive linemen, that your parents are in the stands and they are watching you. Make them proud of your performance.

Treat each child as an individual. Parents and coaches should never compare a player to their brother or sister. Allow them the freedom to be their own person.

- **Winning is fun, but building positive team values is most important**

Everyone wants to win, and winning is certainly more fun than losing. However, when we really think about it, the total experience of being part of a team and working toward a common goal is what is most important. The commitment, persistence, dedication, responsibility, and other values reinforced from being part of a team

> *"The thrill isn't in the winning, it's in the doing."*
> **Chuck Noll**

provide learning experiences that will be with the participant forever.

In fact, dealing with defeat or bouncing back from adversity, can serve as a life-long lesson. By concentrating on doing the little things right, the participant learns the value of paying attention to detail. Winning is what happens when preparation meets opportunity. The concept of winning is most meaningful when it is taught that being well prepared, and doing your best in every situation is what really counts.

- **Find the time to be an avid booster of school activities**

Many schools have booster clubs or other organizations to assist in promoting school activities. Make it a point to be a member, and play an active role to guarantee the group stays positive. Unfortunately, some boosters may become overzealous, and make unkind remarks or place undue pressure on the coach during seasons when the team is struggling. The coach and team need the greatest amount of support during the challenging years. Help channel the booster club in the proper direction.

- **Help students keep jobs and cars in proper perspective**

High school activities provide students with the opportunity to learn the many values of team membership. As a teenager matures, it is possible for materialistic values to get in the way. Too often the appeal of a car or truck will cause young people to make bad decisions. It bothered me greatly when an athlete would choose not to participate as a junior or senior. Upon questioning, the answer usually came down to earning money to buy and support a vehicle.

Other students may reply that they need to save money to go to college. Often the money is used for transportation, clothes, electronics and other goodies. Former students have told me they made a mistake by dropping out of school activities. The saying, "You have the rest of your life to work" holds true today. The advice of the parent can assist the student to make the correct decision. Some parents take the position, "It's his decision to make." I always felt this was the parent taking the easy way out. Sixteen and seventeen year old students, when left to make their own decision, will usually take the route that assures the most immediate and materialistic reward.

- **Athletes must attend all practices and contests**

This seems very understandable, but I have memories of parents speaking with me and asking permission for their son to miss the first week or ten days of practice so they could go on a family vacation. I sent the football practice schedule home in the spring so parents could plan ahead. It undermines the program and the need to build continuity when players miss practice.

> *"Individual commitment is a group effort – that is what makes a team work, a company work, a society work, a civilization work."*
> *Vince Lombardi*

It is all about teaching the meaning of commitment and teamwork. Parents need to plan their lives around the activities of their children. The school years fly by rapidly, help your children make the most of those years.

- **Emphasize the importance of well-balanced meals and regular sleep patterns**

An athlete needs a high level of energy. One of the biggest battles coaches have to fight is to get their athletes to drink proper fluids and eat correctly. Everyone knows what needs to be done, but getting the student to do it is a big challenge. Parents can help by preparing proper meals and having nutritious snacks available.

I recall an outstanding track athlete who missed the opportunity to compete at the state meet because he was up most of the night before the sectionals at a graduation party and didn't perform up to his ability. Parental guidance and encouragement can make a big difference.

- **Many athletes enjoy participating in several sports**

For some reason, perhaps it is the perceived potential for a scholarship, some parents encourage their child to concentrate on only one sport. There are benefits to participating in several school activities, or in being a multi-sport athlete. I've always felt the opportunity to be influenced by a number of different coaches is beneficial. In many ways, making a commitment to a team is similar to the type of commitment necessary to be a successful employee.

> *"Success is a piece of mind which is a direct result of self-satisfaction in knowing that you did your best to become the best you are capable of becoming."*
> *John Wooden*

There is also some value to interacting with a different group of students. Multi-sport competition requires organization and flexibility on behalf of the participant. I used to tell the players that football doesn't have to be your favorite sport, but make the commitment to be the best you can be. Perhaps the best response I ever heard in this regard was, when asked what his favorite sport was, the athlete replied, "Which ever sport is in season."

- **Persistence and being able to accept a role are extremely important for the team to be successful**

Not everyone will be a starter, but everyone is important to the team. At times players may become frustrated because they are not getting enough, "Playing time." Some players may not develop until their senior season. Encourage them to be persistent. Late in my teaching career, the boy's basketball team was struggling because everyone wanted to be a scorer, and what was needed most was a playmaker. Shockingly, in a big game later in the season, a seldom-used reserve started and played the entire game at point guard. The team went on to win the game and the state championship. When asked why he didn't quit after being on the bench for the first ten games, the senior playmaker replied, "I was a valuable member of the team, by doing my best at practice I was helping everyone else get better."

Win – Win – Win

Following these points has proven to be helpful in building the proper parent – athlete – coach relationship. Too often insufficient communication leads to misunderstandings and relatively minor indiscretions may be exacerbated to the degree where they become barriers to success. By effectively implementing the sixteen tips, everyone benefits. It is a win – win – win situation!

Hot Tip! *During my first years of coaching I thought the best way to get along with parents was to have little to do with them. That was what I was taught early in my career. Eventually I discovered a required preseason meeting was a valuable time to communicate and clear up any misconceptions. Every August I am still asked to address different parent groups about positive parenting and keeping sports in perspective.*

A Look Back - It's Funny Now

I went to the first *Rocky* movie when it came out in the late 1970's and left the theater so pumped up that I felt I could run through a wall. That fall we had a good football team and were in contention for the conference championship. It was the time of the year when practices were routine and a change of pace was welcomed. We had a bright group of players, and I was positive they would respond well to my plan.

We had a huge game coming up on Friday against a big rival. The coaches planned the entire week so we accomplished a little more than normal at each practice. Then instead of having our regular pre-game practice on Thursday, which was usually a non-contact day,  we loaded the varsity team on a school bus and transported them to Green Bay. The players had no idea what was going on, and when we began unloading in front of the theater with the *Rocky* poster displayed, they were excited. We had rented the theater for a private showing. The team hooted and hollered through the fight scenes and bobbed and weaved as Rocky refused to stay down. It was inspirational!

Returning to school, we had a chalk talk and made sure everything was ready to go for the big game. I went to bed confident of victory and proud of the motivational experience we provided for the players. The next day in school a number of the players came by to tell me they were "ready to go" and had "the eye of the tiger." As the players dressed for the game, the theme from *Rocky* played in the locker room. Every player was tuned in during the pre-game talk. Once again I was reassured of a Herculean effort when we executed warm up drills with purpose and precision. As the National Anthem played every player appeared to be concentrating on the theme of my pre-game talk, "Let's play like Champions!"

> *"Football is a game played with arms, legs and shoulders, but mostly from the neck up."*
> *Knute Rockne*

We played the worst game of the season and lost by three touchdowns! The word around town was, "If they would practice instead of going to movies, maybe they could win a championship." My conclusion – gimmicks and gadgets are fun, but you still have to play the game. When you are coaching 16 and 17 year olds you never know how they will react. That is why before every game I was as nervous as a cat in a room full of rocking chairs. But I did my best to convey an image of calm, cool, confidence.

> *"It is paradoxical that many educators and parents still differentiate between a time for learning and a time for play without seeing the vital connection between them."*
> *Leo Buscaglia*

Hot Tip! *The forms relating to sportsmanship on page 201 and 202 have been used with coaches and athletes. The contents also pertain to parents.*

My Personal Commitment to Positive Parenting for Success in School
(Check the items that apply to you.)

☐ *I keep an open mind and maintain a positive attitude when working with children.*

☐ *I remain calm in high-pressure situations.*

☐ *I communicate effectively with parents and other educators.*

☐ *I value education throughout the curriculum including extracurricular activities.*

☐ *I set a good example for my children and students.*

☐ *I provide my children with the opportunity to participate in a variety of activities.*

☐ *I find the time to be a booster of my children's and school events.*

☐ *I emphasize the value of eating well-balanced meals and getting an appropriate amount of sleep.*

☐ *I realize that teaching is coaching and coaching is teaching.*

☐ *I manage to control my emotions and remain calm in stressful situations.*

Meeting the Standards

Chapter 11

Hang in There!

"The Cognitive Taxonomy Continuum, Rubrics, Standards, Paradigms, Criteria, Benchmarks, Guided Practice, Systemic Instruction, Yada, Yada, Yada."

➢ **"I cannot teach anybody anything; I can only make them think."**
   Socrates

➢ **"The standards movement is pushing teachers and students to focus on memorizing information, and then regurgitating facts for high test scores."**
   Alfie Kohn

➢ **"Education is not the piling on of learning, information, data, facts, skills, or abilities --- that's training or instruction --- but is rather a making visible what is hidden as a seed."**
   Thomas More

Objectives

- **To reflect on the changes that have taken place in training teachers**
- **To list the Wisconsin Teacher Standards and suggest how to meet them**
- **To provide methods for self evaluation and student feedback**
- **To relate personal experiences citing the application of the above**

Standards, Goals and Objectives

"Learning is not attained by chance, it must be sought for with ardor and attended to with diligence."
Abigail Adams

Years ago at UW-La Crosse we called it "practice teaching." During our senior year of college, students had the opportunity to go into neighboring schools and teach under the supervision of a veteran teacher. The experience varied, and the value was usually directly related to the ability of the cooperating teacher. I remember driving to Onalaska with three other student teachers. On the way to our destination, we discussed our classes coming up and on the way back we compared experiences. I was fortunate because Bill Merwin, who was considered to be one of the best in the area, was my mentor. He had a reputation for taking special interest in each student assigned to him. He was a creative individual with outstanding people skills and a commanding presence. Mr. Merwin provided me with the necessary assistance to almost guarantee a great experience. His insistence on experimentation and developing my own style, forced me to expand my thinking and made me aware of the many types of intelligence in the classroom.

Student Teaching

Another student wasn't as fortunate. His supervisor was a stern, cold person who had little regard for anyone who didn't do things the way he did. He was insensitive to the uniqueness of the teacher's style and dwelled on what was done wrong. The best example of this was when he devised a light bulb and a toggle switch that he would man from the back of the room. Whenever the student teacher used  a particular word that was considered a verbal crutch, the teacher flipped the switch. This became quite a distraction as the students kept turning around to see when the light was shining. My friend became a nervous wreck; he eventually did make it through the experience, but dreaded every day.

"Too Charming"

An attractive woman with a warm personality and potentially an outstanding teacher, almost was driven out of the profession by a supervising teacher who considered her "too charming." The students preferred the refreshing approach of the student teacher to the cynical and negative style of the veteran. Obviously the type of experience one gained was influenced greatly by the attitude and actions of the cooperating teacher. Years later these memories were helpful in empathizing with students who were having their field experience under my guidance.

Change is a Challenge

Teaching has changed, and the immersion into teaching is more gradual, but it is still beneficial to have a mentor or two who are master teachers. When I graduated the operative words were "goals and objectives." We had to have unit goals

> **"Never doubt that a small group of thoughtful, committed citizens can change the world."**
> *Margaret Mead*

and daily objectives with a plan to reach those objectives. Those comprehensive plans were "lesson plans" and one was encouraged to not stray very far from the plan for the day.

Mr. Merwin supplemented his high school income by teaching a "methods" class at UW-La Crosse in the evening. Under his supervision I was able to put into practice the theories he shared with his college students. It was an ideal arrangement and a valuable opportunity to experience personal growth. Mr. Merwin eventually became Dr. Merwin and the president of Gulf State University in Florida.

Philosophy of Education

Prior to student teaching I took a required class in the Philosophy of Education. The professor, Mr. Drab, was a brilliant man, knowledgeable in the subject, but about as enthusiastic as a cement block. We studied epistemology and axiology and numerous other educational terms, but I seldom understood what he was talking about. His voice seemed to blend in with the purr of the ventilation unit. He implored students to "ask questions from the cognitive taxonomy continuum." Whatever that was. A semester later Mr. Merwin insisted that we ask a wide range of questions and gave examples of each. He modeled the Socratic method and emphasized the value of asking follow-up  questions. I still remember his outlook, "We all have the answers within us, it is just a matter asking the right questions."

Within one year I was exposed to two teachers with completely different styles. One was active and innovative; the other was just passing on information. It was during this period in my life that I made a commitment to do everything possible to get students excited about learning. I became a teacher constantly in search of more knowledge and teaching techniques.

Requirements to Teach

Today's requirements to earn a license to teach are more comprehensive than in the 1960's. To be a certified teacher in Wisconsin, a graduate must complete an approved program and  demonstrate proficient performance in the "knowledge, skills and dispositions" under established standards. While some educators may believe this is a revolutionary step, it seems to me they are consistent with the practices expressed and modeled by Mr. Merwin. Perhaps the most dramatic change is that the educational community has reached a common agreement as to the characteristics and components necessary for effective instruction.

Let's take a look at the ten Wisconsin Teacher Standards and what can to done to apply them in the classroom.

Ten Teacher Standards

- **Teachers know the subject they are teaching.**

The teacher understands the central concepts, tools of inquiry, and structures of the disciplines she or he teaches and can create learning experiences that make these aspects of subject matter meaningful for pupils.

Practical experiences: Teachers must remain current in their subject area. Classes and workshops are helpful, but the dedicated professional must find the time for specialized reading in his or her subject area. Set aside a minimum of thirty minutes a day to stay contemporary in your field. Every teacher has a personal responsibility to build a professional library. While this may be financially challenging for young teachers, I know a number of teachers who drop

> *"Everyone has a risk muscle. You keep it in shape by trying new things. If you don't, it atrophies."*
> *Roger von Oech*

145

good hints to their parents about meaningful birthday and Christmas presents. If you acquire four or five books a year, after five years you have built a substantial reference library. The Internet also offers a wealth of resources for inquisitive instructors. You are only as good as your resources and your ability to find pertinent material to apply to making your classroom a more exciting and challenging place.

Teachers know how children grow.

The teacher understands how children with broad ranges of ability learn, and provides instruction that supports their intellectual, social, and personal development.

Mel Levine's book *A Mind At A Time* explains how parents and teachers can encourage a child's strengths and help a child overcome weaknesses. The book, directed at parents, is down to earth and offers many practical suggestions that can be applied in the classroom. Drawing on numerous case studies and his research, Dr. Levine states that the problem often isn't a lack of intelligence, but a learning style that doesn't match the skills necessary to complete traditional assignments. Another outstanding book on early childhood, *Einstein Never Used Flash Cards* by Kathy Hirsh-Pasek and Roberta Golinkoff, emphasizes the value of creative play during the preschool years. Combined, the books lay a firm foundation on the subject of child development.

Daniel Goleman's groundbreaking work on emotional intelligence is useful for all teachers. One might start with his book, *Emotional Intelligence*. Goleman relates that the master teacher uses "opportunities in and out of class to help students turn moments of personal crisis into lessons in emotional competence." The school must become a "caring community" where students feel respected and cherished.

Teachers understand that children learn differently.

The teacher understands how pupils differ in their approaches to learning and the barriers that impede learning and can adapt instruction to meet the diverse needs of pupils, including those with disabilities and exceptionalities.

Commit the eight multiple intelligences to memory and plan lessons for every unit that relate to each. There are many great books available that clarify the educational application of Gardner's research. David Lazear's work is easy to follow and extremely practical. I like *Pathways of Learning* and *Eight ways of Teaching.*

Sylvia Rimm's, "Laws of Achievement" apply at all grade levels. Her book *Why Bright Kids Get Poor Grades* suggests ways to motivate nonlearners toward achievement. The provocative style influenced me to take a hard look at how I was relating to students. Chapters seven and nine of this book reveal numerous tips for reaching all students.

Teachers know how to teach.

The teacher understands and uses a variety of instructional strategies, including the use of technology, to encourage children's development of critical thinking, problem solving and performance skills.

Make it a point to investigate how you can utilize technology to increase your effectiveness. To encourage lateral thinking, investigate research that has been done in the field of creativity and visual thinking. Eric Jensen's books on successful teaching and Brain-Based learning are outstanding. Look outside the field of education for creative ideas that can be used in the classroom.

I made a great leap forward in the use of technology when I finally mustered the courage to seek assistance from my students. That's how I learned to do research on the Internet, utilize PowerPoint and perform numerous computer tasks.

Teachers know how to manage a classroom.

The teacher uses an understanding of individual and group motivation and behavior to create a learning environment that encourages positive social interaction, active engagement in learning and self-motivation.

Some of the best techniques for motivation and energizing the classroom can be found in the primary grades. Use art, music, and poetry to capture the attention of the students. Understand fundamental educational psychology and utilize time-tested methods as demonstrated by effective teachers. Make an arrangement to observe experienced master teachers in action. Numerous books and manuals are available. I like *Teaching With Love and Logic* by Jim Fay and David Funk. Students sense when the teacher is excited about a project and often rise to the level expected of them. It is important to remove as many barriers as possible and encourage students to use their imaginations to utilize creative methods to display their talents. Many practical ideas are presented in Chapters one, two and three of this book.

Teachers communicate well.

The teacher uses effective verbal and nonverbal communication techniques as well as instructional media and technology to foster active inquiry, collaboration, and supportive interaction in the classroom.

Aristotle's quote, "You learn to play the flute by playing the flute," applies to effective communication. The teacher improves with time, patience, and practice. This is why collegial observation and the use of video technology can be a valuable asset. To eliminate verbal crutches and redundancy, all teachers should on occasion video tape their classes and scrutinize their performance. Many excellent books exist on techniques to command attention and stimulate discussion, but my favorite is *Speak Like Churchill Stand Like Lincoln* by James C. Humes. This book is a treasure chest of fundamental principles of dynamic speaking and all are applicable to education. His "Twenty-one Power Points" are practical and apply to all walks of life. Chapter Three of this book includes a number of Humes ideas and addresses clear classroom communication.

Teachers are able to plan different kinds of lessons.

The teacher organizes and plans systematic instruction based upon knowledge of subject matter, pupils, the community, and curriculum goals.

Once again I would refer to anything by Eric Jensen. *Completing the Puzzle: the Brain-Based Approach*, along with *Super Teaching*, provide numerous options to utilize when providing for individual differences. *The Learning Brain* investigates the brain's capacity for learning and how it processes information. Like his other books, it is user friendly and non-technical. His book

> *"Brain-Based learning is a system-wide approach that is based on how current research in neuroscience suggests our brain naturally learns best."*
> *Eric Jensen*

Teaching with the Brain in Mind balances the research and theory of the brain with successful tips and techniques for using that information in the classroom. The most challenging aspect of teaching is to plan each lesson so it is unique and specific to the day's objective. Reread Chapter Eight of this book and take note of all the ideas presented about Emotional Intelligence and Multiple Intelligences.

Teachers know how to test for student progress.

The teacher understands and uses formal and informal assessment strategies to evaluate and ensure the continuous intellectual, social, and physical development of the pupil.

Effective assessment of student progress is, in my opinion, the most difficult aspect of effective teaching. It is challenging and time consuming for the teacher and it is virtually impossible to design a written test that accurately assesses student competence. This is why I moved toward performance-based assessment and provided students with options instead of only written tests. Unfortunately with the current movement toward standardized testing one must compromise one's own beliefs to align with district, state and national expectations.

> *"Grades are often based on tests, and tests are sometimes justified as a way for teachers to determine how students are doing. There are other ways, less punitive and more informative, to meet this goal."*
> *Alfie Kohn*

For the long-term benefit of the student and to teach critical thinking and problem solving skills, it is important to maintain flexibility in thinking and not fall into the trap of teaching toward the test. A well-designed curriculum that emphasizes common sense standards, checkpoints and benchmarks will help keep the end vision in focus.

My favorite thought provoking books for a closer look at assessment and performance are *Punished by Rewards* by Alfie Kohn and *The Manufactured Crisis* by David Berliner. Kohn writes and speaks widely on education, management, and parenting. He convincingly exposes the destructive effects of using rewards to control children and adults. Kohn argues that rewards are counter-productive in that they destroy a person's drive to do his or her best. Berliner, who is a professor of education at Arizona State, disputes the claim of falling test scores, and praises U.S. schools as being efficient and effective.

Teachers are able to evaluate themselves.

The teacher is a reflective practitioner who continually evaluates the effects of his or her choices and actions on pupils, parents, professionals in the learning community and others and who actively seeks out opportunities to grow professionally.

This standard has been addressed in the explanations accompanying a number of the previous standards. Reflective teaching, collegial visits, mentoring, video technology, enrichment classes and workshops are all important. Building a professional library is helpful, and possessing an insatiable appetite for continual growth is essential.

> *Regrettably, because of budget restraints, fewer teachers are being encouraged to attend professional growth conferences.*

Regrettably, because of budget constraints, fewer teachers are encouraged to attend professional growth conferences. Fortunately, during my career I had the opportunity to participate in workshops on creativity, multiple intelligences, teaching the gifted and talented, classroom management, dealing with problem students, effective communication, peak performance, motivation and numerous other personal development experiences that related to teaching and coaching.

At various times in my career I found it helpful to have students complete an evaluation of me. This topic is addressed in more detail in Chapter One. The form that was used is included in the appendix.

Teachers are connected with other teachers and the community.

The teacher fosters relationships with colleagues, parents, and agencies in the larger community to support pupil learning and well being and acts with integrity, fairness and in an ethical manner.

Once again the concept of collegiality relates directly to this standard. We can learn so much from others in our school, and at conferences by interacting with educators from other schools. With modern technology and the Internet, it is easier to communicate with parents, but we must keep in mind the effectiveness of a hand written note or phone call. Find the time to personalize your relationship with your student's parents.

It takes a lifetime to build a reputation, but only one incident to destroy it. Think carefully and gather all the information before making decisions. Always consider the consequences of your actions before you make decisions.

> *It takes a lifetime to build a reputation. One incident can destroy it.*

Community organizations will contribute toward programs to improve education. Publicize your unique programs in the community and reap the benefits of your hard work by having your students receive recognition and rewards. Consider partnership programs with the public library, city government, police and fire departments, the local museum, businesses, and skilled retirees living in the community. Chapter Ten on Positive Parenting provides excellent advice for communicating with parents and the community in academic and extracurricular pursuits.

Thoughts About the Ten Teacher Standards

I'm encouraged to see the teacher standards are written in everyday language with a minimum amount of educational jargon. Too often professional documents such as these are written in "educationalese," and the average teacher needs a dictionary at hand to convert the code into understandable language. Certainly the standards provide all educators with a common interpretation of the characteristics of quality educators. The DPI refers to the standards as "a framework of best practices in teaching and learning." They serve as the heart of PI 34, the state's

> *"The idea that American schools are now failing is a Big Lie. And like all Big Lies, it has created a great deal of mischief and unhappiness for hard working citizens and educators who deserve better."*
> *David Berliner*

licensing law that intends to improve the quality of teaching through greater emphasis on mentoring, and following through on a professional development plan. While it is not the purpose of this work to analyze PI 34 in any detail, the plans, programs and policies don't guarantee more effective instruction. True success is determined by the positive application of the principles presented. This is where the human factor enters in. When each teacher accepts personal responsibility for being the best they can be, educational excellence is the result.

Mentoring

Administrators and teachers must form a collective mentorship program that guarantees a true exchange of ideas and incentives for professional improvement. Too often schools may have a mentor program in name, but close scrutiny reveals little time is actually set aside for professional development. Schools of education may prepare students with philosophy and psychology and an emphasis on several instructional models, but many of the rudimentary skills of classroom management and instruction can only be mastered through actual practice. As one who interacted with student teachers for years, I often observed the lack of the practice of fundamental skills such as asking follow up questions, and positioning in the room as a means of non-verbal communication. School districts must make the commitment to invest in the improvement of instruction through sustaining a viable mentor program.

> *Too often schools may have a mentor program in name, but close scrutiny reveals little time is actually set aside for professional development.*

Collegial Visits

Theory is much different from practice, and it is important for teachers to continue to grow every year in the classroom. This can be promoted through teachers interacting with other teachers and learning from each other. While at Seymour I proposed collegial visits where teachers from various disciplines could visit other classrooms and observe instruction. The procedure was set up so a teacher had the opportunity to invite others to his or her room when a unique learning experience was taking place. The visiting teacher was provided with an invitation and reaction form with statements to be completed and returned to the instructor. Some of these are as follows: I was impressed with... It was a great idea to ... You were very effective at ... Tell me more about ... and an area for general remarks. The visitor would sign this and put it in the teacher's mailbox. A follow up meeting could take place if desired.

This is a non-threatening way for teachers to exchange ideas, receive positive feed back from colleagues and pick up tips for effective instruction and classroom management. It also provides the inviting teacher with the opportunity to demonstrate time tested techniques and creative skills. All innovative programs are subject to scrutiny and criticism. For this program to be successful it is necessary for the participants to have confidence in themselves and trust in others. It must be handled positively and viewed as an opportunity for personal growth. Teachers were required to give up a preparation period to visit classes or arrange with other teachers to trade classes, etc. Another possibility is to have an administrator take over a class, thereby freeing up a teacher for a visit. This would be a great experience for all individuals and send a positive message to the teachers about the value of the mentoring program.

Integrated Learning

Every faculty consists of talented individuals who possess a great deal of knowledge and unique skills. An ideal mentoring program must foster interaction between disciplines. In other words, the history teacher can learn from observing teachers in the arts, sciences, languages, etc. If one really believes in "teaching the child first and then the subject," much can be gained by collegial visits. Another factor to keep in mind is the concept of integrated learning to observe how students interact and perform in other classrooms. Most often we view students as they perform in our classes and not others. The value of the "team" approach in middle school and the structure of most elementary classes can assist the teacher in understanding more about the student. Certainly we can learn from each other and customize our faculty structure to make the most of the mentoring experience. Too often at the high school level, we teach our classes without much of an idea what is happening in the classroom next door or down the hall.

Individualized Instruction

Respect for the individual is a keystone of current educational philosophy. No two students are exactly the same and ideally teachers should recognize the uniqueness of each individual. My experience has been that certain movements in education don't recognize the individuality and uniqueness of each teacher. The reason for this may be administrators who desire to implement an objective tool to evaluate teacher performance. The greatest asset any educator possesses is his or her uniqueness. People are not the same, and there is no one model for teaching that will guarantee success in the classroom. Each teacher has a toolbox that contains tools acquired through the years. It is important to keep adding to that toolbox, and some people are better at utilizing certain tools than others. Find out what works for you. The best thing an insightful administrator can do is to identify teachers who need assistance and help them acquire the tools necessary to be successful. At the same time, teachers who are

> *"Common sense is not so common."*
> *Voltaire*

intrinsically motivated should be encouraged to interact with other faculty and share their gifts. They have earned considerable personal and academic freedom, and the administration should refrain for erecting hurdles, hoops, and barriers. Treat each educator as an individual, and stay out of the way when creative competence is at work within the constraints of the system.

The Hunter Model

Of all the experiences I had as an educator one of the most frustrating was exposure to and immersion in the Madeline Hunter Method of Instruction. I'm not saying the model is flawed or ill conceived, but what frustrated me was the way it was applied in my system. The Hunter model is an example of many programs that are periodically offered as educational panaceas.

The administration made a decision to require all teachers to experience instruction in implementation of the Hunter Model. Each teacher was assigned four eight-hour days for instruction and a substitute was hired to take his or her classes. The meetings were held in a room at the local bank with "certificated" Hunter disciples providing the instruction. The instructors were dull, dry and dreadful, and certainly didn't model what they were teaching. Questions were discouraged and a premium was placed on "getting through the material."

An Evaluation Instrument

Later I discovered the Hunter Model was used as an evaluation instrument in our district, and all lesson plans were to be designed with Hunter in mind. This came at a time when I felt good about my teaching style, relationship with my students, and profession as a whole. Some of the Hunter materials were useful, but the requirement to construct comprehensive lesson plans consistent with the model was a real time waster. It was simply busy work, and I was not being treated as an individual or a professional. Being a "team player," I expressed my dissatisfaction, but didn't lead a rebellion.

Perception Vs. Reality

Closer investigation revealed that Madeline Hunter did not create a seven-step lesson plan model. She suggested various elements that might be considered in planning for effective instruction. Others constructed a seven-step checklist that **must** be contained in each lesson. Even though I discovered Hunter preached not all elements belong in every lesson, when observed, our teachers were evaluated based on the inclusion of the seven steps. For example, Hunter insisted on teaching to the objective. That sounds great, but in our school, all teachers were required to write their objective on the board. I refused to do it! In a social studies class why limit the student thinking to the objective on the board? Often times the students will transcend the teacher's views and introduce stimulating thoughts that inspire critical thinking.

One of the main objectives in any social studies class is to stimulate thought, analysis, synthesis, and the ability to evaluate through comparing, contrasting and appraising. By simply directing students to the objective on the board, the teacher is manipulating rather than inspiring.

Perhaps this was best summed up by my senior daughter who came home from school during the height of the Hunter movement and said, "If I see another objective on the board, I think I'll throw up!" Students and teachers love variety - one size doesn't fit all!

> *By simply directing students to the objective on the board, the teacher is manipulating rather than inspiring.*

Terminology

Teachers were required to have an "anticipatory set." The purpose was to grab the student's attention and focus student attention on the lesson. It seemed to me this was a logical procedure utilized by most teachers. Why not call it "getting the student ready to learn" or "motivation," but no, more education jargon had to be introduced. Certainly input, modeling, and checking for understanding, are logical steps, and integral parts of the Hunter Model. My favorites were the concepts of "transfer" and "monitor and adjust." In other words, how does this apply to this situation, and if it isn't working, use another approach. Neither of these is revolutionary, but both are excellent pedagogical practices.

"Guided practice" (helping them do it) and "independent practice" (allowing them to do it) are sound methods. But then we come to "closure," which teachers were told was required for every lesson. What a preposterous concept! The purpose of closure was to bring the lesson to an appropriate conclusion so the students theoretically could make sense out of what was taught for the day. It is the act of reviewing and clarifying the key points in a lesson, to tie things together to guarantee student

> *Why stifle the creative juices by terminating discussion prematurely by rushing to closure?*

comprehension. This sounds good, but why does it have to be done daily? Why destroy the emotional impact or "flow" of a lesson by going to closure by the end of the period? It is perfectly acceptable to continue the lesson the next day and offer some thoughts to consider as time expires. Knowledge should not be rushed; it must be allowed to ferment. Why stifle the creative juices by terminating discussion prematurely by rushing to closure?

Teachers are Different Too

I'm certain if I had had the opportunity to speak with Madeline Hunter, she would have agreed with me that the big picture of what was happening in the classroom, and the outcome of each unit was most important. That makes more sense than daily checking off the steps.

In my travels throughout Wisconsin making staff development presentations any mention of Madeline Hunter is met with a groan. It is unfortunate. What could have been positive program lost credibility because of the way it was administered. Since this happens with other "canned" programs as well, what is the solution? If we believe that "People support what they create," and if we accept the commonly held leadership principle, "The people doing the work should have input as to how the work is done," we would agree teacher input is essential in decision-making.

Shared Decision Making

A few years ago the concept of "shared decision making" was introduced. Unfortunately at some schools this meant forming committees, getting faculty input, but then administrators making the decision they wanted, then sharing it with the staff. I don't think this is the true spirit of "shared decision making." All it does is destroy

> *Unfortunately at some schools this meant forming committees, getting faculty input, but then administrators making the decision they wanted and then sharing it with the staff.*

initiative and lead to the development of the attitude, "Why serve on a committee? They will do what they want anyway."

Common Goals

With the ten teacher standards all schools have common goals for the staff. To truly improve the quality of education in school, programs must be established to assist all teachers in personal improvement. These programs must be aligned with the standards and made available to all teachers through staff development activities. One unique and economically feasible way to do this is by tapping into a great resource that exists in every school, the most proven and accomplished teachers. Through creative planning, communication, and teamwork, experienced staff can be utilized effectively to teach others. Since these are respected colleagues, credibility is guaranteed, and the staff members will feel good about participation. It will take courage and mutual planning, but it can be done. After all, we are all educators, members of the same team with common goals.

> **💣 Hot Tip!** *A few of my colleagues had the opinion that it was best not to volunteer for anything. They felt it just created more work for them. These were usually the same people who complained the loudest when new policies were put into effect. Find the time to make the commitment to serve on committees where you can make a difference.*

Patience and Understanding

Being cognizant of the fact that all students have different gifts and interests, teachers must understand there will be assorted degrees of motivation for various subjects. Some students will be excited about math while others may be turned on to social studies. While a teacher may utilize diverse methods to capture the attention of the student, seldom will all students share the same enthusiasm as the teacher. Our educational system expects at least proficiency in all subjects, which is very idealistic. In his best selling book, *A Mind At A Time*, the well known educational expert and pediatrician, Mel Levine, points out that, "Vastly more extensive and strenuous use of memory is required for school success than is needed in virtually any career you can name. Students must store and retrieve mounds of facts, skills and concepts across unrelated subject areas and topics."

Teachers must take into account, because of diverse learning styles and brain dominance; the cognitive differences in the classroom are as varied as the physical appearances. Patience and understanding is necessary to provide the type of classroom atmosphere essential to insure the proper learning environment for all students.

> *"Vastly more extensive and strenuous use of memory is required for school success than is needed in virtually any career you can name."*
> *Mel Levine*

Student Achievement

A few years ago the opportunity came up to hear nationally known educational authority Dr. Sylvia Rimm speak on student achievement and gifted students. I had just finished reading Dr. Rimm's book *Why Bright Kids Get Poor Grades* and looked forward to meeting her. Her presentation was outstanding. Dr. Rimm has devoted her life's work to studying why average, above average, and even gifted students, many from homes where education is valued, have not performed up to their capabilities. I recommend her book to teachers and parents to better understand the complexity of the task to reverse the "underachievement syndrome." After

> *"Children must have the opportunity to utilize their learning style strengths."*
> *Sylvia Rimm*

listening to her speak I made copies of her handout "Rimm's Laws of Achievement" and gave one to each of our three daughters who are parents and teachers. Notice how many of the "Laws" relate to and supplement the "Ten Teacher Standards."

Rimm's Laws of Achievement
(Used with permission)

1. Children are more likely to be achievers if their parents join together to give the same clear and positive message about school effort and expectations.

2. Children can learn appropriate behaviors more easily if they have effective models to imitate.

3. What adults say to each other about a child within his or her hearing dramatically affects that child's behavior and self-perception.

4. If parents overact to their children's successes and failures, the children are likely to feel either intense pressure to succeed or despair and discouragement in dealing with failure.

5. Children feel more tension when they are worrying about their work than when they are doing that work.

6. Children develop self-confidence through struggle.

7. Deprivation and excess frequently exhibit the same symptoms.

8. Children develop confidence and an internal sense of control if they are given power, in gradually increasing increments, as they show maturity and responsibility.

9. Children become oppositional if one adult allies with them against a parent or teacher, making them more powerful than an adult.

10. Adults should avoid confrontations with children unless they are reasonably sure they can control the outcomes.

11. Children will become achievers only if they learn to function in competition.

12. Children will continue to achieve if they usually see the relationship between the learning process and its outcomes.

===

Rimm's laws of achievement fill in the missing blanks for guaranteeing academic success. Notice how Dr. Rimm places much of the responsibility for learning on cooperation between the teacher and the parents. Let's go back to the last teacher standard:

Teachers are connected with other teachers and the community.
The teacher fosters relationships with colleagues, parents, and agencies in the larger community to support pupil learning and well-being and acts with integrity, fairness and in an ethical manner.

By being "well-connected" the teacher may draw upon all resources available. This means having the support of other teachers, support staff and school administrators in addition to the parents. As Harvard educator and author, Roland Barth said, *"The nature of the relationship of the adults in a school has more impact on learning than any other factor."*

Cooperation between all parties is a must to provide each student with the best education possible. This includes all three legs of the educational stool: educators, parents and all citizens. It is preposterous to conclude that by raising standards, and testing more often, no child will be left behind. To be effectively educated, students need dedicated, knowledgeable teachers who care enough to find the time necessary to reach all students in the classroom. From what I have witnessed, educators in Wisconsin have always made the commitment to do everything they can to help their students excel. Educators must be given the financial support and responsibility necessary to be able to utilize the proper educational tools. As Winston Churchill said early in WWII, *"Give us the tools and we will finish the job."*

A Look Back – Exceeding the Standards

In 1987 to commemorate the bicentennial of the Constitution of the United States, the Seymour High School Social Studies Department sponsored a "Constitution Super Bowl." It was an original program designed and administered by Seymour teachers and was a huge success. The competition was organized into three levels elementary, middle school and high school. Teachers at each school helped organize teams of four and promoted the program. The top four teams in each division qualified for the finals that were held on the stage in the high school auditorium.

It was a classy competition. The high school technical education department designed game boards with lights, buzzers and bells. We sent letters out inviting parents and grandparents, and teachers encouraged students to attend. Each team came up with a unique historical name, and some even designed uniforms. Several of us compiled the questions and served as hosts. An art teacher helped with the set, and drew up the brackets. Merchants from the community donated prizes. It was a fantastic evening!

We ended up with about 250 people in the auditorium for the final competition. The spectators really got into the theme of the evening and even applauded the teams that were eliminated. We put in many extra hours at school getting ready for the program. At that time teachers were required to turn in weekly lesson plans. Because of all the extra time devoted to the constitution experience, I didn't take the time to submit lesson plans. On Monday, when picking up my mail in the office, I noticed a note from the principal. Certainly it was a compliment and thanks for the commitment of time and leadership in providing the students with a great learning experience! No, it was a reminder that my lesson plans hadn't been turned in. I thought, "Of course I didn't turn in my lesson plans. I was spending every available minute working on the constitution program."

> *"No good deed goes unpunished."*
> *Clare Booth Luce*

Unfortunately, sometimes people who **should** won't recognize your extra effort. Maintain your enthusiasm by identifying with the benefits for the students. An experience such as this should serve as a reminder to give your colleagues a pat on the back to recognize their extra efforts. They will appreciate it!

My Personal Commitment to Teaching Excellence
(Check the items that apply to you.)

☐ *I look upon change as a challenge.*

☐ *I have appreciation for individual differences in students and teachers.*

☐ *I constantly strive to meet or exceed the ten teacher standards.*

☐ *I recognize the need to continually experience professional growth.*

☐ *I engage in self-evaluation and follow a personal improvement plan.*

☐ *I realize my greatest strengths as an educator are my uniqueness and desire to transcend previous levels of performance.*

☐ *I enjoy discussing educational concepts with my colleagues and appreciate their commitment to the profession.*

☐ *I welcome and appreciate the opportunities for input in determining school policy.*

☐ *I believe in* **Rimm's Laws of Achievement** *and apply them in my personal and professional life.*

☐ *I communicate with colleagues, parents and the general public, about the necessity to work together to provide an outstanding educational experience for all students.*

Views from the Top

Chapter 12

"The seeds we plant today will determine the harvest of tomorrow."

➢ "We cannot always build the future for our youth, but we can build our youth for the future."
Franklin Roosevelt

➢ "It is better to light one candle than to curse the darkness."
Eleanor Roosevelt

➢ "If you believe you can be ignorant and free, you believe in something that never has been and never willl be."
Thomas Jefferson

Objectives

- To identify the personal characteristics of top teachers
- To share the results of teacher surveys
- To determine how experienced educators view their profession
- To present the views of teachers who have earned state and national recognition

Views from the Top

"Liberty without learning is always in peril and learning without liberty is always in vain."
John F. Kennedy

The purpose of this chapter is to consider the viewpoints of teachers who have been recognized for excellence and how they responded to the principles that have been introduced in previous chapters. I've tabulated the results of over 100 surveys of teachers with more than ten years experience. Teachers surveyed emphasized certain critical attributes of effective teaching. I've included in narrative form a number of the survey results from teachers of distinction. The most satisfying and delightful rewards of a career in education are the friendships that are formed. A special "attaboy" and "attagirl" goes out to everyone who found the time to respond, and in particular those who gave permission to be identified and quoted.

The majority of educators I know are dedicated people who go above and beyond what is required of them. Teachers are often so busy preparing lessons, correcting papers, writing recommendations, communicating with parents, entering grades into the computer, coaching and advising, etc. that they don't take the time to reflect on their impact on students. When speaking at staff development programs or teaching at workshops, I like to ask the participants to reflect

> *The majority of educators I know are extremely dedicated people who go above and beyond what is required of them.*

on their lives and think of the individuals who have had the greatest influence on them. Invariably, other than mom or dad, most people include two or three teachers. I remind them that they are now in the position to have that same kind of influence on youth. Teaching is an awesome responsibility, tremendously rewarding, but challenging and exhausting work.

The Influence of Teachers

The survey asked the respondents why they became teachers. Two dominant themes emerged. By far most people entered the profession because they were influenced by a teacher to become an educator. Others possessed a deep down desire to take up a profession where they could make a positive contribution to society.

By interacting with quality educators I've come to realize that the most effective teachers share common characteristics. There is no one right way to teach and no computer design program exists that allows us to build the perfect teacher. However, based on interviews with experienced teachers, top educators cite the following traits as keys to their success.

Personal Characteristics of Top Teachers

1. **A Constant Desire for More Knowledge** –Top teachers are life long learners. They constantly work to increase knowledge of their subject and to improve implementation skills.

2. **Preparation Precedes Performance** - Even though they may seem to be "winging it" at times, top teachers do a massive amount of advance planning. Proficient educators have built up an extensive foundation of knowledge that allows them to digress and elaborate on diverse topics.

158

3. **Little Time is spent on "Classroom Discipline."** – Actually top teachers spend considerable time on classroom management. This means they "manage" their classroom to the point where students are engaged for the entire period. I like to call this "classroom leadership."

4. **Passion, Vitality, Energy, Enthusiasm and Inspiration** – These words come up again and again when experienced teachers are asked to list personal characteristics that are essential for successful teaching. Obviously a person must be upbeat and positive to be an effective role model.

5. **Empathy, Caring and Concern** – Top teachers are connected with their students to the point where they take interest in their well-being and future.

6. **A Sense of Humor is a Must** – Because of the demanding nature of the profession, a sense of humor is helpful to reduce stress, maintain attention, and anchor learning.

7. **Well Developed Communication Skills** – Many teachers pointed out how important it is to be a good listener in effectively relating to students and parents.

These seven traits were mentioned most often. To elaborate on these and other aspects of teacher excellence, let's look at the survey results in more detail.

- A vast majority of the teachers said they became educators because of the influence of one or several teachers. About 10 per cent surveyed stated the profession provided good job security, and several others replied they were encouraged by parents who were teachers. Many people mentioned they enjoyed working with youth. No one said they went into education to make a lot of money!

- When asked why they were effective educators, most teachers stated that they cared about every child. Other common responses referred to being enthusiastic about the profession and having fun learning.

- It was interesting to note that almost everyone believed that "classroom management" is an ongoing thing. The classroom is organized with the purpose of keeping the students on task, consequently very little time had to be spent on "discipline." Clear expectations, open communication, consistent and fair discipline, knowledge of subject, how students learn, humor, and providing students with a sense of ownership, were all cited as reasons for effective classroom management.

- Teachers consistently viewed the ideal principal as someone who shows appreciation, supports teachers during controversy, and is accessible and visible in the building. Dedicated principals visit classrooms, assist teachers who need help, don't micromanage, and "Stay out of the way" of the most effective teachers. Most educators see the principal as an educational partner who helps maintain a school environment conducive to learning.

Challenges and Frustrations

When asked to comment on the most challenging and frustrating aspects of teaching, almost all responses referred to situations where educators have little control. These usually have something to do with funding, federal mandates, or undesirable conditions in the student's home. The following list includes the issues that were mentioned most often.

1. Large classes
2. A lack of preparation time.
3. Attempting to teach students with drug or alcohol problems.
4. More and more paperwork.
5. Lack of parental support.
6. Students who lack motivation to learn.
7. Finding enough time for my family.
8. Many extra hours with no overtime pay.
9. Too many students want to be entertained.
10. Being treated unprofessionally.
11. Negative colleagues.

In a similar vein, but with a different emphasis, teachers were asked to comment on the most serious problems facing education in Wisconsin. As one might expect numerous references were made about the Qualified Economic Offer (QEO) and overemphasis on testing.

1. The QEO is unfair to teachers
2. Teachers are being encouraged to teach to the test.
3. Low teacher morale.
4. Hiring and keeping quality teachers.
5. Being asked to do more with less.

Rewards of Teaching

Educators cited many rewards associated with teaching. The dominant response included some reference to the joy and satisfaction one receives through witnessing students achieve or "get it." Overall the message picked up most often was a feeling of joy and self-satisfaction in being a teacher and having a positive influence on youth. These five responses were most common when asked to list the rewards associated with teaching.

1. Students finding success through self-realization or exploration. Watching the lights come on. Seeing the student reaction when they "get it."
2. Receiving a "thank you" from a student or parent.
3. Making a difference in the lives of young people.
4. Students returning from college and giving positive feedback.
5. Teaching life-long lessons.

Reading the survey results from over 100 teachers was gratifying. Time and time again the comments teachers made about the love for their profession, and in particular the commitment to their students touched me. Here are a number of examples.

Testimonials on Effective Teaching

"To be an effective teacher, teaching must be your passion. It has to come from the inside, (your heart) and come out from there. That way you will never get burned out or discouraged by external factors because you will continue to find ways to grow and change internally. Change is good, it forces you to grow."

6th Grade Special Education Teacher - 20 Yrs. Exp.

"A teacher's job is never done – it's 24/7 because you are always thinking about how you could have taught a lesson differently, could you have reached this child by using another strategy? Etc. Teaching is one of the least respected career choices, but one of the most rewarding. I wish I could ask every person who has a negative attitude toward teachers and education, to follow me for one entire week from morning to late night and then acknowledge if my job is so easy.

"As a teacher I've learned that the only people I have to be accountable to are my students and their parents. My job is to foster a positive attitude in my students, help them acquire knowledge and have fun while learning. I want my students to love coming to my room and school."
1st Grade Teacher – 24 Years Experience

"Teaching is an occupation filled with contrasts: In the classroom teachers must motivate and inspire, but control and calm their students. They must have empathy and compassion for their diverse students, but maintain high expectations and set tough standards. They must work long days and weekends planning and evaluating during the school year, but recharge and reenergize during the change-of pace summer break. They must individually plan most daily lessons and activities, but satisfy the desires of federal, state, and local groups.

"They must model the highest standards, academic and social for their students, but read and hear mean spirited criticisms of their profession from parents and politicians. They must know how it has always been done, but stay ahead by learning new methods and technologies. For some, it's a tough, unfulfilling, stress-filled job, for others a job presenting daily opportunities to help youth meet their dreams. Teachers must be able to laugh and cry – and enjoy both!"
9-12 English Teacher – 25 Years Experience

"I believe teachers have one of the most important jobs in the world. We have so much influence on children and their families. We have the ability to encourage, inspire, and change lives for the better. We have the ability to make kids feel they are special and important, and what we say does make a difference. Last week I received a thank you note from a student I had in the first grade. I can still picture him in my mind… No money can reward you like seeing your students achieve or send you a thank you note. Teaching and caring go hand in hand. It's like the bumper sticker says, "I Care – Therefore I Teach."
Elementary Teacher – 13 Years Experience

"Being a true lifetime educator is a calling. Teaching is hard work, and becomes who you are, not just your career. Both my husband and I teach at the high school level. I don't think we have ever taken a vacation in our 27 years of marriage that we haven't been someplace or have seen something when one of us doesn't say, 'Hey, we could use that for this unit, project, essay, lab, etc.'

"As much as I have always wanted to be a teacher, and most days I love what I'm doing, I'm not sure I would suggest going into the field right now. Our state is making education harder and harder to get into. They keep putting up more hoops for students in education to jump through, but we are being treated less and less like professionals. We are being told that we have to do more with less to pay for all the programs/concepts and curriculum we are mandated to teach. Being a good teacher is hard work! But I love it!"
11-12 English Teacher – 25 Years Experience

"Teaching has to be the most rewarding career of all. A mutual gift of love and respect between student, teacher and parent is a beautiful thing. As long as teachers remember that; like clothing, education is cyclical, they will always be on the cutting edge. Continuing education is invaluable in striving to be the best one can be."
K-4 Teacher – 11 Years Experience

"When I graduated from college I felt that education was the most rewarding profession to go into. I still feel that way today. We, as educators, are often attacked by all sides of society. I find it ironic that the most avid critics of education have never taught a class. Therefore we have to have thick skin and keep doing the job that we have always done in the classroom. Our children deserve the best and we have to keep doing the great job that we have always done. Whether I'm coaching or in the classroom, I always remember that my job is to help kids and have fun doing it! That's what I will continue to do."

11-12 Social Studies Teacher – 13 Years Experience

After going through the surveys and reading comments such as these, I felt all teachers would like to read more from the very best in our profession. I've included people who were recognized for excellence and are educators I've gotten to know quite well over the years. Consideration was given to including people teaching different subjects at several levels. Interacting with educators such as these helped me stay fired up and enthused throughout my career. I'm certain you will find their remarks meaningful.

Jim Flora, High School Social Studies Teacher
Experience: 38 Years at New Holstein High School

I first met Jim Flora in the mid 1970's at the Wisconsin Council for the Social Studies Convention. Gregarious and dynamic, Jim was discussing social issues with a number of teachers. I introduced myself and joined the discussion. A tall man with a booming voice, he had a commanding presence and struck me as someone who would be a master at engaging students in the classroom. The next day Jim chose to attend the sectional I was presenting on "Effective Strategies for Teaching U.S. History." I was impressed that this master teacher would find the time to attend my program.

My sectional presentation included a considerable amount of humor with slides supplementing the handouts. Jim was impressed with the program and at the conclusion approached me and suggested we get together over an adult beverage. He inquired about the possibility of me speaking at the New Holstein High School Athletic Banquet. I was pleased, but lacked the confidence to speak in public and expressed that to him. Jim gave me some of the best advice I have ever received. He said, "If you only do the things you are absolutely certain at being successful at doing, you will limit yourself for the rest of your career." He suggested that I think it over and get back to him in a few days.

After reflecting on our discussion I gave Jim a call and told him I would do it. That was my first paid public speaking experience. Thanks to the big guy with the booming voice, charismatic personality, and confidence in me, I now became Bill Collar, Teacher, Coach and Speaker. Jim later became the president of the WCSS and lined me up as a speaker several times including a keynote presentation at the convention and a K-12 staff development program for his school district.

Why I Became A Teacher – Jim Flora

I liked having knowledge, skills and abilities that could be shared with others, to help them learn. It was important to me to be able to take something of interest and put it in a context so that others could understand and enjoy it. I liked the role of being someone who could find ways for others to see things they wouldn't have been able to see without my assistance.

I came of age (emerging into a career choice) in the late fifties and early sixties when there was a need for teachers (the baby boomers were upon us) and consequently there was an ethic and an attitude that promoted this profession ("Ask not what your country can do for you...").

Finally, teaching at that time represented a good deal of security and that is a value that was highly regarded by my family and by my generation in general.

Effective Teaching and Rewards

An effective teacher will exhibit a number of personal characteristics:

1. Enthusiasm – Perhaps even passion for your profession.
2. Empathy – The ability to know what the other person is feeling.

3. Humor – An absolute must!
4. Communication skills – Listening as well as speaking.
5. Be a confirmed continuous learner – I know people who earned a master's degree early in their career and have avoided learning ever since.

It is important to have the ability to make changes, to have endurance and not get caught up in every educational fad that comes along. One gains respect by making a commitment to the profession by assuming roles of leadership, being well read and aware of what is going on in the world.

> *One gains respect by making a commitment to the profession by assuming roles of leadership, being well read and aware of what is going on in the world.*

Don't be too pedantic or dogmatic, develop people skills, good writing skills and make it a point to maintain a great sense of humor. The greatest rewards in the profession relate to seeing students succeed at whatever endeavor they choose. It is gratifying to see former students become good members of the community and quality parents. Feedback from former students tells me I played a part in their achievement.

Classroom Management

Very little time is spent on classroom management on a daily basis, but I've made a serious commitment to this over time. Have brief but essential standards that are enforced as consistently as possible. Intervene early and strictly. Be responsible for the management of your classroom and don't foist this responsibility off on the administration. Allow students the opportunity to make choices and subsequently assume the responsibility for their decisions.

Don't save them from consequences that are the results of their choices. Even good medicine often tastes bad but it usually makes us better. Did you ever chew an aspirin? You must firmly believe that the long term is more important than the right now. Kids don't have to like what we are particularly doing at this time, but need to see the value of it later. If people want to get strong they have to lift weights for themselves. No one can do it for them, but we can be their "spotters" to ensure they don't damage themselves. This metaphor applies to learning. Students have to do the learning, but teachers can be there to spot for them.

The Role of the Principal

A good principal is essential to the success of the school. He or she has to be able to understand and manage the culture of the school. School culture is important and sends a message of what is essential. It is demonstrated by 'walking the walk' rather than 'talking the talk'. If the focus is to be on trust and high expectations, this has to be illustrated by the behavior of the entire staff. We can't expect kids to perform at the highest levels if the staff routinely comes to school improperly dressed, poorly groomed, behaves in an unprofessional manner, hands out materials that are misspelled, produces materials for students that are poorly done, or arrives late and unprepared.

The principal needs to trust the staff to meet the expectations and vision of the school, and this needs to be clearly and repeatedly articulated. They need to illustrate their trust by allowing the teachers to achieve the goals of the school through the means that each teacher finds to be most effective given their individual personality and style. The one size fits all approach is counterproductive. The principal needs to be supportive of the staff and be an advocate for teachers. He/she needs to select the best people they can, nurture and encourage them, and retain the very best and eliminate those who do not have the requisite skills and attitude.

The Most Serious Problems and Challenges Facing Education Today

The belief that the educational system is faulty and in terrible trouble, and needs radical change, originates in legislative chambers and in the ivory towers of academia. They create standards that are too lofty and convoluted, and then hold kids and schools to them while testing at the wrong time on the wrong material. There certainly are problems, most of them located in large urban districts that are under funded and under supported.

We know what works in schools; we just don't use what we know. We know for instance that all kids learn at different rates yet we put every student on the same schedule; start at age five and get done by age 18, no matter what. Everyone must get through high school in four years, but can take as long as needed to get through college. We know boys and girls learn differently but we teach them all the same. It seems there is something wrong with this.

Twenty years ago when **The Nation at Risk** report was published, educators were held to the same ineptitude that occurred 25 years before when Sputnik spun around space. The schools have failed! We went on to dominance in space and have in the last ten years far exceeded the economic achievements of Japan. This was accomplished by maintaining the educational system that we developed slowly but surely over the years without having to have 220 days in the school year and a high rate of student suicide. We are still the Mecca of higher education that attracts the best and the brightest from all over the world. We produce more international patents than any nation on earth; we must be doing something right.

Advice for Beginning Teachers

Be the teacher. Do the things that a teacher needs to do. It is more important that kids come to respect you than it is that they like you. You don't need to be their friend; you need to be their teacher. Don't worry that they don't listen to you, worry that they are watching you. Know what they will need to learn and acquire, and help them. They are not consultants; 15-18 year olds should not be establishing cultural or educational values, but should be learning those values that existed when they came on the scene. Maintain high standards and expect them to rise to that level. Doing too much for them is to give them a vote of no confidence.

Help students accept correction without allowing them to see it as criticism. Help them to learn to assess themselves realistically. Don't get sucked into the self-esteem quagmire. People develop self-esteem by confronting difficulty not by avoiding it. Have a set of core values and stick to them; kids will pick up on it. Do whatever you do with care and empathy. Don't use classroom activities such as showing movies as a reward

> *People develop self-esteem by confronting difficulty not by avoiding it.*

for good behavior. Show movies because they have the requisite learning aspects. Don't accept inappropriate behavior or language. It is not debatable. Think long term, what we do here will be appreciated in retrospect. You want students to come back to you later in life and say they found value in what they learned and intend to promote these values to their kids. Keep incentives close for the young. Telling a freshman that this will be good for them when they are in college is way too far out.

Jim Flora is the personification of the professional educator. Through taking classes, attending workshops, traveling, working as a consultant, and extensive reading, Jim is constantly in search of more knowledge. A History major at UW-Platteville, Jim has graduate credits from Western Michigan

University, DePauw, Macalester, UW-Madison, Marquette, Harvard, University of Virginia, MIT, University of Alaska, Abilene Christian, Montana State-Bozeman, William and Mary, and Roosevelt University in Chicago.

A former Social Studies Teacher of the Year, Jim has received many awards in education including the Freedoms Foundation National Award, Award for Excellence from the Joint Council on Economic Education, Kohl Foundation, Baird Excellence in Teaching Award and several other honors.

He has taught and presented at the elementary, secondary and university levels at schools in the Ukraine, Czech Republic and Croatia. Jim developed curriculum materials in economics to be used in American and Eastern European classrooms. He is a frequent presenter at state and national workshops, conventions and professional conferences in the areas of Economics, Alcohol and Other Drug Abuse and Civic Literacy. Jim is a certified trainer for Student Assistance Programs and has conducted workshops in SAP and leadership in Wisconsin, Illinois, Iowa, Kentucky and Georgia.

A man of many talents, Jim writes for The Master Teacher and has done corporate training for countless Wisconsin businesses. The DPI, State Social Services Department and over 40 school districts have utilized Jim's services as a consultant, speaker, and trainer in the areas of AODA, adolescent depression, and teenage suicide.

Most significantly, in spite of all his travels and national recognition, Mr. Flora's most challenging task is teaching and motivating juniors and seniors at New Holstein. He considers it a labor of love and convincingly states he is still having fun after 38 years in the classroom.

George Conom, High School Social Studies Teacher
Experience: 42 Years at Sun Prairie High School

George Conom was the president of the Wisconsin Council of Social Studies during the 1970's. I attended a conference at Oconomowoc and managed to socialize with a number of the members of the Board of Directors. The WCSS was one of the top educational organizations in the nation claiming over 1,000 members. Through active participation in the WCSS, the chance to interact with some of the top social studies educators in the nation provided me with the opportunity for personal growth and influenced the shaping of my educational philosophy.

George was one of the people who impressed me with his intelligence and dedication to the improvement of education. In 1978 he challenged the social studies educators in the WCSS newsletter with an article titled "The Good Teacher." I cut it out and had it on my desk for years.

The Good Teacher

"It's that time of year again, each of us getting our classrooms and thoughts together for another school year. Starting my twentieth year as a teacher has not diminished the feeling of 'butterflies' in my stomach nor has it stopped me from still wondering just what characteristics a good teacher ought to possess.

If I may, I would like to share with you a characteristic of a good teacher that has great meaning to me. A good teacher is not merely a master of subject matter and teaching skills in the classroom. These two components are certainly important, but a good teacher is also a person and as such, influences students. Your students may not know much about your life outside school, but whether they do or not, it will color your relationship with students in many important ways. Your attitude toward life, your way of thinking, your friendships, your prejudices, your capacity for enjoyment, your very habits of speech and dress are as inevitably a part of your teaching as any technical method. A teacher who is not timid, but curious, who takes part in community affairs and professional organizations, a teacher who is not afraid to hold social views, who contributes to work on his or her own subject, but also branches out into others, adds a dimension to a student's life that is vital.

As I start this new school year, I recognize that my whole existence must make one rich pattern in which my hobbies, my home life, my community participation, must each have a meaningful place. This vitality of my life outside the classroom enters the classroom, and it is my belief that a teacher with a great vitality for life adds a dimension to the classroom that is invaluable.

I wish your students and you an enjoyable and educationally fruitful school year."

George's comments from years ago are just as pertinent today as they were back then. His advice stayed with me for years and formed the foundation of my belief to teach who you are first and then the student and your subject.

Why I Became A Teacher – George Conom

I wanted to have a career that made a difference in people's lives. I wanted to impact the most precious things that most people have, their children. I wanted to engage my intellect with young curious minds. Teaching allows me to do all these things. I wanted a profession that gave me a sense of purpose.

Effective Teaching and Rewards

I believe I am an effective educator because of my overwhelming desire to be an advocate for students, my dedication to being the best economics teacher that I can be and my burning desire to improve my knowledge of my subject and teaching strategies. There are a number of personal characteristics that are essential for successful teaching:

A. Scholarship   D. Vitality   F. Passion

B. Compassion   E. Dedication to continual improvement

C. A commitment to being an advocate for students rather than an advocate for teachers.

The rewards are many. One being the relationship and bonding I have with my students. Another being the joy I experience when my students discover or understand a concept or challenging material. Another being the joy I receive when my students are successful in life's endeavors. There are a few personal rewards such as being energized by my students and the warm fuzzies I receive.

Classroom Management

Less than five per cent of my time is spent on classroom management. I come to class prepared to teach for the entire hour. My teaching style sends a strong message, that message being, I, the teacher am working very hard dealing with important material, and you the student need to work as hard in order to allow learning to take place. Students sense my preparedness and my love for my subject, it becomes contagious.

The Role of the Principal

A principal may assist teachers by minimizing disruptions in the school day, by limiting absences and by encouraging me to be innovative in my approach to meeting individual needs.

The Most Serious Problems and Challenges Facing Educators

Funding is not the greatest problem; it is a lack of accountability of teachers and a poor process for training teachers. My greatest frustration is with other teachers, the teachers who do not comprehend the awesome responsibility of teaching someone else's children. The teachers who really don't like students and who do not have a passion for their subject matter. In other words, what bothers me the most is the lack of dedication and lack of scholarship in a growing number of teachers. This is why I have always felt that education is too important to be in hands only of educators.

My greatest frustration is with other teachers, the teachers who do not comprehend the awesome responsibility of teaching someone else's children.

There are a couple of challenges, one being the competition of the work place on the students, meaning most of my students have jobs. This means there is less time for serious scholarship. Another challenge for me is the political nature of public schools. Public schools are a model of socialism, because of very little accountability and very little nurturing that leads to excellence regarding teaching; an excellent teacher becomes excellent in spite of the system, not because of the system. This results in mediocrity in schools. In order for a teacher to strive for excellence one must develop a mindset that shuts out the day-to-day dynamics of the school setting. This is unfortunate.

Advice for Beginning Teachers

- Never forget that teaching is a privilege. Each day parents send us their children trusting us to educate and nourish their most precious possession.

- There is no substitute for scholarship, become a master of what you teach, both content wise and strategy wise.

- Have a passion for what you do. Have compassion for who you teach.

George Conom always impressed me as an intellectual with common sense and the ability to communicate effectively with anyone. His longevity, 42 years as a teacher, reflects his love for the profession and dedication to students. George earned a Master's Degree in economics with graduate credits from Purdue, Michigan State, Stanford, Georgetown and Emory Universities. Overall he attended 31 different graduate schools and was a Fulbright Scholar to Israel and India.

He is the past president of the Wisconsin Council for the Social Studies and in 1992 was named Wisconsin Social Studies Teacher of the Year. In the early 1960's George was a head basketball coach and for many years worked as an assistant in football. He has been active in writing economics curriculum for the state of Wisconsin and served as the chairperson of a high school committee dedicated to making positive internal changes to the school day.

Carol Banaszynski, High School Life Sciences
Experience: 31 Years Deerfield High School

Carol Banaszynski and I were members of the planning committee for the Wisconsin Teacher Forum in the late 1990's. The Teacher Forum was a program to encourage teachers who had been recognized for excellence to interact and share success principles with teachers who were relatively new to the profession. It was an outstanding program that provided excellent opportunities for professional growth, but after several years it fell victim to budget cuts.

Carol was selected as a lead teacher because of her recognition for excellence including a Kohl Fellowship and Wisconsin Teacher of the Year award. She had been a pacesetter in numerous professional organizations and recognized at the national level for excellence in teaching science. From the time we first met, Carol impressed me with her intelligence, communication skills and commitment in assisting teachers to develop their full potential. She had a practical, no nonsense approach to teaching, but still possessed a great sense of humor and unbridled enthusiasm. I learned a great deal from working with her.

Why I Became A Teacher – Carol Banaszynski

I always enjoyed working with children and found it easy to motivate them to achieve. As a teacher I have been able to make a career of motivating students to be successful.

Effective Teaching and Rewards

My success as an educator is based on a knack for being able to motivate students of all ability levels to achieve. I don't really know why I am so successful with this, but students tell me my enthusiasm is contagious. They are also motivated by my teaching style. To experience success in the classroom a teacher must possess the following characteristics.

A. Organizational skill
B. Enthusiasm
C. Humor
D. Responsibility
E. Respect

F. Inspiration
G. Good work ethic
H. Kindness
I. Patience
J. Empathy (But not an enabler!)

Teachers work in an environment where they are frequently isolated from their peers. Those who are new to the profession have the same responsibilities as veteran teachers. The challenge is to create an effective new teacher-mentoring program, based on quality teaching, to support learning.

The rewards in teaching are intrinsic. Seeing the twinkle in the eye of a student who finally "gets it" is the ultimate reward. When students say, "Thank you for teaching me how to learn," that is also a great reward.

Classroom Management

I spend very little time on classroom management. Less than one per cent of my time is spent disciplining students. My classroom is arranged so students can be collaborative with each other and the teacher. When they are in a non-traditional classroom, are not expected to sit in rows, and are quiet while I talk, they really don't cause many problems. They are active and in control of their own learning, so they tend to use the time to their advantage.

The Role of the Principal

He/she needs to provide support for both school and classroom policies when necessary. I like to handle my own issues because I need students to respect me and each other, not an alternate authority figure. The principal needs to establish his/her own respect. All I need is support, so the respect I have established can be maintained.

The Most Serious Problems and Challenges Facing Educators

Education has become so political; it is almost impossible to ignore the politics and just teach. I wish education could just focus on what is best for students. Failing to talk about and address the growing diversity in our schools is a serious problem. The loss of a large number of veteran teachers to retirement is a concern. Revenue caps negatively affect education, and if not lifted will become an even more serious issue. Education lacks sufficient leadership on many concerns.

Change is occurring in education, but not at a fast enough pace to keep up with the demands of an ever increasingly technological work world. New information is being added so quickly, it cannot be taught as fast as it is discovered. Educational reform must include training students to be better thinkers so they can deal with large volumes of information

> *Educational reform must include training students to be better thinkers so they can deal with large volumes of information that have not yet been discovered, and in many cases can't even be imagined.*

that have not yet been discovered, and in many cases can't even be imagined. Education must facilitate change so students are motivated to be lifelong learners. To do this, education must focus on how to learn, not what to learn.

Advice for Beginning Teachers

Maintain your love of learning, model it, and provide daily opportunities for students to experience it; and you will be the best teacher you can be. Education is becoming more about teaching students to be adaptable than about teaching facts. It is human nature to resist change, but change can energize you. Education needs to encourage acceptance of change so the teaching profession and society continually move forward.

Carol Banaszynski is a human dynamo and has had a variety of unique experiences in and out of education. She has coached volleyball, basketball, and track and field, in addition to advising the Science Club. Carol has volunteered as a tutor, is active in scouting and 4-H, served as an Adopt-A-Highway co-chairperson, and has presented at state, regional, and national conferences. She has assisted in landscaping the school grounds, maintaining the school forest, and even did the announcing for high school football games.

Carol's professional activities include belonging to numerous organizations. She served as a Key Leader for the Wisconsin Science Network and completed the training program as a Wisconsin Academy Staff Development Initiative Lead Teacher. Carol was a member of the Wisconsin Teacher Forum Planning Committee, participated in the National Teacher Forum, has worked for the DPI on "Proficiency Assessment," completed astronaut training at International Space Camp, and been active in training new teachers at the university and local level.

In addition to the Kohl and Teacher of the Year Awards, Carol has been recognized by receiving the Monsanto Biotechnology Fellowship, Radio Shack/Tandy National Outstanding teacher award and the National High School Association's National Educator of the Year.

Married to a technology teacher for over 30 years, Carol earned a B.S. in Physical Education and Biology from UW-La Crosse, M.S. in Professional Development from UW-Whitewater and a M.S. in Educational leadership from Cardinal Stritch University.

Keith Gundlach, Agriculture Teacher – Grades 7-12
Experience: 27 Years at Randolph High School

In the late 1980's Keith Gundlach invited me to speak at Randolph High School's Future Farmers of America Banquet. Since Randolph was a school of about 200 students I anticipated a rather small audience event though Keith informed me that they usually provide a meal for about 400 people. It seemed like the entire community turned out for the banquet. There was a large buffet meal followed by an impressive program featuring the recognition of students for various levels of achievement ranging from local to national awards.

I was told that Randolph had the largest FFA organization in the state with 150 members in grades 7-12. (The Cambria-Friesland FFA has merged with Randolph and at this writing Keith is responsible for 316 students). The evening included the awarding of numerous scholarships, a silent auction and outstanding food prepared by the high school food service and parents. Students, with organizational help from Mr. Gundlach, ran the entire program. Keith explained to me how important it was for them to get the experience speaking and orchestrating the program. Even though a number of the students struggled with their roles, he patiently allowed them to recover and succeed. It was intriguing to witness the recognition of alumni and the appreciation expressed toward community businesses and organizations.

I was overwhelmed when Keith explained the organizational structure of a foundation he established. Its purpose is to advance the role of the FFA through supporting community projects. Keith was pleased with my speech, and I was invited back three more times over the next twelve years. During my last visit in 2003, Keith proudly explained the new football bleachers were courtesy of the FFA and the next project was irrigation and a new playing surface for the football field. Recently he informed me the *football field project was completed, the tennis courts were resurfaced, and several other foundations have been started with a total value of over $400,000.00 at this printing!*

Keith is an amazing teacher, who has made a tremendous impact on the city of Randolph and the school system. During my visits his influence on students was obvious as numerous alumni stopped to shake his hand and catch up on school news. We connected to the degree that he arranged to have me speak at a K-12 staff development program and twice utilized my services for the State Agriculture Teacher's Convention. He helped provide me with the experience and confidence to launch a professional speaking career after I retired from teaching.

Why I Became A Teacher – Keith Gundlach

My middle school teachers were good role models and excellent educators. They influenced me to become a teacher. *Keith not only became a teacher, but also was named the Outstanding Agriculture Teacher in Wisconsin and the National Agriculture Teacher of the Year.*

Effective Teaching

It is very important to know your subject. When you respect students, they respect you. Be patient, understanding and by all means maintain a sense of humor. Have a constant desire to learn more. Honesty is also essential for success. It is very rewarding when former students stop back and visit or remain in touch. It is really great to hear their success stories. The use of technology has been a boon to instruction. The move by many education programs to have the teacher be a "facilitator" bothers me. Teachers still need to teach and use methods, which allow **all** students to learn. I have always believed that **all** students need recognition and any small successes of the challenged students will be remembered by them long after they leave the educational system. As an agriculture teacher I can make that happen with job visits and award applications and then tie those things back to the classroom.

> *I have always believed that all students need recognition and any small successes of the challenged students will be remembered by them long after they leave the educational system.*

Classroom Management

Make it a point to inform students what is expected of them and what routine to follow. I spend less than five per cent of my time on classroom management. In a certain sense students are like cows in that they need to be trained to fit your classroom management plan. All students want discipline and structure and will behave in the manner of the expectations you have established for them. This is a maxim more teachers need to be aware of and follow. Teaching is fun when you aren't distracted with excess management tasks.

The Role of the Principal

It is impressive when the principal stops by the classroom for something other than evaluation. When the principal finds the time to learn all he or she can about each class it sends the message that he/she will support the teacher if assistance is needed in dealing with an unruly student.

The Most Serious Problems Facing Education Today

Funding is an increasingly more serious problem in Wisconsin. It is difficult to convince good young teachers to stay in the profession. Sometimes pay is frustrating and it is nerve racking to have budgets cut and see programs affected in a negative way. Overall I can't complain too much because I am treated well.

Advice for Beginning Teachers

Spend a lot of time in preparation and get to know as much as you possibly can about your subject area. Keep learning as you gain more experience and work hard to stay out of a rut. Learn and use technology to assist you to become the best you can be. Be organized when you start and know both the student and teacher handbook. Take the time to look through the school district policy book and don't be afraid to ask experienced teachers for assistance.

Keith Gundlach is the type of person who makes everyone else around him better. He doesn't like recognition, prefers to give credit to others, but possesses an intense drive to get things done and make a difference. Keith was born in Dodgeville, was educated in the Highland School District and earned a BS Degree in Social Studies and a BS Degree in Agriculture from UW-River Falls. He was active in cross country and track and continues to be interested in sports through being treasure of the booster club and spearheading various projects such as the rebuilding of the football field. He has been president of the Randolph Education Association three times and was active on the negotiating committee for 13 years.

Changes and Challenges

Chapter 13

"Better than I was yesterday, but not as good as I will be tomorrow."

> "Character is much easier kept than recovered."
> *Thomas Paine*

> "Keep on beginning and failing. Each time you fail, start all over again and you will grow stronger."
> *Anne Sullivan*

> "Get excited and enthusiastic about your own dream. This excitement will burn like a forest fire."
> *Denis Waitley*

Objectives

- To review the changes and new challenges facing teachers
- To pass on advice for beginning teachers from experienced educators
- To provide insight on educational issues from skilled teachers
- To summarize the contributions of teachers of distinction

Changes and Challenges

"Books are the carriers of civilization. Without books, history is silent; literature dumb, science crippled, thought and speculation are at a standstill."
Barbara Tuchman

In the previous chapter, veteran teachers who have managed to maintain a positive attitude toward their profession passed on valuable tips. In spite of the QEO, budget cuts, and undeserved criticism, these educators continue to be leaders in their schools and in state and national organizations. They have participated in numerous changes and have seen the responsibilities of teachers and the expectations of schools increase dramatically. When I started teaching in Antigo in 1966, parents were held responsible for sending their children to school ready to learn. Each child was expected to comply with the teacher's requests, or face the consequences later at home. There were few special programs and many students fell through the cracks. Gradually, throughout the course of my teaching career, schools were expected to provide more and more of the services that previously were the responsibility of the parents.

The nature of the family has changed, society has changed and the schools have changed. Schools are much more comprehensive, and of course teachers are required to find the time to implement the changes. This has resulted in a huge challenge for the educator, since the amount of time available to teach content has gradually been reduced. For example, with the advent of the computer, and the Internet, grading and communication with parents was supposed to be more efficient. In reality, each innovation requires a support system and follow-up. Many teachers spend a considerable amount of time entering grades into the computer and communicating with parents through e-mail. Consequently, a common complaint from teachers is the lack of time to prepare lessons and implement strategies. The number of changes is overwhelming.

Educational Changes from 1966 to Present

1966 – The Basics	Added in the 1970's & 80's	Most Recent Additions
Reading	Special Education	At Risk Programs
Writing	Drug and Alcohol Abuse Ed.	Stranger Danger Ed.
Arithmetic	Parent Education.	Sexual Abuse Prevention
Social Studies	Character Education	Child Abuse Monitoring
Science	Environmental Education	State Standards
Health	Keyboarding	High Stakes Testing
Citizenship	Computer Education	Teacher Accountability
Vocational Arts	Global Education	Career Education
Physical Education	Ethnic Education	HIV-AIDS Education
Driver's Education	Multicultural Education	Bus Safety Education
Foreign Language	ESL Education	Computer Grades & E-mail
Music	Full Day Kindergarten	Gang Education
Art	Pre-School Education	Death Education
School Lunch	Consumer Education	Wellness
Immunization	Nutrition	Grief Counseling
Safety Education	School Breakfast	Child Care
1 Day = 24 Hrs.	**1 Day = 24 Hrs.**	**1 Day =24 Hrs.**

I'm sure you can add a number of additional responsibilities to the "Most Recent Additions" list. The amount of time a teacher must dedicate to his or her students outside of teaching content has increased significantly. Certainly it is impressive that the schools fill so many needs of society, but it does place greater demands and stress on the teachers.

Advice for Beginning Teachers

Keeping in mind the many changes and challenges facing teachers, the veteran educators who were surveyed, provided the following advice for beginning teachers. After reading their comments, it is obvious their wisdom applies to all educators.

- Keep a warm fuzzy file. Remember all the good things that happen.
- Be fair and consistent at all times.
- Find time for yourself and family away from school.
- Always maintain a sense of humor.
- Give yourself at least three years before you make a decision on your career.
- Work hard during the year and use the summer to recharge.
- Do everything you can to establish trust with your students and parents.
- Make every student realize he/she is special. Look for the gifts in every student.
- Education is a calling. You must be passionate about your profession.
- Support student activities outside of the classroom.
- Respect and appreciate your colleagues.
- Always maintain your cool.
- Keep searching for new activities and teaching strategies.
- Remember, the students are not your peers. Earn their respect but be cautious of friendships.
- Help students accept correction without allowing them to see it as criticism.
- Have a set of core values and stick to them; kids will pick up on it.
- Students develop self-esteem by confronting difficulty, not by avoiding it.
- Do whatever you do with care and empathy.
- Assist students in learning how to assess themselves realistically.
- Establish high standards and expect students to live up to them. This pertains to language, relationships, homework and class activities.

Wow! That is quite a list and some superb advice. An excellent follow-up activity for staff development is to have a group of teachers generate a list such as the above and prioritize it. Teachers then can challenge themselves to work on implementing at least one of the tips every day. Often when schools plan time for professional development, "experts" from outside the school are contracted to help the staff experience professional growth. Each faculty possesses greatness within. The mission of administrators and teachers should be to awaken the sleeping giant and encourage all educators in the school to communicate with each other and share expertise.

> *The mission of administrators and teachers should be to awaken the sleeping giant and get all educators within the school communicating with each other and sharing their expertise.*

A carefully planned professional day using local talent can stir the pot of educational excellence and stimulate more faculty sharing. Each school staff contains a mixed group of talented professionals, skilled in their particular discipline, but also possessing many other gifts. One of the most incredible observations of my teaching career was the realization that I was interacting daily with many gifted people, and yet most were uncomfortable sharing their genius with colleagues. A key to professional growth is a staff that values each other and is provided with the encouragement, time, resources, and opportunities to interact and communicate. To accentuate this, and the value of learning from each other, let's consider what four more distinguished educators have to say.

Patsy A. Rossman, Intermediate School Teacher
Experience: 45 Years at Madison, Stoughton, and McFarland, mostly in middle school

In the early 1990's I was fortunate to have the opportunity to work with Pat Rossman on the Wisconsin Teacher Forum Planning Committee. She struck me as a bright woman with a wealth of classroom experience and a genuine concern about making a difference every day. A modest woman, it took me a while to discover she had been recognized as Wisconsin's Elementary Teacher of the Year and represented Wisconsin in Washington D.C. at the gathering of Teachers of the Year from all states.

We worked together for several years until the forum was dropped because of the lack of funding. For some reason, even though we taught at different levels, the better I got to know Pat the more I realized our educational philosophies were similar. Pat received a B.S. and M.S. from the University of Wisconsin and earned post masters credits from the UW, Cardinal Stritch, Edgewood College and UW-Eau Claire. She served as National President of the Association for Individually Guided Education and has been president and treasurer and served on the board of directors of a number of local organizations. Pat held several leadership posts for the DPI, served on the Review Board for National Standards for Teachers of Social Studies and edited and reviewed Benchmarks for Science Literacy. Pat has been active as an evaluator and reviewer for the State Evaluation Consortium in various curricular areas and served on the Student Teacher Advisory Board for the University of Wisconsin. Most impressive of all she dedicated her life to classroom teaching.

Why I Became A Teacher – Patsy Rossman

Interestingly enough, I had no clue that I would become a teacher until my senior year in high school. No calling, no family members were teachers and I had none of the usual pulls in the direction of working with kids. My senior advisor and social history teacher asked if I would take an aptitude test. As a fluke I did so. He encouraged me (pushed hard) to go on to school in a "certification" two-year course for teaching in a rural school. He convinced me that I wouldn't be wasting my time and that this "wetting of the feet" would help me know more about whatever talent (or spirit) I had for working with kids.

Effective Teaching and Rewards

My effectiveness as an educator can be traced to the joy I find in the successes of children. Being a life-long learner helps in the quest for newer and more potent ways of learning for children. I am positive in my outlook on life, my profession and the kids with whom I work. The five most important characteristics for effective teaching are enthusiasm, flexibility, curiosity, energy and tenacity.

It is very satisfying to see the "aha" in the eyes of the student who says, "I GET IT." It is also rewarding to have students return after years away and telling me I made a difference in their lives.

Classroom Management

I spend lots of time on exciting lessons, thinking about individual needs, and trouble shooting for children who give clues as to learning and behavior. When those things are in place, I spend maybe 5% or less of class time on words or actions that might be called "management."

The Role of the Principal

The most effective principals I have worked with over the years have been instructional leaders who recognize that the best schools have responsible, learned and dedicated teachers willing to try new things and listen to new ideas. They hire positive, bright, upbeat teachers who are team players. They support me and listen to my ideas. They value what I can do for children and what it takes for me to make the school a better learning environment.

Principals who are **NOT** effective can be very nice, caring people but have an already set agenda. They listen but do not hear. They sometimes have a small cadre of "in folks" which causes rifts in the school community. They do not support teachers when the chips are down, but rather go with the squeaky wheel.

The Most Serious Problems and Challenges Facing Education Today

For many of us, it sometimes seems as though poorly funded mandates, paperwork, a focus on state testing requirements, and group test results negates our looking at an individual child and what that child needs to succeed. There is also the issue of some very vocal parents who read a little of this and a little of that and know immediately how the school should be changed according to the latest "hot" author. These brush fires take lots of time and energy away from making the classroom a better place for kids. However, I think the ultimate challenge is knowing what some of these kids go through in abusive, broken homes and knowing we can't change much of what prevents some children from having a happy and learning childhood.

Problems specific to Wisconsin include the "graying" of teachers, money problems for schools and vouchers for unregulated schools.

Advice for Beginning Teachers

Each day begin with the thought that **today** you will make a difference in someone's life. Choose a different child each day for special focus and observation to help you not lose sight of the small, quiet child in the corner. Put a positive spin on **every** situation and consider it a time for learning. Be **flexible** and look for the

> *Each day begin with the thought that today you will make a difference in someone's life. Choose a different child each day for special focus and observation to help you not lose sight of the small, quiet child in the corner.*

teachable moment, even if the lesson to be learned isn't in the state standards! Find a mentor who will be a good listener to your ideas as well as to your disappointments. Relax and enjoy the most wonderful opportunity to serve the community of children who are lucky enough to have **you** for a teacher.

After reading Pat's remarks I'm sure you will agree she provides outstanding and pertinent insight for educators. What stuck me the most was her advice for a beginning teacher that certainly applies to educators at all grade levels and years of experience. "Be flexible and look for the teachable moment, even if the lesson to be learned isn't in the state standards!" Pat reminds us that the process is important and emotional intelligence, even though it is difficult to assess, is essential for success in life.

A member of many professional organizations, Pat has shared her educational expertise with others through presenting at numerous seminars and workshops. In addition to the local and state teacher of the year awards she has been honored with national recognition for the teaching of geography, the Herb Kohl Award for Excellence, Representative Scott Klug's Friend of Education Award, the

Wisconsin Instructional Leadership Award and the Bicentennial Commission Outstanding Contribution recognition.

Pat has taught in Sweden and Japan, worked in the UK on their Authentic Assessment Project in Wales and contributed to three books. Her professional interests have generated over 25 articles published in journals with an educational focus. Married, with two children and six grandchildren, Pat's favorite activities include traveling each summer on "Grandma and Grandpa's Educational Theme Trips."

Kris Fritz, High School Physical Education and Health Experience: 34 Years at Sheboygan South High School

I first met Kris Fritz in the 1990's when I was a participant in a DPI and WIAA program called "Turning the Tide." It was a three-day experience where high schools sent a team of students and faculty to a workshop to develop an action plan to be proactive in promoting leadership and combating drug and alcohol issues for teenagers. It was an impressive program with over 200 participants that took place twice a year. Unfortunately it fell victim to the budget cuts.

The conference had been going on for some years when I was asked to give the opening presentation. Part of being a keynote speaker is to understand the composition of the audience and the objectives of the conference. Kris emphasized the importance of providing students with the tools necessary to make a difference in their schools. She was extremely valuable in helping me understand my role.

Before long I noticed how much we had in common. Kris also is a UW-La Crosse graduate with a compelling interest in coaching. She views athletics as an avenue where teachers and coaches can develop the critical attributes of leadership and teamwork. A dynamic woman with excellent communication skills, Kris has spoken at state, regional, and national conferences.

Why I Became A Teacher – Kris Fritz

A middle school teacher was an influential role model and as I went through high school there was a young PE teacher who was also a role model. My cooperating teacher during my internship was also a big influence as was a colleague who mentored me during my first years in Sheboygan. As a young teacher, I like others, thought "I could change the world" and now as a seasoned veteran, realize I probably can't change the whole world, but I have met many challenges and at least "made a difference" on a somewhat smaller scope.

Effective Teaching and Rewards

Effective teaching begins with a passion and enthusiasm for what you do. Other critical attributes include:

- Caring about others.
- Setting and maintaining high personal standards and expectations for yourself and those you teach.
- Honesty and commitment.
- Organizational skills.
- Willingness to take risks, become involved, and go beyond the norm.

When students know you care about them and perceive you are knowledgeable, you will be effective. I would agree with Madeline Hunter who says, "Teaching is a constant stream of making decisions and implementation of those decisions which will increase the probability of learning."

The rewards of teaching come with seeing a student move from "I can't or I won't, to I'll try or wow, I'm doing it!" At the high school level, seeing a student go from a timid freshman to a senior award winner is gratifying.

Classroom Management

It takes time to establish clear expectations and consequences at the start of the year or semester. Once that has been done and the teacher follows through, management issues are lessened. Teaching, like sport, another of my favorite involvements, can cause one to be at both ends of the emotional spectrum – exhilaration or exasperation. Yet while teaching, I have never been without a challenge to aspire higher or without the opportunity to show others how to do the same.

The Role of the Principal

I taught with two outstanding principals who became Superintendents in different districts. They provided me with encouragement and flexibility and communicated interest in me as a person, not just an employee. The principal is an integral part of the school TEAM/climate with which I work.

The Most Serious Problems and Challenges Facing Education Today

It bothers me whenever I witness a lack of respect among those with whom I interact. This may be student to self, student-to-student, student to staff, staff to student, staff to staff, parents to staff, staff to parents, administration to staff, students and parents, and they to administration. I have little tolerance for overloaded classes, not enough space or equipment, mindless paperwork, and meaningless supervision assignments. I would prefer to have this time to create lessons, develop grants, communicate with parents, make business contacts, etc.

> *I have little tolerance for overloaded classes, not enough space or equipment, mindless paperwork, and meaningless supervision assignments. I would prefer to have this time to create lessons, develop grants, communicate with parents, make business contacts, etc.*

Many good teachers are retiring. It will take dedicated young people with experienced mentors to replace them. A lack of funding, but more mandates and requirements and a lack of connectedness between the home and school have created problems. By overemphasizing standards and assessment less time is spent teaching.

Advice for Beginning Teachers

Be prepared. Make a commitment to what it is you believe in and do what it takes to bring those dreams to reality for self and others. Dialogue often with those you respect and admire. Become involved in ongoing professional development through a professional association or classes.

Set goals, evaluate or reflect upon those goals and be flexible and empathetic in your evaluation of yourself and your students. As teachers, we are part of what is often termed a "service profession." And, if we serve others well, as Robert Greenleaf suggests, we will not only be leaders, but teach others to lead as "servant leaders" making others better as we go.

Kris Fritz teacher, coach, leader, mentor, referee, organizer, writer and speaker, has truly affected the lives of many people. Her influence has even been felt internationally, going back to the early 1970's

when she participated in a tour of the U.S. by a Scottish field hockey team. More recently, she has been a chaperone and coach for youth track teams that competed in Europe and Australia, and has assisted in bringing international track and basketball teams to Sheboygan.

Kris' expertise comes from more than 30 years involvement with students and student-athletes in school sports settings. In Sheboygan she has coached volleyball, basketball and track on the junior high and high school levels, and has worked as an official in several sports. Kris is a native of Monroe, WI and was a Dean's List member and three-sport athlete at UW-La Crosse. She earned a Master's degree in physical education from the University of North Carolina – Greensboro and has over thirty credits beyond her Master's from various universities.

Currently retired from classroom teaching, Kris is using her career knowledge by developing and implementing a Pre K program for physical activity involving over 600 four year olds. For years she served as the citywide grade-level P.E. chair for the Sheboygan Area School District. Kris is a frequent speaker at regional and national conventions of the American Association for Health, Physical Education, Recreation and Dance (AAHPERD) and has had numerous articles published in professional journals.

The recipient of many honors and awards, Kris was named "WAHPERD Secondary School Educator of the Year," served as president of WAHPERD, was named to the Lifetime Achievement Award Hall of Fame for the Women's Sports Advocates of Wisconsin.

Jeff Elmer, High School Physics Teacher
Experience: 17 years, Oshkosh North High School

Jeff Elmer was a member of the Wisconsin Teacher Forum Planning Committee in the late 1990's. He was a Kohl Award winner and one of the younger members of the committee. As I got to know him better I was impressed with his attitude toward education and life. A fun loving person, Jeff struck me as an engaging and entertaining teacher. After several conversations there was no doubt in my mind that Jeff was an outstanding educator and his students were very fortunate to have a person with such a great attitude as their physics teacher.

Jeff comes from a challenging background. He is the youngest of four children. His mother passed away when he was nine months old and his father died when he was 13. Neither of his parents attended college, but all four children are college graduates. Both parents were deceased at a young age, his mother at 34 and his father at 49. Jeff attributes his success to the outstanding parenting by his father for 13 years, close-knit siblings, (he lived with an older sister and her husband during his high school years) and the outstanding coaches and teachers he had at Evansville High School.

In his comparatively short teaching career Jeff has received the MSOE Excellence in Teaching Award, UW-Oshkosh Sigma Xi Excellence in Teaching Award, WCATY Excellence in Teaching Award and has been named Teacher of the Year at Oshkosh North. He has been active in starting the Fox Valley Physics and Physical Science Share-Group and taught at UW-Oshkosh in the Modeling Physical Science Institute. Jeff believes in being a life-long learner and encourages teachers to take more subject matter course work than is required to be as well prepared as possible. He feels at the minimum, students deserve a well-prepared and highly qualified (more than just "certified") teacher.

Why I Became A Teacher – Jeff Elmer

I wanted to develop in my students a zest and enthusiasm for learning similar to what my own teachers inspired in me.

Effective Teaching and Rewards

To be a truly effective teacher, an educator must concentrate on developing the following characteristics.

- **Enthusiasm** – Enthusiasm is contagious! Successful teachers must be excited about the subject matter and enthusiastic about the challenge and honor of helping students become better thinkers through using the subject matter as a medium.

- **Dedication** – Teachers must be dedicated to providing the best learning experiences they can for their students. This means going to whatever extreme is necessary to create meaningful discourse and maximize the total learning experience.

- **Professionalism** – Teachers must continuously search for the best techniques to utilize with their students. This includes attending workshops, conferences, share groups, as well as journal reading and the latest research. In addition, teachers should never be satisfied with just being "certified," but should challenge themselves to be as knowledgeable as possible in their field of study.

- **Patience** – Rome was not built in a day! I was once told if a concept seemed easy, I had not looked hard enough…ideas are fuel for the soul! Teachers should view the year "not as a destination, but as a journey."

- **Humor** – A veteran teacher once advised me to have at least one belly laugh each day. I have always believed that we all need to lighten up sometimes and not take ourselves (and our subject) too seriously. Humor has been a part of my repertoire since I began. My students have lists of Elmer quotes from over the years.

There are numerous rewards in education:

A. The continued development on my part to meet the needs of the students, of which, no two are exactly alike.

B. The glow of the students who struggle and **finally get it!**

C. The former students who go on to accomplish wonderful things and attribute their success to my making them think!

Classroom Management

With Physics I and Physics II being upper level electives, very little of my time is spent on classroom management. An educational professional will have the lesson designed and ready to go before the students enter the room. Any managerial items (seating charts) are completed ahead of time and placed down on tables or on an overhead so students do all the moving before class actually begins. This way I maximize the use of class time!

The Role of the Principal

An effective principal would encourage me to experiment with new activities and new methodologies, and would trust that anything I do is for the betterment of my students. In addition, when parental concerns arise because of a new method or an activity that doesn't go as planned, the principal should support the instructor and divert some of the flack.

The Most Serious Problems and Challenges Facing Education Today

The biggest problem facing education in Wisconsin is the politicians creating educational policy. Rebate checks and tax freezes are political gimmicks for reelection. Unfortunately, these have damaging effects on the educational structure in Wisconsin. It is obvious what the politicians are against (taxes), but what are they for? It amazes me that people will spend thousands of dollars to have children, thousands to clothe them, thousands for material goods (cell phone, cars, computers, dish television), etc., but we can't ask people to pay for schools which form the backbone of this wonderful state.

The greatest frustration with being a teacher is not being able to reach every student. I realize that many times students have other priorities and/or interests as opposed to learning physics, but I still feel a little empty when such a student leaves without feeling the exhilaration associated with exercising the brain. In particular, when a student does not take me up on my offer

> *The greatest frustration with being a teacher is not being able to reach every student.*

for after school or lunch help, I often wonder why the person would not want to take full advantage of every opportunity to try their hardest while on this earth for a relatively short time.

The most challenging aspect of teaching is trying to balance what you have to do (standards and district employment requirements), what you want to do, what you should do (educational research), and the available resources to do all these items, with the time required to do it.

Advice for Beginning Teachers

As mentioned earlier, teaching is a journey, not a destination. Do not expect to do it all the first year of teaching. On the other hand, expect to continually tweak what you do, as teaching is more of an art than an exact science. I hate to say it, but I am working as hard or harder now than I was as a first year teacher. However, the work now isn't what to teach, it's deciding the **best** way to have students learn it! A teacher must be enthusiastic about his/her subject and students learning the subject. Enthusiasm is contagious! Do your best to utilize research based techniques and pedagogy.

Jeff managed to overcome youthful adversity to graduate from college and become a highly regarded educator. He continues to contribute to his profession through sharing his expertise with others. His warm, outgoing personality serves him well in interacting with students and colleagues. He enjoys running marathons and "just about any athletic activity I can do with my kids." He is married and is the father of two children. He and his wife have found remodeling their home to be "therapeutic," along with running and cheering on the Wisconsin Badger football team

Keith Swett, AP English, Alt. English, and Literature and Composition Teacher
Experience: 32 Years at Seymour High School

Keith Swett impressed me in the late 1960's when I was Assistant Director of Housing and Head Freshman Football Coach at UW-La Crosse. Keith was a member of the football team and the following year he was hired as a resident assistant in a men's residence hall. His well-developed leadership and communication skills along with an imposing physique served him well in earning the respect of the rambunctious underclassmen. After a year in Seymour I was looking for an assistant coach who would also be an effective teacher and disciplinarian. Fortunately, Keith was graduating, and his English major and interest in football and wrestling made him a perfect fit at Seymour.

We worked as colleagues for 28 years. He became the head wrestling coach and eventually gave up football to spend more time with his family. However, our working relationship intensified as we originated a "Great Issues" class, which we team-taught. Even though it was necessary for one of us to give up a preparation period, the popular elective continued for twenty years. With two teachers in the classroom, we placed an emphasis on developing higher level thinking skills. A principal, who had confidence in both of us, provided the degree of academic freedom that allowed us to examine controversial issues in great depth.

The class transcended traditional structure and encouraged student debate and creativity. I developed tremendous respect for Keith's intelligence, ingenuity and ability to connect with students. We modeled proper argumentation techniques through heated discussion and intellectual discourse. Then we stepped aside and the students took over. It was a fun experience! We received much positive feedback from the students. All three of my daughters took the class and found it stimulating and loved it!

Keith, who has been inducted into the State and National Wrestling Coaches Hall of Fame, is a unique educator in that he teaches the highest advance placement classes and classes of students who are academically challenged. His unique style, great sense of humor and ability to bring out the best in each student, makes his classes very popular. Keith's infectious laugh can be heard all over school as he implements a variety of motivational techniques in his classroom. Students respond positively to his enthusiastic and dynamic approach to learning as evidenced by the large percentage of AP students who earn college credits.

Why I Became A Teacher – Keith Swett

Teachers and coaches had a positive influence in my life and three generations of my family have taught. I enjoy working with ideas and helping young people to achieve their dreams. Teaching and coaching provide me with the opportunity to make a difference in the lives of kids.

Effective Teaching and Rewards

I believe the following personal characteristics are essential for effective teaching:

1. Come to class prepared.

2. Have a discipline plan

3. Accept student responses.

4. Laugh at yourself and situations, but not at students.

5. Be a flexible thinker. Continue to learn.

6. Have high expectations for yourself and the students.

7. I love kids and they can tell it.

8. Stay positive.

As both a teacher and a coach I'm willing to give all the time necessary for students to be successful. I measure my success through their success. I push the kids hard, but I push myself harder. Education has been the center of my life for over 30 years. I love teaching and coaching. I see myself as a bridge between the past and the future. Part of my mission is to transfer norms and values to the next generation. As a teacher I want kids to think, so we write 70-80 papers a year. Using great literature as our starting point, we explore problems facing teens, their parents, and our society.

It is very rewarding when kids come back from college and tell me my class prepared them to be successful. Wrestlers tell me the sport changed their lives. It is not uncommon to hear them say, "I wouldn't have graduated without wrestling." or "You are my favorite teacher or coach."

Classroom Management

My classroom is energetic with activities changing quickly. Because of that I don't have many problems with discipline. I have simple rules that are enforced consistently. I don't depend on others to discipline my students. Parents and principals are aides in my plan. I try to know my students, so I am often able to avoid public confrontation.

The Role of the Principal

I hold in high regard a principal who will value my judgment and give me ownership of my programs. I expect support on budgets, class size and getting all the materials necessary to experience success. An effective principal will correct me in private while publicly supporting me.

The Most Serious Problems and Challenges Facing Education Today

An emphasis on meeting state standards and testing is a waste of money when budgets are being tightened. Cutting the budget and cutting programs will destroy education. I hate the negative media and hypocritical politicians. I work with too many students who are inadequately prepared. It seems like administrators worry about paper results. I take kids where they are and move them as far forward as possible.

You can't measure anything worth teaching with an objective test. State standards are a cruel joke. For example we'll **all** run an eight-minute mile, the fit and the obese, those with two legs and those with one leg, those with no legs and no interest. My point is that you don't fatten a pig for the fair by weighing him more often. I know when a kid is having problems. His reading level doesn't help me. Great teachers are dynamic, creative, flexible, concerned and disciplined. Great teachers hate a standardized curriculum and measurable objectives. Standardization kills the soul.

I'm a follower of Socrates and Emerson. The answer lies within the student. My job is to ask the right question. For a good question right answers are unlimited and individual. We talk about diversity but is it an accident that white kids with college educated parents and a high social economic status perform well on tests?

> *I'm a follower of Socrates and Emerson. The answer lies within the student. My job is to ask the right question. For a good question right answers are unlimited and individual.*

Advice for Beginning Teachers

Prepare twice as much as you think you will need during the period. Be yourself, but be your best self. Accept student thinking and then through questioning help them explore alternatives. It is good to like the kids, but they are not your friends. Avoid personal attacks or jokes. Kids break easily. Get help from veterans and parents. The parents are not the enemy. Most attacks from students have nothing to do with you. They might be angry with their parents or their date. Be sure to discuss with the principal how you want different kinds of situations handled.

Clearly communicate your expectations. Don't let students compare their grades to other student grades. Offer to discuss their work with them. Be visible in the hallway and attend co-curricular events. Kids want you to be interested in them. Your job is to give kids tools to help them persevere. Don't do too much for them, but help them earn their successes.

Kids are Wonderful

When my son was killed in a tragic accident, my kids, wrestlers and students stepped up. A boy I had to call everyday to get him to school called me. Forty-eight year old kids joined with 15 year olds. When I couldn't stand they held me up. When life seemed empty they filled it with hope and dreams. They welcomed me at weddings, invited me to birthday parties and stopped over on Father's Day. Karma is very real. What we give we have forever. They can't all read and write equally well, but they all passed the only test that counts.

Keith Swett was born and raised in Marshfield where he was a three-sport athlete and graduated with honors. He continued his athletic pursuits at UW-La Crosse where he also

coached wrestling and graduated with honors. Keith has been named to "Who's Who" as a student and a teacher. He has coached football, wrestling for over 30 years, and power lifting.

An avid reader, Keith enjoys Shakespeare, in particular, Macbeth, Hamlet and Othello, biographies of coaches and athletes, and psychological thrillers by James Patterson. He writes a column, "Panache," for the local paper, and coaches USA Wrestling during the summer. Coach Swett has helped train several wrestlers who went on to become Olympic medal winners.

I enjoyed reading the surveys of over 100 experienced educators. What impressed me most was the zest and enthusiasm these individuals still have for teaching. Many of the teachers have been in the classroom for over 25 years. These individuals realize that change is constantly taking place and welcome it as a challenge. Experienced educators know that change just for the sake of changing isn't a good thing. They have the skills to hang on to what is good and let go of that which is no longer effective.

Virtually everyone mentioned that the major motivation for teaching is the internal joy and satisfaction of seeing students learn. Numerous references were made to "seeing the light bulb go on" or "knowing that he got it." Teachers of distinction agree that teaching is a commitment to life long learning. It is an intense burning desire to make a difference everyday. Teachers are bridge builders who help young people discover their gifts. For years I've concluded my staff development programs with William Dromgoole's poem *"The Bridge Builder."*

The Bridge Builder

An old man going down a lone highway
Came in the evening cold and gray
To a chasm vast and deep and wide
Through which was flowing a sullen tide.

The old man crossed in the twilight dim;
That swollen stream held no fears for him;
But he turned when safe on the other side
And built a bridge to span the tide.

"Old man," said a fellow pilgrim near,
"You are wasting your strength with building here;
Your journey will end with this ending day;

You never again must pass this way;
You have crossed the chasm deep and wide-
Why build you this bridge at the eventide?"

The builder lifted his old gray head.
"Good friend, in the path I have come," he said,
"There followeth after me today
A youth whose feet must pass this way.

This swollen stream which was naught for me
To that fair-haired youth may a pitfall be;
He, too, must cross in the twilight dim;
Good friend, I am building the bridge for him.

Maintain your PMA and keep building bridges everyday!

Appendix

Determine Your Leadership Potential

Common Characteristics of Leaders - "All The Way With PMA!" www.billcollar.com

Instructions: Respond to each item by placing an (X) in the space that best expresses how the statement describes you. If the statement is not like you at all, check space number one. If it fits perfectly, check space five. The spaces in between allow you to indicate various degrees of fit. If you are torn between feeling it does or does not apply, check space number three, the halfway mark.

Unlike Me   Like Me
1   2   3   4   5

__ __ __ __ __   **1. Goals** - I am a goal setter. I have a strong sense of purpose and know where I am going with my life. I have written goals.

__ __ __ __ __   **2. Positive Mental Attitude** - I possess a high degree of confidence and self-worth. I begin every day with positive expectancy.

__ __ __ __ __   **3. Persistence** - I have the ability to bounce back from failure. I view failure as a learning experience rather than a setback.

__ __ __ __ __   **4. Risk Taker** - I am willing to attempt new tasks and welcome a positive challenge even if I am not certain of success.

__ __ __ __ __   **5. Decision Maker** - I understand the decision-making process. Making decisions usually comes easy for me.

__ __ __ __ __   **6. Courage** - I am able to take a firm stand even when my position is not popular. I am in charge of my life.

__ __ __ __ __   **7. Seek New Learning** - I find it rewarding to acquire new skills and information. I plan to be a life-long learner.

__ __ __ __ __   **8. Enthusiasm** - I get excited about projects I believe in and possess a great deal of energy to complete them.

__ __ __ __ __   **9. Focus On Success** - I can accept constructive criticism and value the opinions of people I respect.

__ __ __ __ __   **10. Seek To Serve Others** - I am able to work with other people and find teamwork enjoyable.

__ __ __ __ __   **11. Sense of Humor** - I realize the importance of humor and am able to laugh at myself.

__ __ __ __ __   **12. Integrity** - I take pride in being truthful and in keeping my word.

__ __ __ __ __   **13. Communication** – I express my thoughts in a clear, concise manner. I am an active listener and show interest in what is said.

__ __ __ __ __   **14. Initiative** – I am a self-starter.

_____-----**My Score**

Scoring: Add up your total points to determine how prepared you are to be a positive leader. The following scale will give you some idea of your leadership potential at this time.

60 – 70 Outstanding leadership potential! You are ready to take on major tasks.
50 – 59 An impressive score! You possess the key characteristics of leadership.
40 – 49 Improve in several categories and you will become an excellent leader!
30 – 39 Much potential exists. Keep working on a self-improvement plan.
Below 29 – It is up to you to alter your attitude and lifestyle to develop more leadership ability.

Developing and Maintaining a Positive Mental Attitude

Bill Collar, "All The Way With PMA!" www.billcollar.com

1. **Greet each day with a smile** and look forward to making a difference in the lives of others.

2. When introducing yourself in any new association, **take the initiative and volunteer your name first,** extend your hand for a firm handshake, and maintain eye contact when you speak.

3. **Be enthusiastic!** Move vigorously and use expressive gestures when talking. Walk with a confident stride.

4. **Speak in a loud, clear, voice.** Always use affirmative statements. Work the phrases "I Can" and "I Will" into conversations.

5. Concentrate on viewing yourself as a successful person. **You become that which you think about the most.** It becomes a self-fulfilling prophecy.

6. Look for good in the actions of others. **Treat everyone with dignity and respect.**

7. Be polite and considerate in your communication with others. Say, "Please" and "Thank You" and "You're Welcome." **Compliment others on their good points.**

8. **Remember the "Golden Rule" in all your actions.** This means more than doing unto others, as you would have them do unto you; it means refraining from doing unto others that which you would **not** like them to do to you.

9. Demonstrate interest in the ideas and actions of others. **Be an active listener.**

10. **Have a plan to deal with criticism.** Consider the source and act accordingly.

11. **Be yourself.** Forget about impressing others, be the person you are most comfortable with – you.

12. **Always maintain your composure and self-control.** Consider the consequences before taking action and take personal responsibility for your actions.

13. **A difference of opinion should be expressed in a constructive manner.**

14. **Exercise your mind and body on a regular basis.**

15. **View mistakes as learning experiences.** Realize that failure is often a test of your belief and conviction. Most of the great people in history have failed often. The most important thing is to be able to bounce back when things are not going well.

16. **Accept the things about yourself that cannot be changed.** This includes the shape of your face, the sound of your voice, the color of your skin, your height, etc.

17. When someone pays you a compliment, **accept it and reply with a simple, "Thank You!"**

18. Condition your mind to look for the positive things in your life. "Instead of seeing barriers, see hurdles; instead of obstacles, see opportunities; instead of problems, see solutions." **Begin each day with a positive expectancy!**

Charles Garfield of the Peak Performance Center in Berkley, California has studied over 2,000 peak performers in the United States and has identified ten qualities they most often possess. Read each description and rank yourself from 1 (low) to 5 (high). This activity will help you identify your strengths and weaknesses.

_____ **1. Foresight and the ability to carry out effective planning.**
Do you set goals and develop a plan to follow to reach those goals? Do you always have a practice plan? A game plan?

_____ **2. A drive toward transcending previous levels of accomplishment.**
Are you willing to commit yourself to rise above previous performances? Do your teams show consistent improvement as the season progresses?

_____ **3. High levels of self-confidence and self-worth.**
Do you view yourself as an effective coach? Would you be difficult to replace?

_____ **4. A high need for responsibility and control.**
Do you like to take action and be in charge? Do you enjoy competition and the opportunity to make critical decisions?

_____ **5. Well developed communication skills in both personal and professional areas.**
Are you capable of effectively communicating your ideas? Do your players understand what you expect of them?

_____ **6. An effective use of mental rehearsal.**
Do you visualize the process and desired outcome of your task? Do your players understand how to practice visualization for success?

_____ **7. Little need of outside praise or recognition.**
You must have an internal feeling of accomplishment. Are you driven by attitude motivation rather than fear or reward?

_____ **8. A superior ability to take risks.**
Are you willing to break out of the comfort zone? Do you welcome new challenges?

_____ **9. The ability to accept feedback and to self-correct.**
Are you able to use information from respected sources to improve? Do you attend clinics and conferences for personal improvement?

_____ **10. A willingness to accept ownership of creative ideas.**
Are you willing to "go for it" and initiate action on your ideas? Do you take the time to study your opponent and make proper adjustments to counter their strengths?

·········· Suggestions for Personal Motivation ··········

A. Identify one of your biggest strengths. This is an area that you have ranked as a five. Build on this strength to help you develop to your full potential.

B. Pick an area that you have ranked one or two and make a commitment to show maximum improvement within the next several months. Actually develop a written plan to build this weakness into a strength.

C. Accept personal responsibility for your strengths and weaknesses, and develop a plan to deal with each. Pick out the key factors that have the greatest impact on your profession and build up these areas first.

Eleven Keys to Coaching Longevity

Bill Collar, Seymour, WI "All The Way With PMA!" www.billcollar.com

1. **Keep a Positive Mental Attitude!**

   After the Bay of Pigs fiasco President Kennedy remarked, "Victory has many fathers, defeat is an orphan." Unfortunately, this is often true in sports. You will find the true content of your character by how you react to adversity. Stay positive after a loss and during a difficult season.

2. **Coach with Passion.**

   Emerson stated "nothing great was ever accomplished without enthusiasm." Coach on the run and speak with confidence and conviction. Attitudes are contagious; make yours worth catching.

3. **Have a Plan for Criticism.**

   Be prepared for unjust comments from people who are quick to find fault. Consider the source of the comment; if you respect the person speak with him to get to the root of the problem. If you don't respect him, ignore it.

4. **Never Expect Gratitude from Teenagers.**

   Seldom do teenagers realize the amount of time, effort and commitment the coach puts in to help them reach their full potential. They tend to focus on their own lives and rarely express appreciation. Your gratitude will come from the personal satisfaction in building a cohesive team.

5. **Work Smarter not Harder.**

   Concentrate on the tasks that bring the greatest return on the time invested. Too often a coach will work hard, but much of the effort does not bring about the desired result. Do a task analysis to determine a list of priorities. Be sure to delegate proper tasks to assistants.

6. **Know Which Battles to Lose.**

   Be flexible when dealing with others. At times you may have what seems to be great idea, but there is a time when you have to redirect your efforts when your idea is met with too much opposition. This is important to remember when working with administrators and faculty members.

7. **Find Time for Your Family.**

   You spend so much time working on your sport and building a championship team, but make sure you schedule in time for your wife and family. During the season set aside a certain time for family concerns. Your children will grow up in a hurry--- invest in them now!

8. **Keep a Sense of Humor.**

   Be passionate about your sport, but make sure you and your players are having fun. Enjoy the light moments in practice and have a good laugh when the opportunity comes up.

9. **Teach Life-long Lessons.**

   Much has been said about the building of character through participation in athletics. This is not an exaggeration. Many of the characteristics necessary for success in life can be reinforced through athletic competition. Today's society places a premium on workers with interpersonal skills and problem solving ability. You will feel good about emphasizing positive values.

10. **Don't Discuss Playing Time with Parents.**

    Explain to the players and parents if there is a question about playing time it is the responsibility of the player to speak with the coach about this concern. Communication is part of the maturation process. Parents must honor the relationship that develops between the coach and players.

11. **Keep the Game in Perspective.**

    Realize that you expect the best from yourself and the players. What more can you give? Your health, family, integrity and career must not be compromised in pursuit of victory.

Goal Setting for Success: Use this form to write out your goal and establish a success plan.
Bill Collar, "All The Way With PMA!"

Goal – Write your goal here. It must be personal, positive and deal with the present

Your goal relates to what category of your life? _____
See Chapter Five

Deadline: I will reach my goal on or before _____
Write in the specific target date

Obstacles to achieving your goal – List everything that stands between you and reaching your goal.

Solutions to the Obstacles listed above

Expected Benefits – Reaching this goal will benefit me in these ways.

Verbal Affirmations – Write several statements utilizing positive self-talk to convince yourself you are capable of reaching this goal.

Goal Checklist – Refer to your "Goal Checklist" to guarantee you are prepared to reach this goal.

_____ Stated Clearly?	_____ Deadline Established?	_____ Time Commitment?	_____ Personal?
_____ Challenging?	_____ Visualization?	_____ Belief?	_____ Handle Setbacks?
_____ Measurable?	_____ Written Affirmations?	_____ Personality Changes	_____ Patience & Determination

Is it worth it to me? Am I willing to invest the time and effort to obtain the expected benefits? _____ Yes _____ No

GOAL CHECKLIST

Bill Collar – "All The Way With PMA!"

This simple checklist is designed to help you focus in on your goal and make sure it has been thoroughly thought out. When you can answer "yes" to all of the questions, you have a workable plan. Remember, thought must precede action, but taking action on your plan is the real key. This is up to you!

<u>Yes</u>   <u>No</u>

___ ___ **1.** **Have I stated my goal clearly? Do I really understand what I plan to accomplish?**

___ ___ **2.** **Is this goal challenging for me and yet realistic for a person with my potential?**

___ ___ **3.** **Can this goal be measured? Will I be able to tell when I have reached my goal?**

___ ___ **4.** **Have I established a deadline to aim for in reaching this goal?**

___ ___ **5.** **Do I understand the <u>visualization</u> process well enough to use it to help me reach my goal?**

___ ___ **6.** **Have I written <u>affirmations</u> to help develop a positive attitude toward reaching my goal?**

___ ___ **7.** **Am I willing to take the time necessary to drill and practice as I work toward my goal?**

___ ___ **8.** **Do I honestly <u>believe</u> I am capable of reaching this goal?**

___ ___ **9.** **Am I willing to make the personality changes necessary in order to reach this goal?**

___ ___ **10.** **Is this goal really mine? Do I have the desire to achieve it?**

___ ___ **11.** **Am I prepared to view ridicule, failure, and temporary setbacks as stepping-stones toward reaching my goal?**

___ ___ **12.** **Do I possess the patience and determination necessary to maintain a concentrated effort toward reaching this goal?**

CONGRATULATIONS! You have answered the twelve most important questions a person must deal with when setting goals. Select the appropriate statement below and act on it.

- *I have checked "yes" on all twelve questions and I'm excited about getting started on my plan of action to reach my goal.* <u>**I'm ready to go for it!**</u>

- *I have checked "no" on one or more of the questions. Before I may begin my plan of action, I must revise my goal plan so l am able to answer, "yes" to all twelve questions. If necessary, I will seek help in revising my goal plan.*

Determine Your H.Q. (Humor Quotient)

Bill Collar "All The Way With PMA!" www.billcollar.com

Instructions: Respond to each item by placing an (X) in the space that best expresses how the statement describes you. If the statement is not like you at all, check space number one. If it fits perfectly, check space five. The spaces in between allow you to indicate various degrees of fit. If you are torn between feeling it does or does not apply, check space number three, the halfway mark.

Unlike Me   Like Me
 1   2   3   4   5

__ __ __ __ __ **1. Laughter** – I laugh often and have a lot of fun.

__ __ __ __ __ **2. I am capable of laughing at myself** – It is easy for me to laugh at my mistakes and shortcomings.

__ __ __ __ __ **3. Humorous Stories** – I enjoy a well-told and appropriately humorous story. I will repeat jokes or stories that I have heard.

__ __ __ __ __ **4. Feelings** – I consider the feelings of others before attempting any humor. I realize it is not humor if others are offended.

__ __ __ __ __ **5. Life Stories** - I like to share humorous stories from my life with others.

__ __ __ __ __ **6. Stress** - I use my sense of humor to help combat stress. I am in charge of my life.

__ __ __ __ __ **7. Play** - I find it rewarding to break away from the daily routine and fine the time to engage in activities I find entertaining.

__ __ __ __ __ **8. Unpleasant Times** – I use my sense of humor to cope in unpleasant times. This serves as a diversion from the prevailing problem.

__ __ __ __ __ **9. Have Fun** - I enjoy interacting with people and find that I can have fun without trying to be funny.

__ __ __ __ __ **10. Chill Out** - I am tolerant of mistakes made by others and am more likely to see the humor in a situation than to criticize.

__ __ __ __ __ **11. Spontaneous Comments** – I have developed the ability to engage in off-the-cuff banter with others.

__ __ __ __ __ **12. Silly Ideas** - I see original ideas as stepping-stones to solving problems. I encourage others to voice their opinions.

__ __ __ __ __ **13. Communication** – When I am asked to speak or express my thoughts I am comfortable working in humorous examples or references.

__ __ __ __ __ **14. Health** – I believe the more I laugh, the healthier I am.

_____ -----**My Score**

Scoring: Add up your total points to determine your humor quotient. The following scale will give you some idea of your level of humor at this time.

60 – 70 An excellent level of humor. You have a great attitude and are fun to be around.
50 – 59 An impressive score! You utilize humor to stay in control of your life.
40 – 49 Improve in several categories and raise your H.Q. to a point where it will be an asset.
30 – 39 Lighten up and laugh more. Keep working on a self-improvement plan.
Below 29 – You are at risk of being humor impaired. Act now to welcome more fun into your life.

Keys to Maintaining Self-Motivation

Bill Collar – "All The WAY With PMA!"   www.billcollar.com

Motivation may be defined as: "A desire held in expectation with the belief that it will be realized."
Consider the points below to build belief in your ability to transcend previous levels of accomplishment.

1. **Invest in yourself.** Pay the price for self-improvement. Make it a point to take classes, attend workshops and do professional reading.

2. **Believe in yourself and your ability to improve.** Make sure you realize the value of your profession and see yourself as being essential to the success of your organization.

3. **Establish goals** in all areas of your life and develop a plan for reaching them.

4. **Make a list of your five most important current wants or desires.** Next to each put down what benefit or payoff you expect from each.

5. **Concentrate on the benefits of reaching your goals.** Use the powerful goal of visualization to see yourself accomplishing your goals.

6. **Always use positive, affirmative language** as you communicate with others and in your self-talk. Replace the word "can't" with "can", and "try" with "will" in your daily vocabulary.

7. **Surround yourself with personal and professional winners.**

8. **Keep your problems in proper perspective.** Break them down into small manageable parts so they will be easier to handle.

9. **Know where you stand.** Do a self-evaluation to determine your strengths and weaknesses. Celebrate your successes, minimize your weaknesses and maximize your strengths.

10. **Put yourself in other people's shoes.** How do you see yourself from their perspective?

11. **View criticism as a learning experience.** If your belief is weak, your reaction to criticism will be emotional or irrational. Have a plan to deal with criticism and consider the source.

12. **Develop a "constructive discontent" with the way things are.** Use your imagination to come up with a plan for improvement.

13. **Get into the habit of avoiding procrastination** and develop a "do it now" mentality.

14. **Remember the lessons of history.** The greatest people in history are those who failed most often. Persistence often turns adversity into greatness. It is not how seldom you fail in life that counts, it's how often you rise after a setback.

15. **Learn to stay relaxed and receptive to new ideas.** Always be in control of your emotions.

16. **Minimize the amount of time you spend watching television.** It can be a huge time waster.

17. **Constantly work to improve your communication skills.** Speak with confidence and emphasize critical points by varying your voice and using proper gestures. Make an effort to be an active listener. This will reaffirm your desire to be the best you can be.

18. **Walk with an animated stride and convey confidence in the way you carry yourself.**

19. **Analyze people of achievement** and learn from the way they handle themselves and how they deal with various situations.

My Strengths

Bill Collar – "All The Way With PMA!"   www.billcollar.com

Directions: Circle a minimum of ten personal traits that you consider to be your greatest strengths. Use the form at the bottom of the page to prioritize what you consider to be your five most valuable characteristics.

Attractive	Healthy	Well-groomed	Courteous	Patient
Content	Tolerant	Calm	Considerate	Peaceful
Sensitive	Assertive	Persuasive	Ambitious	Creative
Intelligent	Friendly	Wise	Decisive	Happy
Enthusiastic	Mature	Caring	Understanding	Generous
Honest	Dependable	Attentive	Sincere	Fair
Open-minded	Cheerful	Energetic	Loyal	Organized

Prioritize Your Selections
(Rank from 1 to five)

Directions: List what you consider to be your most important trait first, etc., then explain how you   will apply that trait in your personal life.

Trait # 1 _____ Application: _____

Trait #2 _____ Application: _____

Trait #3 _____ Application: _____

Trait #4 _____ Application: _____

Trait #5 _____ Application: _____

Parenting for Success in School

Bill Collar, "All The Way With PMA!"   www.billcollar.com

1. **Be positive with your child.** Positive expectations lead to positive results. Focus on the accomplishments and exercise caution when dealing with lack of achievement. Always concentrate on improving the performance and not ridiculing the individual. Parenting can be very difficult and tough decisions must be made. Remember, you must do what is best for your child and not what your child wants you to do. You are the adult with mature problem solving ability and a solid foundation of self-esteem.

2. **Establish a time schedule.** Illustrate to your child how to make a list and establish priorities. Schedule in key activities and explain the need to minimize time wasters such as television, computer games and telephone time. Establish a certain amount of time when television is acceptable. Don't turn off the TV or throw it out, but exercise your parental responsibility to establish proper guidelines.

3. **Keep extra-curricular activities in perspective.** All research indicates students who participate in school activities achieve more academically than those who do not. Encourage music, drama, sports, etc. but stress that doing their best in the classroom comes first. Help your child to make good decisions in this area and never threaten to take away participation as a punishment for poor grades. Seldom will a student study during the time normally spent practicing for an activity.

4. **Homework is essential.** Much has been written about students being burdened with excessive homework. Most often the problem is more one of procrastination and poor time management. Check with your son or daughter to guarantee they have a workable time schedule and help them eliminate time wasters. Many teachers provide students with work time in class or often a study hall is available. Getting a jump-start on homework during the day can be a big help in reducing frustration with a lack of time at home. Talking with friends and straying off task at school can be a tremendous time waster.

5. **Make the commitment to find time to take interest in schoolwork.** When you ask, "What did you do in school?" or "How is school going?" the customary reply is "nothing" or "good." Ask follow up questions and express interest in seeing your child's daily work and special projects. It is easy to get wound up in your work and have a busy social schedule at the expense of spending quality time with your children. Find the time to schedule the children in your day.

6. **Tell your children you are proud of them.** Unconditional love is essential and must be expressed, but communicating a sense of worth to your son or daughter is most meaningful. Stress you are proud of who they are, and not what they accomplish. Too often children compare themselves with others and invariably come up short. Emphasize that doing their best is more important than being the best.

7. **Help your child find his/her gifts.** Students will display a variety of talents in and out of class. Work with the teachers to help provide your child with opportunities to develop their skills. Music, drama, art, athletics, etc. provide them with valuable learning experiences.

8. **Part time jobs.** Many students work too many hours while attending high school. About two thirds of U.S. high school students hold part-time jobs and work an average of 15 to 20 hours a week. This concept is unique to the United States. Explain to your teenagers that their number one job is to do their best in school. Too often the money earned is used to purchase materialistic goods that are not needed. "Putting money aside for college" is often the stated reason for working, but mostly it is spent in less essential ways. Be sure to investigate the availability of scholarships and financial assistance to attend college.

9. **Spending time with friends.** Students may spend 20 to 30 hours a week just "hanging out" or wasting time with friends. Your influence as a parent must be greater than the influence of friends. Socializing may take the time that could be devoted to homework. Obviously teenagers shouldn't be locked in their room, but parents must accept the challenge of positive leadership. Numerous studies indicate teens feel they need restrictions and value parents who are willing to establish specific guidelines for them to follow.

10. **Introduce yourself to teachers.** Make it a point to get to know your child's teachers. Too often parents feel they have this responsibility during the primary grades, but become less visible as the student matures. It is important to continue to monitor your child's progress throughout high school. Always attend parent conferences, and if you are unavailable, make an appointment to visit with the teacher at another time.

11. **Support the school professionals.** If an incident takes place where there is a serious difference between the teacher or principal and the student, have confidence the school professionals are doing what is best for your child. Listen to your son or daughter, but follow up by communicating with the teacher before you jump to conclusions. Set up a conference with the people involved and establish a plan to work out individual differences. If the teacher has made a mistake in judgment, realize the complex nature of the profession and maintain your decorum while tactfully working out a solution.

12. **Allow your child to make decisions.** Students develop self-confidence and a sense of ownership when they help make the choices that influence their lives. Be sure you have taught the proper steps to making good decisions prior to giving your child that responsibility. By providing them with incremental decision making experiences you are building a foundation for future growth. Simply saying. "It's your decision to make" doesn't take into consideration the vital steps of gathering information and evaluating the evidence. Emphasizing the value of considering the consequences and accepting personal responsibility is important.

13. **Stay calm and keep failures and successes in perspective.** Overreaction by parents to achievement or disappointments, can lead to a feeling of intense pressure to succeed or the inability to deal with failure. It is important for children to learn at an early age that failure is never fatal and success is never final. Each setback should be viewed as a learning experience.

14. **Always have logical consequences.** Maintain control of the outcomes when discussing consequences with your children. Too often decisions are made in haste and emotion is involved. Simply grounding someone, banning television, dropping extracurricular activities, or invoking some other unrelated penalty is punitive in nature and doesn't teach any life-long lessons. The consequence must be a learning experience and relate to the indiscretion.

To maximize your performance in any activity it is important to win the mental game. Rank yourself from 1 (low) to 5 (high) in each of the qualities below to determine your strengths and areas for improvement.

_____ 1. **Peak Performers Set Goals.** They have the ability to break their dreams down into small manageable parts and are able to work on them on a daily, weekly and monthly basis. Peak performers have precise objectives in mind and always keep their eyes on the prize.

_____ 2. **Peak Performers Practice Mental Rehearsal.** Mental rehearsal is often called the "master skill" because the development of many other skills depends on the ability of the individual to picture being successful at the desired task. Mental rehearsal means focusing on a goal to the point where the individual actually practices the activity in his or her mind. Research has determined the mind does not distinguish between real and imagined experiences.

_____ 3. **Peak Performers Practice With A Purpose.** Every practice session is viewed as an opportunity for personal improvement. Peak performers truly believe positive preparation and practice means perfect performance. They always practice with a purpose and never just to get it over.

_____ 4. **Peak Performers Strive For Excellence.** They believe they are capable of bettering their previous performance. Peak performers are capable of evaluating their accomplishments and determining how they can improve. As they push themselves to new levels they have the ability to relax and stay "in the zone."

_____ 5. **Peak Performers Are Confident.** They have the ability to rise above fear, worry, doubt and anger, and concentrate on controlling the emotions that will help them accomplish their task. They thrive on pressure situations because through the practice of mental rehearsal they have been there before.

_____ 6. **Peak Performers Take Educated Risks.** This means they are not being foolhardy or reckless, but accept the challenge and possibility of failure that is necessary for achievement to take place. They focus on success and know that in order to rise to their full potential, perseverance is essential.

_____ 7. **Peak Performers Are Team Players.** They are unselfish in team situations and are willing to play a lesser role to bring out the best in the team. When working with others peak performers demand the same type of commitment from team members and will encourage others to elevate their level of achievement. In the ideal team setting peak performers give support to others and receive it themselves.

_____ 8. **Peak Performers Focus On The Present.** Whether in sports, music or drama they have the ability to learn from, but rise above past mistakes and concentrate on the task at hand. While they tend to be perfectionists they are tolerant of error to the point where they will not allow previous flaws or setbacks to hinder future performance.

_____ 9. **Peak Performers Are Positive Thinkers.** They see what can be done and communicate in a manner that conveys belief. Peak Performers understand that thoughts control feelings, feelings control actions and actions become habits that influence attitudes and determine behavior. True believers control their minds to think constructive thoughts and visualize success.

_____ 10. **Peak Performers Have Little Need For Outside Praise Or Recognition.** Since they are internally motivated and driven by the desire to excel, peak performers often give credit to others. Of course they appreciate a pat on the back, but they derive a great deal of satisfaction and fulfillment from their accomplishments.

Selling Yourself and Your Product

Bill Collar, "All The way With PMA!" www.billcollar.com

> **Basic Premise:** Whether you are selling real estate, transportation, insurance, or teaching a class, first you must convince the customer you are trustworthy and committed in doing what is best for them. They don't care how much you know, until they know how much you care. A successful salesman knows people do things for their reasons and not yours. In other words, the recipient of your product must see the benefits involved and how losses may be avoided. Consider these tips for success.

1. **It's your attitude that makes the difference.** Attitude is everything. When you are enjoying yourself, the clients can sense it. Great attitudes are contagious; make sure yours is worth catching. Emerson said, *"Who you are speaks so loudly, I cannot hear what you say."*

2. **Personal motivation is a must.** You must have an intense burning desire to constantly improve your drive and determination. Learning as much as possible about your product and how you may help the customer benefit will increase your level of belief. Belief in your product helps maximize the faith you have in yourself.

3. **Self-Confidence is a given.** When you control your feelings and utilize attitude motivation, the end result is self-confidence. Confidence gives you the energy necessary take on challenging tasks. When you successfully complete a demanding mission you experience personal growth. To build trust you must exemplify competence and character.

4. **Have a deep down desire to succeed.** Internal motivation to be the best you can be will assist you in developing the courage necessary to overcome obstacles and take advantage of opportunities. Use the powerful tool of visualization to see yourself being successful. *"All our dreams can come true – if we have the courage to pursue them." Walt Disney*

5. **Persistence is a valuable characteristic.** Have a plan to deal with criticism and rejection. Understand that rejection may mean correction, and that follow-up is critical to reaching some prospects. Have that attitude Susan B. Anthony had when she said, *"Failure is impossible."*

6. **Do Your Follow-up.** Develop a master list of prospects and determine the best approach to use for each. Keep thorough records and read your latest entries so you know what you need to do next.

7. **Know your product.** Make an effort to continually work on building your knowledge base. Classes, workshops, and reading about your product will enhance your degree of belief.

8. **Be a goal setter.** Goals give direction to our dreams. Ben Franklin said, *"Going through life without a goal is like shooting without a target."* Short range, intermediate, and long-range goals are essential for success.

9. **Maintain a professional appearance.** Look sharp, be prepared, and get a good night's sleep. When you are interacting with, and serving people, it is essential to have unbounded energy and go the extra mile. You have only one opportunity to make a good first impression.

10. **Master the art of sales.** Study various approaches on how to reach diverse people. Know that different individuals may comprehend facts and statistics differently. Utilize a wide variety of methods to communicate and close. Have as many tools in your toolbox as possible. *"You may have to fight a battle more than once to win it." Margaret Thatcher*

11. **Empathize with the customer.** Put yourself in the other person's shoes. How do you like to be treated? The ability to identify with the thoughts and feelings of others is essential.

12. **Have fun!** Enjoy interacting with people and providing them with the education and service vital to improving the quality of their lives. Always remember Henry Ford's statement, *"Failure is only the opportunity to begin again more intelligently."*

Extracurricular Activities: A Valuable Educational Tool

Bill Collar – "All The Way With PMA!"

Participation in extracurricular activities provides students with the opportunity to develop to their full potential in their relationships with others. Society places a premium on workers with interpersonal skills and problem solving ability. Positive interaction develops personal characteristics that may be utilized later in life.

1. **Teamwork** - The ability to work with others is extremely important.

2. **Commitment** - Students must be positive role models and make sacrifices for the benefit of all participants.

3. **Work Ethic** - Success can only be attained through hard, smart work.

4. **Pride in Performance** - A feeling of accomplishment is realized through positive application of effort.

5. **Friendships** - Lifetime relationships are developed through participation in activities.

6. **Achievement** - Students represent their communities, schools, and families. A feeling of togetherness is experienced.

7. **Enthusiasm** - In order to be successful, both leadership and life must be approached with enthusiasm.

8. **Persistence** - One learns to get up and go again after suffering a setback.

9. **Confidence** - Self-esteem is enhanced through a series of achievements.

10. **Speaking Ability** - The skills essential in one activity are valuable in others.

11. **Have Fun!** – Participation is fun and the quality of life is enhanced.

12. **Identity** - The team or organization provides participants with a sense of belonging.

13. **Courage** - Performance under pressure helps conquer fear.

14. **Challenges** - Participants learn how to overcome obstacles to success.

15. **Better Grades** - Numerous studies indicate students who participate in school activities perform better in the classroom.

16. **Responsibility** – Activities hold individuals accountable for their actions.

17. **Success in Life** - According to the American College Testing Service, participation in H.S. activities is the major indicator of success later in life

SIXTEEN TIPS FOR POSITIVE PARENTING IN EXTRACURRICULAR ACTIVITIES

Bill Collar – "All The Way With PMA!" www.billcollar.com

1. **Be positive with your athlete.** Let them know you are proud they are part of the team.
   *Focus on the benefits of teamwork and personal discipline.

2. **Encourage your athlete to follow all training rules.** Help build a commitment to the team.
   *Set a good example in your personal lifestyle.

3. **Allow your athlete to perform and progress at a level consistent with his ability.**
   *Athletes mature at different ages; some are more gifted than others.

4. **Always support the coaching staff when controversial decisions are made.**
   *The coaches need your backing to keep good morale on the team.

5. **Insist on positive behavior in school and a high level of performance in the classroom.**
   *Numerous studies indicate extracurricular involvement helps enhance academic performance.

6. **Stay calm in injury situations.**
   *Parents can help minimize the trauma by being in control and offering comfort.

7. **Cheer for our team and players. Opponents and referees deserve respect.**
   *Realize that players may make mistakes. Your support is needed during tough times.

8. **Promote having fun and team play. Very few high school athletes receive scholarships.**
   *Concentrate on what is best for the team. Preoccupation with statistics can be very distracting.

9. **An athlete's self-confidence and self-image will be improved by support at home. Comparison to others is discouraged.**
   *Encourage the athletes to do their best regardless of the performance of their brothers or sisters.

10. **Winning is fun, but building positive team values is most important.**
    *The concept of working together to perform a task will have lasting benefits. Winning takes place when all the little things are done correctly.

11. **Find the time to be an avid booster of school activities.**
    *Help build a solid support system for coaches and athletes.

12. **Help students keep jobs and cars in proper perspective.**
    *Materialistic values can detract from the commitment to the team. Teenagers should have the opportunity to take advantage of extracurricular activities.

13. **Athletes must attend all practices and contests.**
    *Stress the necessity to make a commitment to the team. Practice is important.

14. **Emphasize the importance of well-balanced meals and regular sleep patterns.**
    *An athlete plays best when care is taken to consume nutritious food and obtain sufficient rest.

15. **Many athletes enjoy participating in several sports.**
    *Specialization in one sport may prevent an athlete from enjoying great team relationships in other activities.

16. **Persistence and being able to accept a role are extremely important for the team to be successful.**
    *Not everyone will be a starter, but everyone is important to the team. Some players may not develop until their senior season. Encourage them to be persistent.

Sportsmanship for the Coach and the Participant

Bill Collar – "All The Way With PMA!" www.billcollar.com

*Sportsmanship: Conduct of one participating in a sport. This includes
fairness, respect for one's opponent and graciousness in winning or losing.*

1. **Always keep a positive attitude.** Believe in your coach, believe in yourself and believe in your teammates. Belief comes from hard work, practicing with a purpose and making good decisions in your life. *"Ability may get you to the top, but it takes character to keep you there."* **John Wooden**

2. **Communicate in a positive manner.** Explain what should be done, never how not to do it. Studies indicate a person is encouraged to act by his dominant thoughts. Coach by creating a vivid picture of the best way to accomplish the task. Most often yelling or screaming results in a breakdown in communication. There is no place for sarcasm or humiliation is sports. *"Always bear in mind that your own resolution to succeed is most important.""* **Abraham Lincoln**

3. **Coach and play by the rules and in the spirit of the game.** All sports have a specific code of rules to follow. Finding ways to circumvent the intent of the rule results in confusion and unethical play. Example: Intentional teaching of holding in football is wrong and may lead to a distorted interpretation of how to play the game and affect how future decisions are made. *"The ultimate goal should be to doing your best and enjoying it."* **Peggy Fleming**

4. **Coaching is teaching.** Explain, check for understanding, drill and practice through repetition. These are all essential for success. The player and coach must remain patient and realize each learns in a specific manner. Encourage teammates and believe in your ability to perform the task. *"I don't know that there are any shortcuts to doing a good job."* **Sandra Day O'Connor**

5. **Mutual respect is essential.** All coaches and players want the team to be successful. A wide variety of individuals comprise the team. Be aware of different personalities and relate to each person with concern for what is best for them and the team. Players must realize they don't have to "like the coach" to be a good team player. *"The harder you work, the harder it is to surrender."* **Vince Lombardi**

6. **Be a good role model.** Coach who you are first and then what you know. Always be on time and prepared for every practice. Players are expected to make good decisions with regard to training rules and following team expectations. *"If there is no struggle there is no progress."* **Fredrick Douglas**

7. **Do everything with class.** Conduct yourself in a manner that brings credit to the team. Following the game give credit to your opponent and maintain your self-control. There is no place for "trash-talking," demeaning gestures, yelling out of the bus or behaving in a manner that could discredit your opponent. Remember the Golden Rule – treat your opponents the way you would like to be treated. *"Being a great athlete is important to me, but it's more important to be a great person."* **Jackie Joyner Kersee**

8. **Be the best TEAM player you can be.** Whether you are a starter or reserve always practice to get better and see yourself as a valuable member of the team. Coaches must make decisions based on performance, but a hustling, hard working player will get the coaches attention. Play an important role in every practice and expect to play in every game. *"Every player must put the team first—ahead of personal glory."* **Paul "Bear" Bryant**

9. **Team performance is more important than personal records.** Once a game has been decided leaving the "star" in to build stats or break a record is unfair to the rest of the team and shows disregard for the opponent. *"I will not let my teammates down, and I will not let myself down."* **Mia Hamm**

10. **Respect the officials.** Concentrate on the game and your performance. The officials will do their best to see that the game is played within the rules. If you must speak with an official, address them with respect. It shows a lot of class when both coaches recognize a job well done. *"Kind words can be short and easy to speak, but their echoes are endless."* **Mother Teresa**

Do You Practice Good Sportsmanship?

Instructions: Respond to each item by placing an (X) in the space that best expresses how the statement describes you. If the statement is not like you at all, check space number one. If it fits perfectly, check space five. The spaces in between allow you to indicate various degrees of fit. If you are torn between feeling it does or does not apply, check space number three, the halfway mark.

Unlike Me   Like Me   Bill Collar "All The Way With PMA!"   www.billcollar.com

  1   2   3   4   5

__ __ __ __ __   **1. Play By The Rules** – I always follow all the rules

__ __ __ __ __   **2. Respect The Officials** – I concentrate on my play and demonstrate respect for the officials.

__ __ __ __ __   **3. Communicate In A Positive Manner** – I am upbeat and optimistic when communicating with my teammates and coaches.

__ __ __ __ __   **4. Practice Self-Control** – I keep my emotions under control and focus on my performance.

__ __ __ __ __   **5. Be A Positive Role Model** – I set an excellent example for others to follow.

__ __ __ __ __   **6. Make Positive Comments** – I stay away from trash talk and never provoke opponents.

__ __ __ __ __   **7. Admit Your Mistakes** – I take personal responsibility for my play and never make excuses.

__ __ __ __ __   **8. Be A Team Player** – I value the success of the team ahead of individual praise and recognition.

__ __ __ __ __   **9. Always Give 100%** - I play with pride and make a commitment to do my best at all times.

__ __ __ __ __   **10. Credit The Opponent** – Win or lose I give credit to the opponent after a tough   game.

__ __ __ __ __   **11. Play With Class** – I concentrate on properly executing the fundamentals of the game and refrain from showing off.

__ __ __ __ __   **12. Maintain A High Degree Of Integrity** - I take pride in being truthful and in keeping my word.

__ __ __ __ __   **13. Follow All Training Rules** – I exercise self-control and make good decisions in my personal life.

__ __ __ __ __   **14. Have Fun** – I enjoy the spirit of competition and interacting with my teammates.

_____-----**My Score**

Scoring: Add up your total points to determine your level of sportsmanship.

60 – 70 Outstanding sportsmanship. Keep being a positive leader on your team
50 – 59 An impressive score! You possess the key characteristics of good sportsmanship.
40 – 49 Improve in several categories and you will have excellent sportsmanship skills.
30 – 39 Much potential exists. Keep working on a self-improvement plan.
Below 29 – It is up to you to alter your attitude and lifestyle to develop better sportsmanship.

The Teacher's Semester Exam

Bill Collar "All The Way With PMA!" www.billcollar.com

Directions: Read both statements and place a check in the blank of the one that best applies to you. Then add each column and determine your attitude toward your profession by checking the scale at the bottom of the page.

_____ 1. I welcome positive change.	_____ 1. I'm closed-minded toward change.
_____ 2. I encourage classroom humor.	_____ 2. I discourage classroom humor.
_____ 3. I'm cheerful and relaxed.	_____ 3. I'm too serious and stressed.
_____ 4. I enjoy the rewards of teaching.	_____ 4. It's a job and a paycheck.
_____ 5. I believe all students are can learn.	_____ 5. Some students will never learn.
_____ 6. I expect the best from students.	_____ 6. I'm satisfied with minimum results.
_____ 7. I experience much professional growth.	_____ 7. I don't find time for growth.
_____ 8. I'm the "guide on the side."	_____ 8. I'm the "sage on the stage."
_____ 9. I strive to empower students.	_____ 9. I tend to intimidate students.
_____10. I keep cool under pressure.	_____10. I overreact when stressed.
_____11. I promote high self-esteem.	_____11. I ignore student feelings.
_____12. I foster cooperative learning.	_____12. I seldom build teamwork.
_____13. I maintain a colorful room.	_____13. My room is plain and sterile.
_____14. I appreciate uniqueness in students.	_____14. I seldom recognize individual differences.
_____15. I utilize various teaching styles.	_____15. My teaching technique seldom varies.
_____16. I make maximum use of time.	_____16. I waste vital minutes daily.
_____17. I dwell on positive expectations.	_____17. I emphasize what I don't want.
_____18. I allow for student creativity.	_____18. I establish rigid rules for learning.
_____19. I nurture mutual respect.	_____19. I look for student "friends".
_____20. I exhibit enthusiasm for my subject.	_____20. I emphasize covering the material.
_____21. I maintain a high degree of integrity.	_____21. I vacillate on critical issues.
_____22. I forget and forgive past mistakes.	_____22. I dwell on negative experiences.
_____23. I interact with all students.	_____23. I single out the best for attention.
_____24. I support school activities.	_____24. School activities are of little interest.
_____25. I have fun teaching.	_____25. I work at school.
[ ] **Total**	[ ] **Total**

Scoring

1 – 5	Check into early retirement	1 – 5	"All the way with PMA!"
6 – 10	Watch out for T.L.S.	6 – 10	Experiencing excellence.
11 – 15	On the edge of greatness.	11 – 15	Focus on your vision.
16 – 20	You are kindling many flames.	16 – 20	Professional growth is needed.
21 – 25	Share your attitude and expertise with others.	21 – 25	Keep playing the lottery.

1. **Self-Esteem** - You must believe in the value of your teaching and your impact on youth. You are an important person. Feel good about your accomplishments and wear a smile -- it's contagious!

2. **Goals** - Establish a number of concise, written goals and develop a plan to reach them. You should include short range, intermediate, and long term goals. Consider all areas of your life when planning for the future. It is important to keep your "wheel" round.

3. **Imagination** - Set your imagination free. Continually search for new ideas that will help make your lessons more appealing. Develop a "constructive discontent" with the status quo. Utilize various approaches to reach all learning styles.

4. **P.M.A.** - Develop a positive approach to life. Begin each day with a positive expectancy. Program your subconscious mind to expect success and the "law of attraction" will do the rest. An essential ingredient to a great attitude is to maintain a sense of humor. Laughter in the classroom helps promote an atmosphere conducive to learning.

5. **Motivation** - Be a self-starter. Your goal setting plan will help you develop enthusiasm toward each day. Believe in your value to the system. Internal motivation will serve as the spark to get you started for another day of achievement.

6. **Adversity** - Grow with each hardship in your life. Rededicate yourself to overcome fear, worry and doubt. These will sap your strength and smother personal growth.

7. **Decompression Routine** - It is important to get away from school and get your mind off teaching at times. Take a vacation, follow an exercise program, take up a hobby, all of these are important to your mental health. These will help you avoid "burnout." Physical exercise is a must to help combat lethargy. Peak performers are not workaholics.

8. **Relaxation** - Set aside a time each day when you can put your mind at ease by "thinking black." A Fifteen-minute relaxation session can be very refreshing and beneficial.

9. **Gratitude** - Teachers must cultivate a sense of satisfaction for a job well done. This internal reward is vital when working with teenagers who are usually too self-centered to express thanks for all the assistance.

10. **Positive Feedback** - Keep any letters or notes from students praising your teaching or expressing thanks for the efforts you have made. File them in a special place and refer to them when you have a "down day." This will help you realize a sense of purpose and keep your self-esteem high.

11. **Unsigned Letters** - Ignore unsigned letters. Tear them up and throw them away. Part of your plan for dealing with criticism is to consider the source. This is impossible with an unsigned letter. Usually they are from someone attempting to make you feel bad who doesn't have the courage to sign his or her name.

12. **Communicate With Parents** – Telephone, E-mail, or send letters to parents of your better students. They deserve recognition and you will feel good about the positive comments you have made.

13. **Teamwork** - Support other teachers. Congratulate your colleagues for their achievements and the successful programs they generate.

14. **Administration** - Work with the administration to build the best possible learning experience for the students. When you have concerns or suggestions speak with the people responsible. Be persistent with concepts you believe will be beneficial to all.

15. **Respect Students** - Mutual respect between student and teacher is ideal. Exercise caution when students need counseling and refer them to professionals for assistance. Beware of student "friendships" and maintain the proper relationship. Some students will demand an inferior education, we must not allow it!

16. **Extra-curricular Activities** - Students appreciate teachers who are sincerely interested in them. Your support of activities tells them you care about their accomplishments. Find the time to work as a coach or advisor — it keeps you young!

17. **T.L.S.** - Avoid the "Teacher's Lounge Syndrome." Keep your comments upbeat in the lounge. It is easy to become critical of just about everything when you are having a challenging day. Associate with optimistic people and avoid the "if'a, would'a, could'a, should'a, and yeah-buts"!

18. **Professionalism** - Teachers often speak about their desire to be treated as professionals. Make it a point to uphold high standards. Always keep confidential information privileged and school news at school. Use good judgment when socializing.

19. **Community** - Be actively involved in your community. Parents and students will appreciate your interest in local activities. Make it a point to share your unique programs with civic groups such as the Lions and other organizations.

20. **Time** - Make effective use of your time. It is easy to waste valuable time that could be spent in a constructive manner. Keep a daily "will do" list and prioritize your tasks. Consider taking a class in time management.

21. **Personal Growth** - An occasional summer class, clinic, conference or workshop can be very stimulating. Make it a point to have experiences that will enhance your teaching effectiveness. This will keep you fresh and aware of the latest educational research.

22. **Change** - Look at change as a challenge. Modify your classes through using different approaches and various teaching techniques. Make twenty years' experience pay off rather than repeating one years' experience twenty times. Welcome technology into your classroom. It is stimulating and provides you with the opportunity to reach more students.

23. **Student Behavior** - It is your responsibility to maintain a classroom atmosphere favorable to learning. No one has the right to destroy the learning environment for others. Make sure you take the time to establish proper behavior guidelines for the classroom.

24. **Enthusiasm** – Be enthusiastic about your lessons. Enthusiasm is contagious. Make an effort to obtain maximum student involvement in learning. Be the "guide on the side" and not the "sage on the stage." Decrease the gap between what you teach and what students learn.

25. **Patience** - Always keep your composure when dealing with students. It is best to reason things out without resorting to emotion. Allow individuals a way to avoid public embarrassment when they put themselves in a difficult position.

Suggestions for Promoting Creative Thinking

in the Classroom - Bill Collar, www.billcollar.com

1. **Establish a climate of mutual respect between teacher and students.** Students must sense that you care about them as individuals and you enjoy working with them daily.

2. **Encourage all students to participate in class activities through providing a wide range of involvement activities.** Realize that creativity cannot be limited in scope. Creative potential exists in everyone. It is your mission to help turn it loose. Many "gifted" students lack creativity - help stretch their minds.

3. **Withhold judgment of student contributions and ideas.** Allow for a proper fermentation period. Often the best ideas are those that seemed the craziest when they were presented. Hitchhike and piggyback to maximize student output. Some students will transcend your level of thinking. It is your responsibility to *encourage divergent thinking.*

4. **Beware of convergent thinking.** Too often teachers develop a "teach to the test" mentality where students are rewarded when they come up with the answer the teacher has in mind. Divergent thinking allows for new ways to solve problems. Often there may be more than one right answer. *Solving future problems will require the application of innovative techniques and technology.*

5. **Help channel students into creative activities where they will experience a certain degree of success.** This success will help build confidence and stimulate the creative powers for future accomplishments.

6. **Allow students to experience failure.** A great deal of input from the teacher may enhance the possibility of a project's success, but the student may lose ownership in the process. This will stifle the creative process and failure will be blamed on others. *View failure as a positive learning experience and a stepping-stone to future success.*

7. **Find the time to plan your lessons in a manner that allows for student input and original thinking.** Remember, *"How much you teach is not nearly as important as how much students learn."* Students support what they help create.

8. **Be prepared to experience criticism from colleagues and supervisors.** In promoting creative thinking you make break certain long established rules. Breaking rules, which exist, "because it has always been done that way," can be painful to those who demand a high degree of order.

9. **Be a creative teacher!** Everyone possesses certain creative talents. However, we get programmed into doing things in a certain way. We must experiment with new methods of teaching and *learn from our successes and failures.* Change can be painful, but it will often renew a person's enthusiasm. Employ a variety of strategies in your teaching and students will follow your example.

10. **Creativity takes time.** The best ideas must be given time to grow. Don't expect immediate success when using a new method or when utilizing a student-centered project. *Monitor and adjust* to refine the learning experience to make it as valuable as possible.

11. **Maintain Your Uniqueness.** As you utilize the teaching style that works best for you, develop your gifts to the maximum. *Transcend "canned" approaches to the art of teaching.* Some structure gives a person direction, but too much structure destroys original thought.

12. **Challenge yourself.** Break out of your "comfort zone" and dare to be different. Make it a point to attend conferences and workshops, and do enough professional reading to stimulate your mind and encourage "out of the box" thinking.

13. **Have fun teaching!** Look for the positive in your profession. Laugh together, learn together and explore together. *A laughing classroom is a learning classroom.*

Answers to Brain Teaser #1 From Page 53

1. Long Underwear	2. Tricycle	3. Mixed Up Kid	4. GI Over Seas
5. Mind Over Matter	6. Crossroads	7. Split Level	8. Paradise
9. Three Degrees Below 0	10. Neon Lights	11. Touchdown	12. Ring Around the Rosie
13. Man Overboard	14. Scrambled Eggs	15. Circles Under Eyes	16. Just Between You & Me
17. Misunderstanding Between Friends	18. High Chair	19. Backward Glance	20. Read Between The Lines

Answers to Brain Teaser #2

1. M. + M. + N.H. + V. + C. + R.I. = N.E.
   1. ME+MA+NH+VT+CT+RI = New England States
2. "1B. in the H. = 2 in the B."
   2. A Bird in the Hand = Two in the Bush
3. 8D. − 24H. = 1W.
   3. 8 Days − 24 Hours + 1 Week
4. 3P. = 6
   4. 3 Pair = 6
5. H.H. & M.H. at 12 = N. or M.
   5. Hour Hand & Minute Hand at 12 = Noon or Mid.
6. 4J. + 4Q. + 4K. = All the F.C.
   6. 4 Jacks + 4 Queens + 4 Kings = All the Face Cards
7. S. & M. & T. & W. & T. & F. & S. are D. of W.
   7. Sun. & Mon. etc. are Days of the Week
8. A. + N. + A.F. + M.C. + C.G. = A.F.
   8. Army + Navy + Air Force + MC +Coast = Armed Forces
9. T. = L.S. State
   9. Texas = Lone Star State
10. 23Y. − 3Y. = 2D.
    10. 23 Years − 3 Years = 2 Decades
11. E. − 8 = Z.
    11. Eight − 8 = Zero
12. Y. + 2D. = T.
    12. Yesterday + 2 Days = Tomorrow
13. C. + 6D = N.Y.E.
    13. Christmas + 6 Days = New Years Eve
14. Y. − S. − S. − A. = W.
    14. Year − Summer − Spring − Autumn = Winter
15. A. & E. were in the G. of E.
    15. Adam & Eve were in the Garden of Eden
16. My F.L. and South P. are both M.C.
    16. My Fair Lady and South Pacific are both Musical Comp.
17. "N.N. = G.N."
    17. No News is Good News
18. N. + P. + S.M. = S. of C.
    18. Nina + Pinta + Santa Maria = Ships of Columbus
19. 1 + 6Z. = 1M.
    19. 1 + 6 Zeros = One Million
20. "R. = R. = R."
    20. "A Rose is a Rose is a Rose"
21. A.L. & J.G. & W.M. & J.K. were all A.
    21. Abe Lin. J. Garfield, McKinley, Kennedy all Assassinated
22. N. + V. + P. + A. + A. + C. + P. + I. = P. of S.
    22. Noun + Verb + Preposition +Adjective, etc = Parts of Sp.
23. S. + H. of R. = U.S.C.
    23. Senate + House of Rep. + United State Congress

How's Your Attitude?

Bill Collar, *ALL The Way With PMA!*   www.billcollar.com

This is me!	This could be me?	This is not me!	

Directions: The decisions you make help form your attitude. Take this simple self-evaluation by checking the blank that best describes you. Add up the "This is me!" column and use the scale to determine your rank.

___ ___ ___ 1. When my alarm goes off I hit the "snooze button" or shut the alarm off and go back to sleep. I had too little rest and hate to have to get up and go to work.

___ ___ ___ 2. I find something to wear, but realize clothes are just to cover the body. Staying in fashion or matching colors really doesn't concern me.

___ ___ ___ 3. Glancing at the morning newspaper I realize this is the worst condition our country has ever been in and it is just a matter of time before the government or economy will crumble.

___ ___ ___ 4. Most people drive too slowly and they bog me down. I would like to drive a tank so I can get to work on time. Everyone is a terrible driver but me.

___ ___ ___ 5. People are much too happy at work. They must be faking it. When someone says, "Good morning," I respond with, "What's good about it?"

___ ___ ___ 6. When I'm asked, "How are you today?" I proceed to tell about my physical ailments and personal problems. People should know just how tough my life is.

___ ___ ___ 7. I make it a point to complain about co-workers, even though I wouldn't consider speaking with them privately. Many people just don't know how to work.

___ ___ ___ 8. Everyone in the supermarket is conspiring to slow me up.   The express line is closed because they saw me coming.   Why can't people move faster?

___ ___ ___ 9. I go to my child's game and he/she is sitting on the bench because the coach is, "playing favorites again." Someday I'll give the coach a piece of my mind.

___ ___ ___ 10. I'm definitely overworked and underpaid and no one appreciates everything I do. I should have taken up a more rewarding occupation.

___ ___ ___ 11. When playing golf, cards or other games I will do anything to win. A little cheating really doesn't hurt anyone and it is acceptable as long as no one finds out.

___ ___ ___ 12. Anyone who doesn't share my political beliefs really doesn't understand the issues and is poorly informed.

___ ___ ___ 13. I Know pretty much everything there is to know about my job or profession. I see little need to take classes, go to workshops or waste time with more training.

___ ___ ___ 14. I only have a few more years left before I can retire. It really doesn't pay to, "rock the boat."   If I suggest changing some things it will just create more work for me.

___ ___ ___ 15. I'm so busy with work. It is impossible for me to find enough time to spend with the family.

Rate Yourself: *Total the "This is me! column.*

0 – 3 Congratulations! You have a super Positive Mental Attitude!
4 – 9 Your attitude needs work. Develop a plan to improve your daily outlook.
10 – 15 "Attitudes are Contagious." Please stay away from other people.

Positive Self-Talk

Directions: Since we are moved by our dominant thoughts it is important to control our thinking. Read the "I Can" statements out loud and then read the "I Can't" statements. Notice how your attitude changes corresponding to your self-talk. Finish by reading the positive affirmations again.

 I Can - I Shall - I Will

I know I can do it

I feel great

I'm relaxed

I'm happy

I'm in control

I like myself

My life has meaning

I'm proud of myself

I believe in myself

I keep things in perspective

I can I can I can I can

I make good decisions

I feel confident

I'm doing a great job

I can handle anything

I've come a long way

I know what I want

I will reach my goals

I'm a successful person

My life is great

I know I can

I can I can I can I can

 I Can't - No Way - Forget It!

I can't stand this

I'm stupid

I'm worthless

This is awful

Why me why me why me

It's impossible

Nobody cares

I feel lousy

I hate myself

It's my fault

I'm defeated

I feel rejected

This can't be

I don't deserve this

No one likes me

I can't do anything right

I'm miserable

Unfair unfair unfair

I'm depressed

I'm rotten

Teacher Evaluation

Directions: Place an (X) in the blank that most closely indicates your reaction to each question. Please be honest and frank. Don't sign your name.

	Poor	Fair	Average	Good	Excellent
What is your opinion concerning Mr. Collar's:					
1. Knowledge of subject matter	____	____	____	____	____
2. Clearness of Presentation	____	____	____	____	____
3. Fairness (impartial treatment of all students)	____	____	____	____	____
4. Control (orderly, but friendly and relaxed)	____	____	____	____	____
5. Success in stimulating interest in the subject	____	____	____	____	____
6. Personal enthusiasm and joy in teaching	____	____	____	____	____
7. Attitude toward student ideas (do I encourage and respect student opinion)	____	____	____	____	____
8. Sense of humor	____	____	____	____	____
9. Assignments (challenging – but fair)	____	____	____	____	____
10. Appearance (grooming and dress)	____	____	____	____	____
11. Self-control	____	____	____	____	____
12. Effectiveness (overall teaching success)	____	____	____	____	____

A. Describe your attitude toward class. _____

_____

B. What types of the class did you enjoy most? _____

_____

C. What parts of the class did you enjoy least? _____

_____

D. What suggestions do you have to make class more interesting? _____

_____

E. Evaluate Mr. Collar's grading system. (circle one)

Too easy   Fair   Too difficult

F. Other comments: _____

_____

_____

Coaching with a Winning Attitude

1. We will always use a positive approach in our coaching. Positive talk, positive expectations and positive results.

2. Insist that players pay attention when you speak. Up to 85% of communication is non-verbal.

3. Be the first one on the practice field and the last one off. Give encouragement to players during stretching and running.

4. Our coaches will work together as a team. We will support each other on the field. Any difference of opinion should be expressed in coaches' meetings.

5. Be organized. Follow our practice plan and accomplish as much as possible. Coach on the run.

6. Be enthusiastic! Enthusiasm is contagious. Speak in a strong voice. Always give encouragement!

7. Be a good drill coach.
   a. Explain the purpose of each drill.
   b. Drills must simulate game conditions.
   c. Organize your drills so a minimum number of players are standing around.
   d. Coach in a manner that prevents injuries.
   e. Give positive feedback for good performance.
   f. Be certain the area is clear of potential hazards.

8. Always emphasize proper fundamentals. Pay attention to details.

9. If you are tough on a player during practice, visit with him before he leaves the locker room.

10. Keep an open mind toward players regardless of their reputation.

11. Be consistent in your coaching. Some days you may have to push yourself.

12. Make an extra effort to motivate players who are not starters.

13. If you notice a player who is not performing up to his ability, find out why.

14. Communicate with the players that you care about them on and off the field.

15. Keep a close eye on the players during hot, humid, weather.

16. Report all injuries to the head coach before the end of practice.

17. Be proud to be a coach, and realize the tremendous responsibility that goes with the position.

18. Varsity coaches will always meet immediately after practice.

19. Suggestions on personnel, practice organization, and game strategy are always welcome.

20. Make sure we find the time to emphasize special teams.

21. Be a positive role model on and off the field. Have fun coaching!

22. Game Day
   a. Keep calm and appear confident. Our players notice how the coaches react.
   b. Be a positive coach on the sideline.
   c. Make good use of halftime. Make key adjustments. Be organized.
   d. Limit what you say to players during timeouts.
   e. Be concerned about the next play. Nothing can be done about the last one.

Defensive Wins Championships

Study this defensive checklist and **know it**! Be a smart player in addition to a tough one. A team that plays smart defense wins big games.

Defensive Checklist

1. **Always know your responsibility!** Have your head in the game. Know the score, time, down, distance, field position, time remaining, etc. Stay focused and ready on every play.

2. **Be a great Tackler!** Keep your shoulders square, bend your knees, step into the runner, be under control, and drive through the ball carrier. Tackle with the front of your shoulder pad. Rip through with the arms. **Always keep your head up!**
   a. **Dip** – Bend the knees.
   b. **Rip** – Thrust the arms.
   c. **Wrap** – Grab cloth.
   d. **Snap** - Drive through with the hips.

3. **Maintain a good football position** – Head up, back arched, proper hip–shoulder relationship, feet apart, and heels out. Keep your body under control.

4. **Always go across the face of a blocker!** This will keep you in position for proper pursuit.

5. **Pursue to the football and Gang Tackle!** Make sure you understand the proper angle of pursuit. Second and third tacklers will go for the football. We want the ball!

6. **Always keep leverage on the ball carrier.** Recognize where the sideline is, keep a proper angle on the ball carrier, cut him off, but know that a good back like to cut back.

7. **Get rid of the blocker as soon as possible!** Always keep your feet.

8. **Play defense with emotion!** We will be the most physical team in the conference.

9. **Always Hustle!** On every play we will have a team meeting at the ball. We want to build a fence around the ball carrier.

10. **Play with confidence.** When you practice hard you know you are getting better. Always practice with a purpose. **Do the little things right and the big things happen.**

11. **Have fun! Play with Enthusiasm.**

Be a good **TEAM PLAYER!** In order for our defense to be the best in the conference, everyone on the team must make the commitment to be the best they can be.

Reader Evaluation

Your opinion and feedback are important to me. Suggestions and comments will be taken into consideration when I prepare to address various audiences in and out of education. You have permission to reproduce any forms or pages for personal or school use. When copying a document in its entirety please give credit to the source. Periodically additional materials will be added to my website (www.billcollar.com). Click on "Downloads" to access educational materials. If you are looking for quotes or inspirational poems click on "Quotes and Poems" and you will find quite a collection.

Thank you for taking the time to complete the brief survey and mailing it back to me.

1. Your Occupation: _____

   Optional:
   Your Name: _____

2. Experience: _____

   E – Mail Address: _____

3. Please describe the most influential teacher or teachers in your life. What made that person special and why do you still remember him or her? To give permission for me to quote you in a future book please sign your name above. Use the back if you need more room.

4. What is the best book you have ever read about teaching?

5. What do you look for when you attend an in-service program? You are the most qualified person to help me meet the needs of my audience. Please comment.

This Book

1. What part of this book did you find most valuable?

2. What part of the book was least valuable?

3. Why did you purchase this book?

4. Other comments:

Please make a copy of this page, fill it out and mail it to: Bill Collar, 421 Keune St. Seymour, WI 54165   Thank You!

Authors of Quotes

Adams, Abigail – Patriot, women's advocate, wife of our second President and mother of another.

Adams, John – Founding father and second President of the United States

Addams, Jane – Social reformer of the late 19th and early 20th centuries. Nobel Prize for peace - 1931

Alcott, Louisa May – Nineteenth century author of *Little Women* and other books for and about children.

Anthony, Susan B. – Nineteenth and early 20th century reformer, abolitionist and suffragist

Barth, Roland – Modern day Harvard University educator and author.

Beck, Dr. Lee – A professor at the University of California Medical School.

Berliner, David – A Prof. in the College of Ed. of Arizona State U. Author of *The Manufactured Crisis*.

Berra, Yogi – Former New York Yankee all-star and manager. Known for malapropisms.

Borge, Victor – Twentieth century pianist and comedian.

Brothers, Joyce - Twentieth century psychologist and author.

Browning, Robert – Twentieth century English poet.

Bryant, Paul "Bear"- Extremely successful football coach at the University of Alabama, 1958-82.

Buscaglia, Leo – Twentieth century author, renowned lecturer, and USC Prof. An expert on relationships.

Bush, Barbara – First lady for the 41st President and mother of the 43rd.

Carnegie, Andrew – Nineteenth and 20th century industrialist and philanthropist.

Carnegie, Dale – Author of *How to Win Friends and Influence People*, a success manual written in 1936.

Carter Jr., Hodding – Twentieth century author who earned a Pulitzer Prize for editorials on racial injustice.

Churchill, Winston – WWII era Prime Minister of Great Britain. An excellent speaker and author.

Conklin, Robert – Contemporary author and motivational speaker.

Coolidge, Calvin - Thirtieth President of the United States known for his brevity.

Cousins, Norman – Editor of the *Sat. Review*, author of *Anatomy of an Illness* and an advocate of humor.

Curie, Marie – First modern woman scientist. Awarded a Nobel Prize in Physics and Chemistry.

Dangerfield, Rodney – Twentieth century comedian who "didn't get any respect."

Darrow, Clarence – A late nineteenth and early 20th century lawyer who defended unpopular causes.

DeBono, Edward – Twentieth century author and founder of the Center for the Study of Thinking.

Diller, Phyllis – Twentieth century comedienne.

Douglass, Fredrick – A former slave who worked for abolition and suffrage.

Durant, Will and Ariel – Twentieth century historians who authored *The Story of Civilization.*

Earhart, Amelia – Intrepid aviatrix who was lost attempting to fly around the world.

Edison, Thomas – Inventive genius with over 1,000 patents.

Einstein, Albert – A twentieth-century physicist who developed the Theory of Relativity.

Eisenhower, Dwight D. – WWII General and 34th President of the United States.

Emerson, Ralph Waldo – A nineteenth-century author and leader of the transcendentalist movement.

Ferber, Edna – Pulitzer Prize winning author who wrote novels of social significance.

Ford, Henry – An American auto manufacturer who perfected the assembly line and mass production.

Frankl, Viktor – Survivor of Auschwitz who became a well-known psychiatrist and author.

Franklin, Ben – A Founding Father, patriot, diplomat, scientist, author, and inventor known for his wit.

Frost, Robert – An American poet of the 20th century. Best known for "The Road Not Taken."

Fry, Dr. William – A professor in the Stanford University Medical School.

Fulgrum, Robert – Author of the book *All I Really Need to Know I Learned In Kindergarten.*

Fuller, Margaret - A mid 19th century feminist and author.

Gardner, Howard – Modern day Harvard professor and prolific author on Multiple Intelligences.

Garfield, Charles - A NASA scientist and authority on peak performance.

Ginott, Haim – Prolific 20th century author who has written books about parenting and families.

Goleman,Daniel – Modern day author and researcher on Emotional Intelligence.

Graham, Billy – Contemporary religious leader and evangelist.

Graham, Katharine – Dynamic chair of the Washington Post Co. Earned Pulitzer Prize for her autobiography.

Guliani, Rudolph – Former Mayor of New York City, political figure and author.

Hansberry, Lorraine - The first African American playwright to achieve success on Broadway.

Hemingway, Ernest – American 20th century author known for glorifying male exploits such as boxing.

Hill, Napoleon – Hired by Andrew Carnegie to establish a success plan. Wrote *Think and Grow Rich.*

Holmes, Oliver Wendell, Jr. – A Supreme Court justice from 1902-1932 who supported freedom of speech.

James, William – An American philosopher and psychologist of the late 19th and early 20th century.

Jensen, Eric – Contemporary American educator and author and disciple of Brain-Based learning.

Keller, Helen – Blind and deaf from an early age, she became a prominent author and educator.

Kennedy, John F. – Thirty-fifth President of the United States. Established the "New Frontier."

King, Martin Luther – Civil Rights Movement leader of the 1950's and 60's.

Kipling, Rudyard – An English author in the 19th and early 20th centuries. Known for his children's books.

Kohn, Alfie – A Contemporary American author and lecturer who is critical of reward motivation.

Leahy, Frank – An outstanding football coach at the University of Notre Dame.

Levine, Mel – An author and professor of pediatrics at the University of North Carolina Medical School.

Lincoln, Abraham – Sixteenth President of the United States known for his leadership through the Civil War.

Lombardi, Vince – Legendary coach of the Green Bay Packers and noted football author and speaker.

Luce, Clare Booth – A journalist and congresswoman of the mid 20th century

MacArthur, Douglas – Twentieth century military leader who led the Allied Pacific forces in WWII.

Maltz, Maxwell – A plastic surgeon, lecturer and author of *Psycho-cybernetics,* a guide to self-improvement.

Mann, Horace – A 19th century educator known as the father of the American public school.

Maslow, Abraham – Mid 20th century psychologist who established a hierarchy of needs.

Maxwell, Elsa – "The Hostess with the Mostest." America's premier party authority during the mid 1900's

Maxwell, John C. – A contemporary leadership speaker and prodigious author.

McKay, John - Legendary USC football coach who struggled in the NFL with the Tampa Bay Buccaneers.

Mead, Margaret – A 20th century anthropologist who researched and wrote about primitive societies

Meir, Golda – Israeli Prime Minister from 1969-1974 who attempted to lessen the Arab-Israeli Conflict.

Montague, Ashley - An English anthropologist who explored issues such as race, gender and the individual.

More, Thomas – A statesman of the 16th century who was beheaded for his refusal to recognize Henry VIII.

Moses, Grandma – An American artist of the 20th century who began painting in her late seventies.

Mother Teresa – A humanitarian Roman Catholic Nun who received the Nobel Prize for Peace in 1979.

Nash, Ogden – A 20[th]century American writer of humorous and satirical poetry, and light-hearted verses.

Nightingale, Earl – A radio personality who became a giant in the self-improvement field.

Noll, Chuck – He coached the Pittsburgh Steelers to four Super Bowl titles.

O'Connor, Sandra Day – The first woman Supreme Court Justice. Appointed by President Reagan in 1981.

Orben, Robert – One of America's leading authorities on the use of humor.

Paine, Thomas – A patriot and author in the Revolutionary War. He wrote the pamphlet ***Common Sense***.

Patton, George –WWII general known for his aggressiveness and expertise at tank warfare.

Paul, Alice – An early 20th century suffragist and women's rights activist.

Peale, Norman Vincent – A 20th century American clergyman, famous for his writings on positive thinking.

Penn, William – A late 17th and early 18th century Quaker colonist and founder of Pennsylvania.

Reagan, Ronald – Fortieth President of the United States known for his anti-communist foreign policy.

Richards, Ann – Former Governor of Texas. Feminist spokeswoman.

Rimm, Sylvia – TV & Radio personality and head of the Family Achievement Clinic at the Cleveland Clinic.

Robinson, Jackie – In 1947 he became the first African-American to play major league baseball.

Rockne, Knute – Legendary football coach at the University of Notre Dame.

Rogers, Will – An American humorist of the 20th century known for biting political commentary.

Rooney, Andy – Modern day author, commentator, humorist, and TV personality.

Roosevelt, Eleanor – A humanitarian, diplomat, and Ambassador to the U.N. Married to Franklin Roosevelt.

Roosevelt, Franklin – Thirty-second President of the U.S. 1933-1945. Married to Eleanor Roosevelt.

Roosevelt, Theodore – Twenty-sixth President of the United States known for the Progressive Movement.

Rudolph, Wilma – Overcame a childhood illness to win three gold medals in the 1960 Olympics.

Russell, Bertrand – A 20th century English philosopher known for his writings on logic and pacifism.

Schweitzer, Albert – Twentieth century recipient of the Nobel Peace Prize for his medical work in Africa.

Seyle, Hans – In the 1930's he became one of the first researchers to study stress and link it with illness.

Snead, Sam –From 1936-1965 he won 82 PGA tournaments. Known for his smooth swing and class.

Socrates – An ancient Greek philosopher and teacher of Plato.

Spielberg, Steven – Popular 20th century movie producer who fosters much imagination and creativity.

Stanton, Elizabeth Cady – A reformer and feminist who organized the Women's Rights Convention in 1848.

Starr, Bart – All-Pro quarterback who led the Lombardi coached Packers to several championships.

Stevenson, Robert Louis – A Scottish essayist, and poet who became one of the world's most popular writers.

Stone, W. Clement – A 20th century multi-millionaire insurance executive & author. A Horatio Alger story.

Sullivan, Anne – The teacher of Helen Keller

Thatcher, Margaret – English political leader who served as Prime Minister from1979-1990

Thoreau, Henry David – A 19th century American author who criticized social conformity.

Tracy, Brian – Contemporary motivational speaker, author and purveyor of the principles of success.

Truman, Harry S – President of the United States from 1945 to 1953.

Tuchman, Barbara – Twentieth century historian and author.   She wrote *The Guns of August.*

Twain, Mark – A Late 19th and early 20th century American author and humorist. (Samuel L. Clemens)

Valvano, Jim – National champion NCAA basketball coach, speaker and broadcaster

Voltaire – A French philosopher and author during the 18th century. (Francois Arouet)

von Oech, Roger – A modern-day author, speaker and creativity consultant.

Waitley, Denis – A contemporary author, speaker and motivator. Known for his seminars and workshops.

Ward, William – Twentieth century educator and administrator at Texas Wesleyan University.

Washington, Booker T. – An African-American educator of the 19th century who preached economic gain.

White, Byron – All American and All Pro football player who became a Supreme Court justice.

White, Margaret Bourke – A pioneering photojournalist who created defining images of the 20th century.

Winfrey, Oprah – Contemporary social crusader and television personality

Wooden, John – Outstanding basketball coach at UCLA. Know for his "Pyramid of Success."

Woods, Tiger – One of the top professional golfers in the world today.

Bibliography and Suggested Reading

Abernathy, Rob and Mark Reardon (2002) *Hot Tips for Teachers* – Many excellent tips for motivating students.

Adams, James (1986) *Conceptual Blockbusting* – A very good book to promoting creative thinking.

Anderson, P. (1990) *Great Quotes from Great Leaders* – Includes many quotes on leadership.

Armstrong, Thomas (1993) **7 Kinds of Smart – My favorite reference book on Multiple Intelligences.**

Ayres, Alex (1992) *The Wit and Wisdom of Abraham Lincoln* – An insightful look at Lincoln's wit.

Berliner, David ((1995) *The Manufactured Crisis* – A convincing argument that U.S. schools are successful.

Bernikow, Louise (1997) *The American Women's Almanac* – A great reference book for women's history.

Biro, Brian (1997) *Beyond Success – 15 Secrets of Effective Leadership* – A look at Wooden's Pyramid of Success.

Bonder, Jim (1958) *How to be a Successful Coach* – A collector's item. One of my first coaching books. Great tips.

Bryant, Paul "Bear" (1960*) Building a Championship Football Team* – Practical coaching advice. Still applicable.

Buzan, Tony (1983*) Use Both Sides of Your Brain* – Includes much of the early brain research.

Caine and Caine (1994) **Making Connections – An examination of how the brain functions during learning.**

Carlson, Richard (1997) *Don't Sweat the Small Stuff…and it's all small stuff* – Practical advice to reduce stress.

Carlson, Richard (2000) *Don't Sweat the Small Stuff for Teens* – Much good advice for teenagers

Carruth and Ehrlich (1988) *The Harper Book of American Quotations* – A user-friendly reference work.

Covey, Sean (1998) **The 7 Habits of Highly Effective Teens – An outstanding book to use with students.**

Covey, Stephen (1989) **The 7 Habits of Highly Effective People – A must read for all educators.**

Covey, Stephen (1990) *Principle-Centered Leadership* – I like Covey's practical approach.

Covey, Stephan (1994) *First Things First* – More good stuff from Covey

Curtis, John D. (1991) **The Mindset for Winning – Many excellent tips on self-image and mental rehearsal.**

DePree, Max (1989) **Leadership is an Art – A short, provocative, and useful book on leadership.**

Fay, Jim & Funk, David (1995) **Teaching With Love and Logic – Excellent advice for dealing with students.**

Ferguson, Howard (1983*) The Edge* – Motivational pictures and quotes from athletes of the 1960's and 70's.

Gardner, Howard (1991) *The Unschooled Mind* – A valuable book about how children think and how we should teach.

Gardner, Howard (1993*) Creating Minds: An Anatomy of Creativity* – **Outstanding, especially if you like history.**

Gardner, Howard (1995) **An Anatomy of Leadership – A remarkable study of different leadership styles.**

Gardner. Howard (1993) *Multiple Intelligences* – An in depth look at Multiple Intelligences

Garfield, Charles (1984*) Peak Performance* – **One of the first really good books on peak performance.**

Gerber, Robin (2002) *Leadership the Eleanor Roosevelt Way* – Timeless strategies from the first lady of courage.

Giuliani, Rudolph (2002) *Leadership* – Much practical advice about human relations.

Goleman, Daniel (1995) *Emotional Intelligence* – An explanation of the origins of Emotional Intelligence research.

Goleman, Daniel (1998) *Working with Emotional Intelligence* – The practical application of the E.I. principles.

Goleman, Daniel (2002) **Primal Leadership – An intriguing explanation about applying E.I. to leadership.**

Goudey, Pat (2000) *Unofficial Guide to Beating Stress* – **The best book I have read on handling stress.**

Greenleaf, Robert (1977) *Servant Leadership* – The foundation of all writing on the leader as a servant.

Greenstein, Fred (2000) *The Presidential Difference: FDR to Clinton* – A comparative look at modern presidents.

Hall, Doug (1995) *Jump Start Your Brain* – Numerous exercises to stimulate higher level thinking.

Hartman, Dick (1987*) Motivating the Unmotivated* – Practical examples of how to reach the reluctant learners.

Hill, Napoleon (1937) *Think and Grow Rich* – **The first widely distributed book on the formula for success.**

Hirsch, E.D. (1988) *The Dictionary of Cultural Literacy* – An excellence reference book and educational resource.

Hirsh-Pasek, Kathy and Golinkoff, Roberta (2003) *Einstein Never Used Flash Cards* – **Super for early childhood.**

Humes, James (1985*) Podium Humor* – Includes numerous tips about working humor into presentations.

Humes, James (2002) *Speak Like Churchill, Stand Like Lincoln* – **Best book I have read on communication skills.**

Jensen, Eric (1988) *Super-Teaching* – **Outstanding! Every teacher should own this book. Recently updated.**

Jensen, Eric (1994) *The Learning Brain* – An excellent explanation on the latest in brain research.

Jensen, Eric (1996) *Completing the Puzzle: A Brain-Based approach to Learning* – Very well done and practical

Jensen, Eric (1998) *Teaching With the Brain in Mind* –More information how the brain works – great stuff!

Kohn, Alfie (1999) *Punished by Rewards* –A study of incentives and bribing children to learn – provocative!

Kouzes, James & Posner, Barry (2002) *Leadership Challenge* – **A detailed, complex book for the serious reader.**

Lazear, David (1998) *The Rubrics Way* –Using Multiple Intelligences to Assess Understanding

Lazear, David (2000) *Pathways of Learning* – An excellent book on the application of M.I. in the classroom.

Levine, Mel (2002) *A Mind At A Time* – **One of the best books I have ever read about how children learn.**

Lombardi, Vince (Estate) (1992) *Motivation Lombardi Style* – Motivation hints from the master motivator.

Maltz, Maxwell (1960) *Psycho-Cybernetics* – **The second book I read on self-image and success. Outstanding!**

Maltz, Maxwell (1973*) Live and Be Free Through Psycho-Cybernetics* – The practical application of the above.

Mandino, Og (1984) *University of Success* – **Includes 50 lessons from the greatest motivational writers.**

Maxwell, John (1993) *Developing the Leader Within You* – **Great tips for developing your leadership skills.**

Maxwell, John (1998) *The 21 Irrefutable Laws of Leadership* – **More application of the leadership principles.**

Maxwell, John (1999) *The 21 Indispensable Qualities of a Leader* – A summary of characteristics of the ideal leader.

Maxwell, John (2001) *The 17 Indisputable Laws of Teamwork* – **A reference work on the qualities of teamwork.**

Maxwell, John (2002) *The 17 Essential Qualities of a Team Player* – A brief study of what it takes to be a team player.

Maxwell, John (2002) *Your Road Map For Success* – **A practical hands-on workbook to help achieve success.**

Nixon, Richard (1982*) Leaders: Profiles of Men Who Shaped the Modern World* – A thoughtful look at world leaders.

Olsen, Carl (2000) *Energizers: Calisthenics for the Mind* – **Neat activities to energize your class, group or club.**

Orben, Robert (2000) *Speaker's Handbook of Humor* –A good resource for all types of humor.

Palmer, Parker ((1998) *The Courage to Teach* – **An excellent book on student-teacher relationships.**

Peche, W.W. (1994) *Legendary* TEAM *Leadership* – Coaching comments by Bennett, Wooden, Summit, Nelson, etc.

Phillips, Donald (1992) *Lincoln on Leadership* – **My favorite leadership book. Basic principles clearly stated.**

Phillips, Donald (1997*) The Founding Fathers on Leadership* - **A leadership book for those who enjoy history.**

Phillips, Donald (2001*) Run to Win: Vince Lombardi on Coaching and Leadership* – Similar to the above, on Lombardi.

Restak, Richard (1979) *The Brain The Last Frontier* – A classic book investigating the workings of the brain.

Rimm, Sylvia (1994) *On Raising Kids* – **Practical, commonsense answers to fundamental questions.**

Rimm, Sylvia (1995) *Why Bright Kids Get Poor Grades* – **Excellent advice for parents and teachers.**

Robbins, Anthony (1986) *Unlimited Power* – A popular self-help book by a successful consultant and businessman.

Robbins, Anthony (1991*) Awaken the Giant Within* – Explains numerous strategies used in his seminars.

Roberts, Wess (1987*) Leadership Secrets of Attila the Hun* – A somewhat Machiavellian look at leadership.

Robertshaw, Stuart (1995) *Dear Dr.Humor* – **Fun book from the CEO of The Nat. Assoc. for the Humor Impaired**

Simmons, Sylvia (1991*) Life of the Podium* – An entertaining reference book with many suitable stories.

Spinrad, Leonard and Thelma (1997) *Speaker's Lifetime Library* – A variety of resources for the serious speaker.

Stephenson, Fred (2001) *Extraordinary Teachers* – **A superb study of effective teaching at the college level.**

Theibert, P. (1997*) How to Give a Damn Good Speech* – **One of the better books on effective speaking**

Tutko and Richards (1971) *The Psychology of Coaching* – Dated, but much useful advice on the mental side of sport.

von Oech, Roger (1983) *A Whack on the Side of the Head* – **A brilliant and practical study of creativity.**

von Oech, Roger (1986*) A Kick in the Seat of the Pants* – **With *A Whack* and *A Kick* you will reach new heights.**

Waitley, Denis (1983*) Seeds of Greatness* – **A tremendous foundation for success from one of the best.**

Waitley, Denis (1984) *The Winner's Edge* - **More first-rate advice from Waitley.**

Walton, Gary (1992) Beyond Winning: *The Timeless Wisdom of Great Philosopher Coaches* – Hints from the best.

Warren, William (1983) *Coaching and Motivation* – A practical guide for maximum athletic performance.

Welch, Jack (2002) *Jack: Straight From The Gut* – A leadership book that provides a look at the workings of Gen. Elec.

Williams, Linda (1983*) Teaching for the Two-Sided Mind* – The seminal book of brain dominance, etc.

 * **Bold lettering is used to identify my favorite books.**